SAP® Enterprise Learning

 **PRESS**

SAP PRESS is a joint initiative of SAP and Galileo Press. The know-how offered by SAP specialists combined with the expertise of the Galileo Press publishing house offers the reader expert books in the field. SAP PRESS features first-hand information and expert advice, and provides useful skills for professional decision-making.

SAP PRESS offers a variety of books on technical and business related topics for the SAP user. For further information, please visit our website: *www.sap-press.com*.

Richard Haßmann, Christian Krämer, Jens Richter
Personnel Planning and Development Using SAP ERP HCM
2009, ~550 pages
978-1-59229-187-2

Sylvia Chaudoir
Mastering SAP ERP HCM Organizational Management
2008, 348 pp.
978-1-59229-208-0

Jeremy Masters and Christos Kotsakis
Implementing Employee and Manager Self-Services In SAP ERP HCM
2008, 431 pp.
978-1-59229-188-5

Manuel Gallardo
Configuring and Using CATS
2008, 162 pp.
978-1-59229-232-5

Prashanth Padmanabhan, Christian Hochwarth, Sharon Wolf
Newton, Shankar Bharathan, and Manoj Parthasarathy

SAP® Enterprise Learning

A Practical Guide

Galileo Press

Bonn • Boston

ISBN 978-1-59229-269-1

© 2009 by Galileo Press Inc., Boston (MA)

1st Edition 2009

Galileo Press is named after the Italian physicist, mathematician and philosopher Galileo Galilei (1564–1642). He is known as one of the founders of modern science and an advocate of our contemporary, heliocentric worldview. His words *Eppur si muove* (And yet it moves) have become legendary. The Galileo Press logo depicts Jupiter orbited by the four Galilean moons, which were discovered by Galileo in 1610.

Editor   Jenifer Niles
Copyeditor   Lori Newhouse
Cover Design   Jill Winitzer
Photo Credit   Image Copyright Serg64, 2008. Used under license from Shutterstock.com.
Layout Design   Vera Brauner
Production Editor   Kelly O'Callaghan
Typesetting   Publishers' Design and Production Services, Inc.
Printed and bound in Canada

Contents at a Glance

1   Introduction and Market Overview 25

2   Roles in SAP Enterprise Learning 45

3   SAP Enterprise Learning Architecture 59

4   Integration of SAP Enterprise Learning 73

5   Tools for Learners, Instructors, and Managers 95

6   Training Administration 119

7   Virtual Learning Room 203

8   Content Design, Development, and Delivery in the
    SAP Learning Solution 219

9   Enhancing the SAP Enterprise Learning Solution 267

10 Managing an Enterprise Learning Implementation 287

11 Case Studies 303

12 Functionality Comparison by Version 327

Contents

Acknowledgments 17

Foreword 19

Preface 21

1 Introduction and Market Overview 25

1.1   Why Do Organizations Invest in Learning
      Management Systems? 25
1.2   Market Overview 27
1.3   History of SAP Enterprise Learning 27
      1.3.1   SAP Learning Solution 28
      1.3.2   SAP Enterprise Learning (Environment) 28
      1.3.3   Integration with Other ERP Components 28
1.4   Integration of SAP Enterprise Learning with SAP ERP HCM
      Functionality 29
      1.4.1   Role of SAP Enterprise Learning in SAP ERP HCM
              Talent Management 29
1.5   Role of SAP Enterprise Learning in the SAP Business Suite ... 31
      1.5.1   Sample End-To-End Business Process 32
1.6   Product Release Cycles 32
      1.6.1   Enhancement Package Strategy 32
      1.6.2   Enhancement Packages for SAP Enterprise Learning ... 33
1.7   Training and Event Management vs. Learning Solution vs.
      Enterprise Learning 33
      1.7.1   Comparison of the Solution Designs 34
      1.7.2   Comparison of Training Management Capabilities ... 35
      1.7.3   Comparison of Support for Self-Service 37
      1.7.4   Comparison of e-Learning and Content Management ... 38
      1.7.5   Comparison of Workflow and Other Correspondences ... 41
      1.7.6   Comparison of Reporting Function 42
      1.7.7   Comparison of Web Services 43
      1.7.8   Comparison of Product Roadmaps 43
1.8   More Resources on This Topic 43
1.9   Summary 44

2 Roles in SAP Enterprise Learning **45**

2.1   The Learner 46
       2.1.1   Learner Collaboration 47
       2.1.2   Tools Used by a Learner 47
2.2   The Instructor 48
       2.2.1   Instructor Collaboration 50
       2.2.2   Tools Used by the Instructor 51
2.3   The Training Administrator 52
       2.3.1   Administrator Collaboration 53
2.4   The Manager 54
       2.4.1   Tools Used by a Manager 55
2.5   The Content Author 56
       2.5.1   Tools Used by the Content Author 56
2.6   The Content Administrator 57
       2.6.1   Tools Used by the Content Administrator 58
2.7   More Resources on This Topic 58
2.8   Summary 58

3 SAP Enterprise Learning Architecture **59**

3.1   SAP Enterprise Learning Product Architecture 59
3.2   SAP Enterprise Learning Technical Architecture 60
       3.2.1   Learning Portal (LSOFE) 61
       3.2.2   Instructor Role in the SAP Enterprise Portal 63
       3.2.3   Content Player (LSOCP) 64
3.3   Offline Player (LSOOP) 65
       3.3.1   Authoring Environment (LSOAE) 66
       3.3.2   Environment for the Training Administrator 67
       3.3.3   Content Management 68
       3.3.4   TREX Text Retrieval and Information Extraction 68
3.4   Deployment Options 68
3.5   Deployment Best Practices and Recommendations 69
       3.5.1   Purpose of the System: Development Box 69
       3.5.2   Purpose of the System: Quality Assurance 70
       3.5.3   Purpose of the System: User Acceptance 70
       3.5.4   Purpose of the System: Production 70
       3.5.5   Purpose of the System: Disaster Recovery 70

3.6   More Resources   70

3.7   Summary   71

3.8   Contributors   71

4   Integration of SAP Enterprise Learning **73**

4.1   Integration of SAP Enterprise Learning with HCM Application
       Components   74
       4.1.1   Infotypes   74
       4.1.2   Additional Infotypes   77

4.2   Organizational Management   77
       4.2.1   Organizational Management and Enterprise Learning   79
       4.2.2   Organizational Units   79
       4.2.3   Jobs   82
       4.2.4   Positions   82

4.3   Personnel Development   83
       4.3.1   Personnel Planning   83
       4.3.2   Qualifications   83
       4.3.3   Proficiency   84
       4.3.4   Depreciation Meters and Validity Periods   85
       4.3.5   Maintaining Requirements and Qualifications   86
       4.3.6   The Profile Match-Up Report   88
       4.3.7   Essential Qualification   89
       4.3.8   Development Plans   89
       4.3.9   Structure of Development Plans   90

4.4   Performance Management Integration   90
       4.4.1   Integration Points   91
       4.4.2   Features in Enhancement Pack 4   92

4.5   More Resources on This Topic   93

4.6   Summary   93

5   Tools for Learners, Instructors, and Managers **95**

5.1   The Learning Portal   95
       5.1.1   Employees Can Use the Portal to Plan Their Careers   95
       5.1.2   Learners Can Take Appropriate Action to Address
                Skill Gaps   97
       5.1.3   Learning Portal Delivers Training and Collects Feedback   97

	5.1.4	Structure of the Learning Portal	98
	5.1.5	Training Home	99
	5.1.6	Course Catalog and Keyword Search	101
	5.1.7	My Learning Account	102
	5.1.8	Course Booking and Participation	103
	5.1.9	Web-Based Learning	105
	5.1.10	Technical Settings for the Learning Portal	106
	5.1.11	Enhancing the Learning Portal	106
5.2	Content Player		108
5.3	Instructor Portal		112
	5.3.1	User Experience and Structure of the Instructor Portal	112
	5.3.2	Stages of Instruction and Features Used	113
	5.3.3	Provide Access to the Instructor Portal to All Instructors	114
5.4	Managing Learning Activities of a Team		115
	5.4.1	Managing Mandatory Course Assignments	116
	5.4.2	Tracking Progress on Mandatory Course Assignments	117
	5.4.3	Booking Team Members to Courses	117
5.5	More Information		118
5.6	Summary		118

6	**Training Administration**		**119**
6.1	Training Management Process		119
6.2	Key Transactions in Training Management		120
6.3	Course Preparation		122
	6.3.1	Designing the Course Catalog	122
	6.3.2	Course Types and Delivery Methods	126
	6.3.3	Course Type Attributes	129
6.4	Course Offering		131
6.5	Day-To-Day Activities		132
6.6	Follow-up Activities		134
6.7	Configuring Enterprise Learning		134
	6.7.1	Activate Business Functions	135
	6.7.2	SAP Learning Solution	136
	6.7.3	Course Preparation	137
6.8	Course Offering Section		141
6.9	Day-to-Day Activities		142
	6.9.1	Control Elements	142

6.9.2   Booking 143
6.9.3   Versioning 145
6.9.4   Participation Cancellation 146
6.9.5   Workflow and Correspondence 147
6.10   Recurring Activities 150
6.10.1   Completion Specifications for a Course 151
6.10.2   Course Follow-Up 151
6.10.3   Course Appraisals 153
6.11   Basic Settings 154
6.12   Integration 155
6.12.1   Time Management 156
6.12.2   Materials Management 157
6.12.3   Budget Management 157
6.12.4   Billing and Activity Allocation 157
6.12.5   Appointment Calendar and SAP Knowledge Provider 159
6.12.6   Collaboration 159
6.13   Curriculum Types and Course Programs 161
6.13.1   Curriculum Types 161
6.13.2   Creating a Curriculum Type 162
6.13.3   Course Types and Courses Exclusive to Curriculum 164
6.13.4   Scheduling a Curriculum 167
6.13.5   Course Program 170
6.14   Reporting 175
6.14.1   Delivered Reports 175
6.14.2   Business Intelligence 179
6.14.3   Using Ad Hoc Query for Enterprise Learning 183
6.15   The Training Administrator Portal 189
6.15.1   Structure of the Training Administrator Portal 190
6.15.2   Scheduling Courses, Assigning Resources, and
           Managing Participation 195
6.15.3   Configuring the Training Administrator Portal 196
6.16   Development Plans 196
6.16.1   Individual Development Plan function
           (SAP HCM backend) 197
6.16.2   Talent Management and Development 198
6.16.3   Using SAP Performance Management 200
6.17   Summary 202

7 Virtual Learning Room **203**

7.1 Virtual Learning Rooms are Important Business Tools 203

7.1.1 Types of Learning for Which the Virtual Learning Room
is Best Suited 204

7.1.2 A Virtual Learning Room is for Synchronous Events 205

7.1.3 The Virtual Learning Room Can Surpass
Classroom Training 205

7.2 SAP Enterprise Learning Virtual Learning Room 206

7.3 How Adobe Connect is Integrated with SAP Enterprise
Learning 206

7.3.1 Learning Portal 206

7.3.2 Instructor Portal 207

7.3.3 Administrator Interface 209

7.3.4 Tracking of Information with the Virtual Learning Room 210

7.4 Features of the Virtual Learning Room 210

7.5 Installation and Configuration 211

7.5.1 Troubleshooting Tips 215

7.6 Infrastructure Planning for Adobe Connect 216

7.7 More Resources on This Topic 217

7.8 Summary 218

7.9 Contributors 218

8 Content Design, Development, and Delivery in the SAP Learning

8.1 Introduction 219

8.2 Content Design 220

8.3 The SAP Authoring Environment (AE) 222

8.4 Configuration for the Authoring Environment 236

8.5 Third-Party Content and the Authoring Environment 237

8.6 SCORM Course Delivery 237

8.6.1 SCORM Versions 238

8.6.2 SCORM Course Creation 239

8.6.3 Deploying and Launching a SCORM Course 240

8.6.4 SCORM Tests 242

8.7 AICC Course Delivery 243

8.7.1 AICC Course Creation 243

8.7.2	Deploying and Launching an AICC Course	243
8.7.3	Hosted AICC Content	244
8.7.4	AICC/HACP Error Codes	245
8.8	Content delivery	246
8.9	Configuring the Content Player	247
8.10	Offline Player	249
8.11	Tracking and Reporting Progress in e-Learning Courses	250
8.11.1	Progress Tracking in the Learning Portal	251
8.11.2	Learning Progress BAdI	252
8.11.3	Content Reports	253
8.11.4	Publisher Database	254
8.12	Delivering Third-Party Hosted Content	255
8.13	Using the SAP Exchange Infrastructure (XI)	256
8.13.1	XI Examples	257
8.13.2	Master Data Requirements	260
8.13.3	Questionmark™ Perception™ Assessments Integration	261
8.14	Summary	265
8.15	Contributors	266

9 Enhancing the SAP Enterprise Learning Solution 267

9.1	Enhancements and BAdIs	267
9.1.1	Training Management	267
9.1.2	Resource Management	270
9.1.3	Fee Handling	270
9.1.4	Cancellation Reasons	271
9.1.5	Correspondence BAdIs	271
9.1.6	Learning Portal	273
9.1.7	Content Player and Learning Objectives	277
9.1.8	Additional Enhancements	277
9.2	Structural Authorization Techniques	278
9.2.1	Configuring Structural Authorizations	278
9.2.2	Maintain Structural Profiles	279
9.3	Enhancement Case Study: Controlling Access to the Course Catalog	282
9.3.1	Enhancement	283
9.4	Summary	286

10 Managing an Enterprise Learning Implementation 287

10.1 Project Planning 287
    10.1.1 Project Goals, Objectives, and Scope 288
    10.1.2 Project Staffing 291
    10.1.3 Project Timeline 293
10.2 Blueprint 294
10.3 Realization 298
    10.3.1 Content Management 298
    10.3.2 Change Management 299
    10.3.3 Proof of Concept 301
10.4 Go-Live Preparation and Go-Live 301
10.5 Summary 302

11 Case Studies 303

11.1 Case Study 1: Implementing a Standalone Learning Solution
    Using ALE 303
    11.1.1 Background 303
    11.1.2 Implementation Project Planning 304
    11.1.3 Blueprint 305
    11.1.4 Realization 306
    11.1.5 Go-Live Preparation and Go-Live 308
    11.1.6 Team Education and Change Management 308
    11.1.7 The Rest of the Story 310
11.2 Case Study 2: Global Implementation 310
    11.2.1 Background 311
    11.2.2 Global Implementation Readiness 311
    11.2.3 Learning Systems 311
    11.2.4 Planning the Future State 313
    11.2.5 Requirements Gathering 315
    11.2.6 Design 318
    11.2.7 Catalog Design 319
    11.2.8 Realization 321
    11.2.9 End-User Education 323
    11.2.10 Rules of Thumb 324
11.3 Summary 325

12 Functionality Comparison by Version 327

12.1 System Architecture Compatibility 327
    12.1.1 Portal Functionality Comparison 329
    12.1.2 Training Management Functionality Comparison 331
    12.1.3 Authoring Functionality Comparison 332
    12.1.4 Content Management System Functionality
          Comparison 333
12.2 Workflow, Courseware, and Reporting Functionality
    Comparison 334
    12.2.1 Support for External Learners 335
12.3 Standards and Compliance 335
12.4 Virtual Learning Room 336
12.5 Integration 336
12.6 Learning Services for Managers 337
12.7 Summary 338
12.8 Conclusion 338

The Authors 339

Index 341

Acknowledgments

We would like to thank the following people for their valuable insight and support. Hendrik Vordenbaeumen, Vice President of HCM product management at SAP; David Ludlow, Vice President of HCM product strategy; Harry West, Director of HCM product management; Lisa Tinti, Manager HCM product management; Joachim Foerderer, topic lead for talent management; and James Rocha, business development manager for SAP Enterprise Learning.

Jenifer Niles, our editor and publisher, SAP PRESS made the book happen.

We are grateful to the SAP Enterprise Learning product team for their support and contribution. Neha Agrawal, Arijit Barik, Hagen Eck, B R Girish, Aron Kornhall, Pradeep Kumar, Seshatalpasai 'Sesh' Madala, Mandira Mukherjee, Srinivasa 'Srini' Raghavachar, Alessandro Silvestri, Robin Sperle, Jochen Wilhelm, Wenwen Xu, Emira Ylli, Stephanie Rieder.

We thank Simone Buchwald and Tammie Eldridge who managed the SAP Enterprise Learning until version 6.02; Nish Pangali and Diana Hecker, who manage the SAP HCM Performance Management and SAP HCM Compensation Management applications; Judith Roess from HCM product management, who provided valuable inputs on analytics; Debbie Peake, who manages the travel management product, for her advise on the publishing process; Peter Barby, practice manager for SAP Enterprise Learning, for his valuable inputs and insight about the product, and Magesh Mugunthan and Thomas Kunoth, from the SAP RKT team, for their help with system access.

We thank Vad Vayntrub for contributing to the Questionmark integration section, Jason Siesko, Shirish Yadvadkar and Alvin Dohl for their contribution to the Skill-Soft integration section; Jason Ichen, of Learn2Perform and Sapphire Development Group, who contributed his expertise on authorizations and enhancements; Robert Kelly, of hyperCision Inc., who contributed his expertise on reporting and ad hoc query, Frank Hanfland of SAP for his contribution to the section on AICC integration; Barry Vorster of Epiuse who provided case study information; Joe Hoskins, of Fifth Third Bancorp, who provided valuable feedback; Ravi Sekhar, of Ananth Technologies, who provided valuable feedback; Vivek Mahajan, Praveen

Kaushik and Alex Lowrie, of Convergys, who provided valuable feedback, Kate Hutchinson, of hyperCision Inc., who provided valuable feedback and formatting help; and Danielle Morrison, for her valuable insight and help with reviewing the content.

Finally we are grateful to our families who supported us during this long assignment.

Foreword

In different HCM keynote speeches and customer meetings over the last few months, I spoke about the mega trends in today's world and how SAP ERP HCM product teams are partnering with customers to help them address the challenges these trends bring.

As you all know, we are living in interesting times. The financial crisis which started in 2008 is forcing companies to shun risk, reduce their workforce, and focus on survival. Massively disruptive technologies such as Web 2.0 and the mobile web are revolutionizing the consumer markets. The energy supply and climate change are forcing governments and companies to rethink business as usual and focus on sustainable business practices and business models.

At the same time the workforce of the western world is aging and fewer young people are entering the workforce in western countries. Emerging markets are graduating more workers. Yet the quality and cultural fit of these workers vary widely across countries and regions. Meanwhile, the generation that grew up with the Internet is entering the workforce and demanding more flexibility at work, more collaboration with colleagues, more meaningful jobs, and better and different work-life balance than older employees do. If you don't provide what they ask for they have several other places to work and this will increase in the years to come.

While natural resources are dwindling everywhere and the race is on to find renewable resources, I urge you to pay attention to a resource that not only renews itself, but also magnifies multi-fold in value if nurtured with care. I am talking about your people, your human capital.

You are not alone in this race against time and this often-called "war for talent." The SAP Business Suite has software that can help you visualize your talent, attract your talent, grow your talent, and develop your talent. SAP Enterprise Learning is an integral part of the SAP Business Suite and is a key weapon in your "war for talent."

SAP Enterprise Learning is tightly integrated with other talent management and business applications in the SAP Business Suite. Such integration helps you devise, develop, and execute a talent management strategy in the context of your core business, instead of in an isolated training department or HR department.

SAP Enterprise Learning has tools to manage all aspects of learning including classroom- based events, virtual learning programs, and web based courses. It is used by customers with a few hundred learners to customers with hundreds of thousands of learners. In this book Prashanth, Christian, Sharon, Shankar, and Manoj have provided a comprehensive overview of the SAP Enterprise Learning product that will be relevant for both current and future customers.

I hope you enjoy the book and that it helps you understand, use, and strategically plan with SAP Enterprise Learning and the process support is provides. I wish you a great success in your "war for talent" and I'm sure that SAP Enterprise Learning and this book will help you with it.

Sincerely,
Hendrik Vordenbaeumen
VP, SAP ERP HCM Solution Management
Walldorf, Germany

Preface

SAP Enterprise Learning has evolved over the past eight years into a compelling product. Since it was built in multiple phases and made available to customers over various releases, there was no single, publicly available, information source that provided a comprehensive overview for decision makers who wanted to buy the product, consultants who wanted to implement or enhance the product, customers who wanted to deploy upgrades, and SAP partners who wanted to integrate with the product.

We also noticed that IT directors, training managers, implementation project managers and functional consultants attended the three day HR 270 course to prepare for an SAP Enterprise Learning implementation project. Several of our customers and partners told us that they attend SAP HR conferences to prepare for an implementation, respond to an RFP, build a business case, and, more important, make informed decisions about their future direction. While the HR 270 course and presentations at conferences have excellent technical information, no single training program or conference provides a comprehensive overview of the entire product.

Moreover, training programs are only scheduled in certain cities around the world, a few times a year, while conferences happen in two locations twice a year. Only a select group of individuals could afford to travel to these events due to time and cost constraints. So we wanted to do something about it, and decided to provide a comprehensive, affordable, public information source for everyone in the SAP Enterprise Learning ecosystem. This book is not a replacement for a formal technical training program or a conference; however, we believe that this will be a good starting point. It will also be a ready-reference source for all project team members during and after an implementation.

Structure of the Book

Chapter 1 is meant for decision makers and buyers. If you are a CIO, CLO, IT director, HR director, or training manager who needs to make or influence a decision about software purchases, this chapter is for you. It introduces the product and describes a learning management system. It also describes the evolution of training goals in an organization. You can identify the level of maturity of your organization and determine the right approach for your organization. This chapter also clarifies the target market for the product. Finally it describes how SAP Enterprise Learning fits into the talent management strategy of SAP and the SAP Business Suite.

Chapter 2 is about the various roles in a training organization and the tools those roles use. This chapter is meant for decision makers, planners and implementers. If you are a CIO, CLO, or training manager who needs to determine the number of people to staff your team and the number of different licenses you need to buy, this chapter will be of help. If you are an IT director who needs to determine the number of users who will be accessing the various components and portals in the product for implementation planning purposes, reading this chapter will help.

Chapter 3 covers the technical architecture of SAP Enterprise Learning. If you are an IT director, SAP Enterprise Learning consultant, SAP HCM Consultant, or an SAP NetWeaver consultant you should read this chapter. It provides a high level overview of the architecture first, and then describes the technical architecture component by component. It is also a useful chapter to read if you are a customer building a business case for an implementation or a partner answering an RFP for a customer project. More important, it has information about the sources from where this information was derived.

Chapter 4 talks about how SAP Enterprise Learning integrates with other SAP ERP HCM and SAP ERP applications. It explains the various applications first and then lists the integration points. It then explains the relevance of every integration point and tells you if and why you need the integration points. It also provides detailed information about SAP terminology and concepts associated with the integration. If you are an HR director, HCM consultant, or SAP Enterprise Learning consultant, read this chapter.

Chapter 5 talks about tools used by Learners, Instructors, and Managers. This chapter is for SAP Enterprise Learning consultants, training managers, and implementation teams. Consultants can get information about configuring the portals. IT directors and implementation managers can understand the features of the tools meant for learners, and instructors and managers can determine if the tools fit the business needs of their organization without alteration. Most customers customize, combine, or extend the functionality of the portals to suit the needs of their organization.

Chapter 6 covers training administration, the heart of a learning management system. If you are a training manager, read this chapter to understand the administration features and tools. If you are a training administrator or an SAP Enterprise Learning consultant, read this chapter to understand how to prepare the system and create course offerings. The chapter discusses reporting and lists the standard reports available in the system. It then covers the training administration portal and talks about how the portal simplifies administration for those who may not be familiar with SAP systems.

Chapter 7 covers the integration with Adobe Connect, the software that powers the Virtual Learning Room that is part of SAP Enterprise Learning. If you are a CIO, training manager, or HR manager read the first four sections of this chapter to understand how you can reduce training costs and improve training quality using a Virtual Learning Room. If you are an IT director, training administrator, or SAP Enterprise Learning consultant, read the entire chapter to understand the value and understand how to install and configure the software.

Chapter 8 covers E-Learning content design, development, and delivery. It also covers integration with external content delivery systems. If you are a training manager, training administrator, content author, instructional designer, or SAP Enterprise Learning consultant, read the entire chapter. If you are an SAP XI consultant, the last section on integration with external content delivery systems is meant for you. This chapter talks about how an organization should develop its content strategy. It also talks about content development tools, content development standards such as SCORM and AICC, and E-Learning content delivery tools that come as part of SAP Enterprise Learning. The chapter then talks about how SAP Enterprise Learning can launch content from externally hosted content providers such as SkillSoft and assessments software provider, Questionmark.

Chapter 9 covers enhancements that can be done to SAP Enterprise Learning. This chapter is for IT directors who want to understand the opportunities for enhancement and for SAP Enterprise Learning technical consultants who will implement the enhancements. The section on customizing the portal used by learners will be of interest to training managers and implementation managers. The chapter talks about implementing dynamic menus, controlling access to the course catalog, customizing the portal used by learners, and customizing the content delivery tools.

Chapter 10 covers project management of an SAP Enterprise Learning implementation. This chapter is a must read for implementation project managers. Implementing SAP Enterprise Learning is different from implementing a standalone LMS. Project managers need to understand and plan to take advantage of all the integration opportunities available. The implementation will also require understanding the pre-requisites and close coordination with experts from other business and technical areas. Reading this chapter will provide a head start for planning and implementing SAP Enterprise Learning. The chapter also includes a sample high level project plan derived from a real-world project.

Chapter 11 provides two case studies based on projects the authors were involved in. The first one is a case study where SAP Learning Solution was implemented in a standalone mode with the relatively loose integration with SAP ERP and then integrated tightly in a second phase. The second case study is based on a global implementation of SAP Learning Solution for a manufacturing company. The focus in this case study is on the planning and preparation that a large global implementation warrants. This chapter is a must for implementation project managers, SAP Enterprise Learning consultants, and IT directors.

Chapter 12 is for training managers, IT directors, consultants, and business decision makers. This chapter provides a complete matrix of features available in different releases of the product. This information is particularly important for customers who want to determine the version of the software they need to deploy to meet their business goals. It is also helpful for customers who are using an older version of the product and want to build a business case to deploy the current version.

Prashanth, Christian, Sharon, Shankar, and **Manoj**
Palo Alto, CA, USA; Walldorf, Germany; Oak Park, IL, USA; Bangalore, India; Riverside, CA, USA

You may see training as a perk for your employees and not as an investment in your business. You may even wonder what happens if you spend a significant amount of money training employees and then they leave. However, have you wondered what happens if you don't train them and they stay?

1 Introduction and Market Overview

We have written this book based on the assumption that those who will read it are training professionals or executives who know that training your employees at all levels is critical to your business's success. We also assume that you are knowledgeable of learning management systems.

For the purposes of this book, we will define a *Learning Management System* (LMS) as computer software that automates the administration and delivery of training. LMSs register users, track Courses in a catalog, record data from learners, and provide reports to management. LMSs also enable the delivery of Web-based Courses conducted in virtual classrooms.

In 2008, training industry experts and analysts expanded the scope of learning management to also include the management of online user communities that enable informal learning.

1.1 Why Do Organizations Invest in Learning Management Systems?

An organization usually buys a LMS to automate the administration, tracking, and reporting of classroom, online training, and knowledge-related events for employees. Compliance with regulatory requirements is often the initial reason an organization implements an enterprise class LMS, because the software facilitates timely training and provides completion documentation.

A company may also buy a LMS to save money on training. It is not unusual for an organization to have multiple training departments, with some run by business units, some run by country organizations, and others run by departments. Centralizing all of these training management tasks and systems, and even outsourcing them, can reduce the cost and complexity of learning management in your organization.

A final reason that a company may buy a LMS is to develop an employee's internal skills and competency. Giving employees the skills and knowledge they need to do their jobs gives managers windows into the skill gaps of their employees. According to Gartner Research, there is growing interest in a tighter connection between strategic Human Capital Management (HCM) and learning management.

An organization that effectively implements a LMS and then moves on to an integrated talent management approach considers learning management an integral part of its strategy to attract, develop, and align employees with organizational goals.

Once an organization masters integrated talent management, the next step in the evolution of learning goals is to use the learning infrastructure to develop the competencies of partners and customers. The company can then concentrate on enabling, tracking, and harnessing informal learning and community-based learning. After enabling learning within the organization, the company extends community-based learning to its partners and then its customers. Table 1.1 illustrates the evolution of learning management goals and the approach an organization usually takes to achieve those goals.

	Evolution of Goals	Approach
1	Training automation to improve efficiency	Use a LMS to automate routine administration, tracking, and reporting.
2	Compliance	Use a LMS to ensure timely training and maintain required documentation.
3	Cost control	Use a LMS to centralize and outsource training administration activities conducted by various business units, country organizations, and departments. Features to support shared service center personnel is key if you outsource your LMS administration.
4	Employee development and employee alignment with organizational goals	Use a LMS that is tightly integrated with competency libraries, *Human Resource Information System* (HRIS) systems, *Employee Self-Service* (ESS) portals, and *Manager Self-Service* (MSS) portals.

Table 1.1 Evolution of Learning Management Goals

	Evolution of Goals	Approach
5	Integrated talent management. Attract, develop and align talent toward organizational goals.	View learning management as one of the four pillars of strategic human capital management. Use a LMS from a provider who supplies recruiting, performance management, learning management, and compensation management software.
6	Educate partners and customers.	Use a LMS that supports the training and development of people who are not employees of the organization.
7	Enable and track informal learning and community-based learning.	Use a LMS that supports the administration of informal learning and community-based learning.

Table 1.1 Evolution of Learning Management Goals (Cont.)

Although this is the normal Course of evolution, organizational culture, capability, and grassroots efforts may change the way your learning system evolves. Selection of your LMS depends on the current and future goals of your organization. We recommend that you consider your current training situation, your desired future, and your existing infrastructure before selecting an LMS.

1.2   Market Overview

There are different types of LMSs on the market today. There are LMSs from specialized providers who just focus on learning management. There are providers who provide learning management as part of an integrated talent management suite. Finally, there are learning management systems provided as part of a business suite that includes all software to run a business successfully.

SAP Enterprise Learning is part of the *SAP Business Suite* of applications. SAP Enterprise Learning is integrated with several SAP business applications, so customers who run SAP software to operate their human resource functions or their financials will derive the most benefit from SAP Enterprise Learning.

1.3   History of SAP Enterprise Learning

The history of SAP's software for learning management started with the Training and Event Management component in SAP Enterprise Resource Planning (ERP). This module helped customers manage training programs conducted in classrooms. Training and Event Management was and still is an integral part of SAP Human Capital Management (HCM) and interfaces with all of the relevant SAP application components, making it a basis for extending and updating employees' skills and knowledge.

SAP Enterprise Learning is a relatively new term, and the product was known as SAP Learning Solution until March 2007.

1.3.1 SAP Learning Solution

In 2001, SAP introduced the SAP Learning Solution, which offered the management and delivery of *e-learning Courses* apart from the management of classroom-based Courses. Functionality has improved over the last several years and customer adoption has grown. Currently, SAP Learning Solution has more than 700 customers.

1.3.2 SAP Enterprise Learning (Environment)

In 2007, SAP partnered with Adobe Systems to incorporate a *Virtual Learning Room* into the product. The Virtual Learning Room is powered by Adobe Connect Professional, Adobe's online meeting software. The new product was named *SAP Enterprise Learning* (environment)(SAP EL).

> **Note**
>
> SAP Enterprise Learning = SAP Learning Solution + Virtual Learning Room powered by Adobe Connect.

Although SAP Enterprise Learning is the product that SAP actively markets, SAP makes both SAP Learning Solution and SAP Enterprise Learning available for customers to purchase. This is to meet the needs of customers who have early versions of the SAP Learning Solution and may not be ready, organizationally and technically, for SAP Enterprise Learning.

Please note that we will compare all three of these offerings: Training and Event Management, SAP Learning Solution, and SAP Enterprise Learning, in more detail later in the chapter.

1.3.3 Integration with Other ERP Components

From the beginning, the design team focused on integrating SAP Enterprise Learning with other SAP ERP components to enable seamless business processes. The Training and Event Management module was integrated with Personnel Administration, Personnel Development, Organizational Management, Time Management,

Cost Accounting, Payroll, Materials Management, Business Intelligence, and Sales and Distribution (see Figure 1.1).

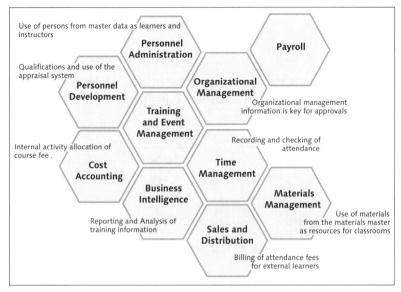

Figure 1.1 The Training and Event Management Solution Shares Data

1.4 Integration of SAP Enterprise Learning with SAP ERP HCM Functionality

SAP Enterprise Learning also inherits the tight integration of Training and Event Management with various functions in SAP ERP HCM. And taking it one step further, the product is integrated with other applications in SAP's Talent Management functionality.

1.4.1 Role of SAP Enterprise Learning in SAP ERP HCM Talent Management

SAP Enterprise Learning is an integral part of the SAP ERP HCM Talent Management component (Figure 1.2). Instead of looking at the value of individual applications to customers, SAP looks at the value of business processes that take advantage of multiple integrated applications within the Talent Management component. Customers who use all of the Talent Management functionality, rather than a single function, will continue to derive the best value of their investments in SAP software.

SAP has defined four main talent management themes:

- Pay for Performance
- Educate and Develop
- Identify and Grow
- Attract and Acquire

There are multiple applications involved in each theme. The tools are integrated with each other and with applications in other components to enable a seamless execution of related business processes.

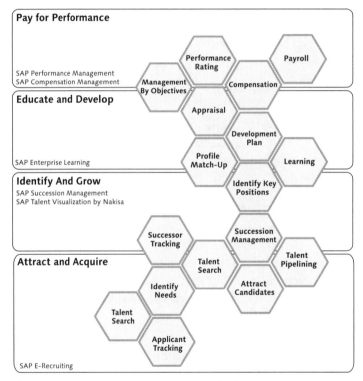

Figure 1.2 SAP Enterprise Learning is Part of Talent Management

Let's look at each theme of Talent Management briefly.

In *Pay For Performance*, an employee's performance is quantified with a rating and then given to compensation management for appropriate decision making. The *Educate and Develop* theme is used for monitoring and identifying the gaps in an employee's qualification profile and providing the employee with a development plan along with the necessary learning resources to follow the plan. *Succession Planning* is the process of identifying successors to key positions within a company, assigning those people as successors to those positions and evaluating the readiness of such successors. Ideally, there should be a pool of successors for all key positions. Succession Planning plays an important role in the *Identify and Grow* theme, which incorporates steps to identify key positions and high potential employees and then enable the development of such employees, so they can fill key positions in the future. Attracting, recruiting, and retaining the right people are the cornerstones of the *Attract and Acquire* theme.

SAP Enterprise Learning is part of the *Identify and Grow* theme and is integrated with other applications such as Performance Management, which allows an appraiser to assign mandatory Courses to an employee while they are in the appraisal document in the Performance Management system. We'll cover this more later in the book.

Now let's see how SAP Enterprise Learning fits in with the SAP Business Suite.

1.5   Role of SAP Enterprise Learning in the SAP Business Suite

SAP Business Suite 7.0 is a comprehensive family of business applications, providing industry-specific functionality for every enterprise. Individually, SAP Business Suite applications help an organization manage critical business processes. Collectively, they form a tightly integrated business application suite that adds value to every facet of an organization.

These are the applications components that make up the SAP Business Suite:

- SAP Customer Relationship Management (CRM)
- SAP ERP
- SAP Product Lifecycle Management (PLM)
- SAP Supply Chain Management (SCM)
- SAP Supplier Relationship Management (SRM)

SAP's product designers, product managers, and consultants paid attention to end-to-end business processes while designing, developing, and implementing the Business Suite. SAP Enterprise Learning, part of the SAP Business Suite, serves several end-to-end business processes in many application components in the Business Suite.

1.5.1 Sample End-To-End Business Process

Let's take a look at an end-to-end business process: *Asset Safety and Compliance*. Asset Safety and Compliance is best achieved by aligning the objectives of key stakeholders and supporting the realization with an integrated solution.

There are several stakeholders with different objectives in this business process. The compliance officer wants to keep the other stakeholders involved and informed. The plant manager wants to keep the environment safe, the safety officer wants to keep the people safe, and the engineering manager wants to keep the assets safe. These objectives cannot be met with one application or a collection of disparate applications that are not integrated with each other. In the case of this business process, SAP Enterprise Learning works in conjunction with SAP ERP, SAP Business Objects, SAP Compliance, and SAP GRC Risk Management to meet the asset safety and compliance requirements of an organization. We'll look at this integration more throughout the book.

For now, let's take a quick look at how SAP deploys new functionality to customers.

1.6 Product Release Cycles

SAP releases new functionality for its ERP platform every eight to nine months via *Enhancement packs*, which are released more frequently compared to the earlier methods of updating.

1.6.1 Enhancement Package Strategy

SAP introduced its enhancement package strategy for SAP ERP as a means to speed up delivery of features, and to simplify the way customers manage and deploy new software functionality. Customers can implement these software innovations from SAP and activate the software based on business demand. As a result, customers can isolate the impact of software updates and bring new functionality online faster through shortened testing cycles (see Figure 1.3).

The enhancement package strategy is part of SAP's ongoing commitment to deliver business innovation to customers without disruption.

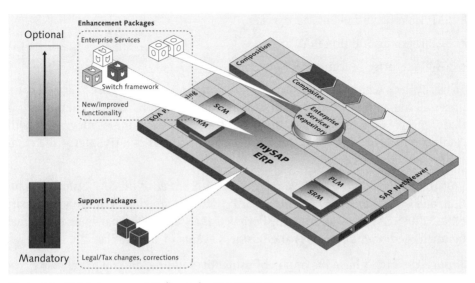

Figure 1.3 SAP Enhancement Packages for SAP ERP 6.0

1.6.2 Enhancement Packages for SAP Enterprise Learning

Significant new functionality was introduced in enhancement pack 2 [2007] and enhancement pack 4 [2008] for Enterprise Learning.

These enhancement packages are cumulative, so each new enhancement package includes new innovations as well as all innovations delivered with prior packages. So, if you deploy Enhancement Pack 4, you will get all the functionality released as part of Enhancement Pack 2.

As of January 2009, there were over 1,000 customers on Training and Event Management, about 620 customers on SAP Learning Solution, and about 80 customers on SAP Enterprise Learning. Customers who use Training and Event Management and need to upgrade to new features often ask how the three products compare. So, let's have a look at how these three products compare in functionality.

1.7 Training and Event Management vs. Learning Solution vs. Enterprise Learning

When looking at the learning management solution offerings from SAP, you will hear three different terms:

- SAP Training and Event Management

- SAP Learning Solution (SAP LSO)

- SAP Enterprise Learning (SAP EL)

To clarify, let's review and compare these solutions. SAP Enterprise Learning comprises all functions and features of SAP Learning Solution. The only difference is that it includes the Virtual Learning Room feature — the built-in integration with Adobe Connect. In this book, the distinguishing features of SAP Enterprise Learning are explained in detail.

SAP Training and Event Management is the forerunner of the SAP Learning Solution, and so, SAP Enterprise Learning. SAP Training and Event Management is part of SAP ERP HCM and was primarily designed as a solution for managing traditional instructor-led training Courses and business events in an organization.

Though customers have the option of using this solution, and there are many customers who still use it, it is recommended that customers choose either SAP Learning Solution or SAP Enterprise Learning for learning management, because future enhancements and developments will be done with these two solution offerings. No further enhancements will be done to SAP Training and Event Management. It will be supported and maintained only until the release of the next version after SAP ERP 6.0 (earlier referred to as *mySAP ERP 2005*).

> **Note**
>
> The SAP note 953832 (*http://service.sap.com*) provides additional details about this.

It is easy to see that the latter two solutions have been designed with a bigger scope in mind, reflecting the current changes and trends in the learning management domain, whereas SAP Training and Event Management (HR-TEM) was designed when organizational training was still mostly based on classroom training. The next section provides a comparison of capabilities of these three solution offerings.

1.7.1 Comparison of the Solution Designs

SAP Learning Solution and SAP Enterprise Learning are designed to support a blended learning approach. The objective of blended training is to enable learners to go through the learning process in a variety of ways — not just through classroom trainings. So it includes traditional classroom based approach and other media, such as Web-based trainings and virtual classroom trainings.

Training and Event Management (HR-TEM) was primarily designed for classroom-based programs and similar business-events (e.g., seminars and workshops).

1.7.2 Comparison of Training Management Capabilities

Let's begin this comparison by reviewing the Course Types and catalogs offered in each.

Course Types and Course Catalogs
SAP Learning Solution: Supports the creation and delivery of Course Types of several delivery methods, including *Instructor-Led Training* (ILT), *Computer-Based Training* (CBT), *Web-Based Training* (WBT), *External WBTs*, *virtual classroom trainings*, and *online tests*.

It is possible to categorize and group such Courses by different factors, such as subject, country, delivery method, or any other category that makes sense to the organization. Within each subject grouping, a variety of delivery methods may coexist, making it possible to create a complete catalog of the entire Course offering of the organization.

It is also possible to integrate Courses from third-party training providers into the catalog, such as training institutes by means of Web services.

SAP Enterprise Learning: Because SAP Enterprise Learning includes all features of the SAP Learning Solution, all features in SAP Learning Solution are also in SAP Enterprise Learning.

Training and Event Management: Course catalogs are limited to classroom-based, instructor-led training events only.

Assigning Resources and Instructors
SAP Learning Solution and SAP Enterprise Learning: The ability to assign resources and instructors is available in the SAP Learning Solution and SAP Enterprise Learning. All types of resources that would be needed for a Course Type, such as rooms (venues), equipment (computers, projectors), and consumables (training Course materials) can be defined and assigned to Course Types along with the units needed (for example, the number of computers needed for a technical training).

Apart from such resources, instructors, who are capable of delivering Courses, and tutors, who can assist in the training process, can also be assigned to Course Types.

Training and Event Management: This feature is also available. Resource types and instructors can be mapped to Course Types.

Course Scheduling and Resource Management
SAP Learning Solution and SAP Enterprise Learning: Facilitate preparing planned schedules of Courses. Resources can be reserved for such schedules.

Later, such planned Courses can be firmly booked, when, for instance, the minimum or optimum capacity (number of learners booked) for the Courses has been reached.

Resource reservations during scheduling automatically takes care of resolving resource booking conflicts. When instructors are assigned to Course schedules, the system also checks an instructor's time schedule against the Course schedule.

Training and Event Management: This functionality is available in Training and Event Management as well.

Bundling and Packaging Courses
SAP Learning Solution and SAP Enterprise Learning: Both solutions enable organizations and institutions to bundle and package together related Course offerings in the form of *Course Programs* and *Curriculum*.

A Course Program offers an excellent method of structurally grouping related Courses into logical learning units called *blocks*. Such blocks can then be grouped and packaged as a Course Program, which provides learning maps and continuous and long-term learning initiatives to learners.

A Curriculum also offers facilities to group related Courses together, which is ideally suitable when such sets of Courses are taken together for overall learning. Curriculums are ideally suitable for employee induction training, where Courses from different areas need to be grouped together.

Training and Event Management: This is not supported in Training and Event Management.

Integrated Collaboration Room
SAP Learning Solution and SAP Enterprise Learning: This is available in SAP Learning Solution and SAP Enterprise Learning. Synchronous and asynchronous collaboration from the Enterprise Portal supports team news, team calendars, team tasks, team discussion, document sharing instant messaging, and chat.

Training and Event Management: This is not available in Training and Event Management.

Employee Training History
SAP Learning Solution and SAP Enterprise Learning: This is available in both solutions. All training history information is available in the Learning Portal and in several standard reports.

Training and Event Management: In Training and Event Management, this is available for classroom Courses. Standard HR-TEM reports display training history.

Course Evaluations/Feedback
SAP Learning Solution and SAP Enterprise Learning: In the SAP Learning Solution and SAP Enterprise Learning, feedback or Course evaluation forms can be created based on configurable templates. Learners can give feedback on Courses they have undertaken through the Learning Portal. The underlying framework of such evaluation forms is that of the appraisal engine from SAP Performance Management.

Training and Event Management: In Training and Event Management, this is available using appraisal from the Personnel Development component.

Support for Regulated Industries
SAP Learning Solution and SAP Enterprise Learning: SAP ERP HCM facilitates attaching rates of depreciation to qualifications, as well as expiration or validity periods for qualifications. Notifications of such expiring qualifications/ certifications are displayed in the Learning Portal for attention and action. Newer or updated versions of e-learning content can also be pushed to learners immediately to ensure the latest content is available on a subject area. And it's also possible to confirm Course participation with an electronic signature, which can be used for other follow-up activities, such as Course evaluation and transfer of qualifications.

Training and Event Management: This is not available in Training and Event Management.

Now let's take a look at how the solutions support self-service.

1.7.3   Comparison of Support for Self-Service

Employee Self-Service Capability
SAP Learning Solution and SAP Enterprise Learning: In the SAP Learning Solution and SAP Enterprise Learning, there is rich functionality available in the Learning Portal.

The Learning Portal serves as the point of access to all training-related activities. With its clear structure, it provides personalized information and a quick orientation to the learning environment. It interactively assesses the learner's current knowledge level, and then delivers the learning objects that are best suited to the situation and task.

A learner accesses the Learning Portal using a PC-based browser. The Learning Portal provides a complete overview of available Course offerings, tailored to the learner's role within the organization and personalized for his use. The relevant Courses proposed for each learner can range from WBT and virtual classroom sessions to CBT or traditional classroom training. Authors develop Courseware in the Authoring Environment by creating and structuring modularized, reusable, learning content.

The SAP Learning Solution Web application is coded using the *Business Server Pages* (BSP) programming model.

The Learning Portal can be integrated into the SAP Enterprise Portal but can also be accessed as a URL in an Intranet or the Internet.

Training and Event Management: HR-TEM provides an HTML-based self-service scenario using the *Internet Transaction Server* (ITS).

Compared to the scenarios in the Learning Portal, HR-TEM provides fewer ESS scenarios, and certain ESS services, based on ITS, are no longer supported in higher releases.

Manager Self-Service Integration
SAP Learning Solution and SAP Enterprise Learning: Both solutions allow the line manager more participation in the learning activity. Within the Manager Portal, it is possible to view qualification gaps of employees. The system also recommends possible Courses that could fill such gaps, which managers can communicate to employees. A detailed training history of individual employees is also shown.

Managers can also directly book team members to Courses, and they can set Courses as mandatory for their team members and to their reporting organizational entities.

Training and Event Management: In the standard scenarios, MSS scenarios are limited to the universal work list for Course request approvals and reviewing the information about classroom training in the MSS scenario.

Next we'll review how e-Learning and Content Management are handled.

1.7.4   Comparison of e-Learning and Content Management

Administration and Use of e-Learning
SAP Learning Solution and SAP Enterprise Learning: SAP Learning Solution and SAP Enterprise Learning are designed to administer and deliver e-learning content.

Training and Event Management: e-Learning administration is not supported in Training and Event Management.

Authoring Environment

SAP Learning Solution and SAP Enterprise Learning: Both solutions have an environment for creating tests and structuring e-learning content. External e-learning content can also be imported into the Authoring Environment and can be made available to learners as Courses. Already-used e-learning content creation tools can be easily integrated into the Authoring Environment.

Training and Event Management: The Authoring Environment is not available as part of Training and Event Management.

Support for Third-Party e-Learning Content

SAP Learning Solution and SAP Enterprise Learning: This is available in both solutions. It is possible to import e-learning content from third-party vendors into the SAP Learning Solution and integrate it with the organization's Course offering. And both solutions support Sharable Content Object Reference Model (SCORM) and Aviation Industry CBT Committee (AICC)–compliant e-learning content.

Training and Event Management: Training and Event Management does not support e-learning.

Content Management System

SAP Learning Solution and SAP Enterprise Learning: In both solutions, the Content Management System serves as a repository of e-learning content and also helps in versioning (when there are changes) of such content. It also provides an open interface to integrate external content management systems if desired (WEBDAV).

Training and Event Management: Training and Event Management does not have this feature.

Content Player

SAP Learning Solution and SAP Enterprise Learning: Both solutions have content players that are intelligent enough to recognize the structure and content of e-learning Courses (contents) created by a wide range of third-party authors, and then play them to learners.

The Content Player is capable of playing SCORM 2004 (also SCORM 1.2) and AICC-compliant content.

The Content Player is also capable of handling and passing significant Course progress data, Course access and completion information, and Course scores (e.g., in the case of an online test) to the solutions, so it is possible to report on such data later.

Training and Event Management: There is no Content Player in Training and Event Management.

Offline Player

SAP Learning Solution and SAP Enterprise Learning: In both solutions, learners can download e-learning content (if it is allowed) locally and go through the Course offline. Later, the progress of learners and completion can be synchronized when the learner is online.

Training and Event Management: There is no Offline Player in Training and Event Management.

Online Testing

SAP Learning Solution and SAP Enterprise Learning: In both solutions, online testing can be delivered as standalone Courses facilitating learners to assess themselves on specific areas. Based on a learner's performance, specific learning objectives can also be imparted to a learner.

Tests can also precede an e-learning Course as a "pre-placement assessment." In such a case, the test can be used to check the current knowledge level of the learner, which the system can use to offer a different view of the e-learning content. If needed, the results of the test can also be used to decide whether the learner can take the e-learning Course or not.

Tests can also be placed as "post-assessment" tests for e-learning content. In this case, the objective of the test gauges the level of learning (from the e-learning content), based on which learning objectives can be imparted to learners.

Qualifications that learners can achieve by undertaking e-learning Courses can also be governed by such tests.

Both solutions also facilitate detailed reporting on test results.

Training and Event Management: Online testing is not possible with Training and Event Management.

Integration to Third-Party Virtual Classrooms

SAP Learning Solution and SAP Enterprise Learning: This is available in both solutions. It is also possible to integrate the solutions to external classroom or meeting room tools such as Interwise and WebEx through SOAP or XI Web services.

Training and Event Management: No such integration is available.

Next we'll take a quick look at how the three solutions handle workflow and other correspondences.

1.7.5 Compare Workflow and Other Correspondences

Workflow Capabilities

SAP Learning Solution and SAP Enterprise Learning: Both solutions use the Business Workflow engine in the WebAS ABAP stack.

Training and Event Management: Training and Event Management uses the Business Workflow engine in the WebAS ABAP stack

Workflow Approvals for Course Booking and Cancellations

SAP Learning Solution and SAP Enterprise Learning: In both solutions an employee booking a Course can be configured to either seek a manager's approval or not.

In the case of approvals: For time-dependent Courses (e.g., classroom trainings), the system can be configured so that the approval is to be done before "n" days before the Course date. If the manager does not take action before this period, the booking is automatically taken as approved. For time-independent Courses (e.g., WBTs), the booking is made only when the request is approved. In a similar manner, Course cancellations by employees can also be sent to managers for approval.

Training and Event Management: The standard HR-Training and Event Management ESS allows for a single level approval in the standard workflow template. The workflow can be modified according to the specific business requirement.

Correspondence

SAP Learning Solution and SAP Enterprise Learning: This is available in SAP Learning Solution and SAP Enterprise Learning. It is possible to generate automatic correspondence when business processes are carried out (e.g., send confirmation of booking). The standard system supports the generation of correspondence based on Adobe Forms, Short Message Service, and email.

Training and Event Management: This is also available in Training and Event Management. Automated generation of correspondence and other documents such as certificates, and attendance sign-up sheets based on pre-defined templates in SAPscript is possible.

Another important function of these solutions is their reporting capabilities, so let's see how they compare.

1.7.6 Comparison of Reporting Function

SAP Learning Solution and SAP Enterprise Learning: Standard reports and Business Intelligence (BI) content are available in both solutions. BI reports are available on information such as Course participation and attendance statistics, learning objectives achieved, and training costs.

Training and Event Management: In Training and Event Management, standard reports and BI content are available.

User Interface

SAP Learning Solution and SAP Enterprise Learning: In both solutions, learners can access their learning related activities through the Learning Portal. The Learning Portal can be, for instance, integrated with a company's internal portal or website.

Managers can access an employee's training history details and training recommendations through MSS, which runs over SAP Enterprise Portal.

Instructors and tutors can access their training-related activities via the Instructor Portal, which runs over SAP Enterprise Portal (7.0 and above; an integral part of SAP NetWeaver 04s).

Training administrators can manage training through the backend ECC system. Additionally, they have a dedicated portal interface for performing their regular, day-to-day activities.

Training and Event Management: Training and Event Management provides a Web browser for employees as part of ESS. SAPGUI is for administrators.

Because HR-TEM does not support e-learning, standard ESS scenarios only allow the employee to browse the catalog, search for Courses, do profile match-ups, and enroll online.

Now let's take a quick look at the web service offerings.

1.7.7   Comparison of Web Services

SAP Learning Solution and SAP Enterprise Learning: Both solutions have standard integration scenarios to communicate with external content (e.g., content hosted in external servers), through SAP NetWeaver's XI (Exchange Infrastructure) interface.

This facilitates seamless integration between solutions and the external content provider for regular training activities such as booking and cancelling Courses, launching Courses through the Learning Portal, and also to update a learner's progress back into the solution system.

Use of SAP XI sets up a communication and data exchange between solution system and any other external system without the need for too many interface modifications and customizations, either on the SAP solution side or on the external content provider's side.

Training and Event Management: Training and Event Management does not provide Web services.

Now let's wrap up this section with a roadmap comparison.

1.7.8   Comparison of Product Roadmaps

SAP Learning Solution and SAP Enterprise Learning: SAP Learning Solution is SAP's primary solution to support learning and training management. All developments around the learning management process will be centered on the SAP Learning Solution.

SAP's new release strategy is to serve on SAP ERP 6.0 (formerly known as SAP ERP 2005). It is planned that, until 2010, further enhancements to SAP solutions will be delivered as a series of enhancement packages for SAP ERP 6.0.

Training and Event Management: Support for HR-TEM will continue only until ERP 6.0 (formerly known as SAP ERP 2005). No additional development effort is planned by SAP. Maintenance will be provided.

1.8   More Resources on This Topic

▶ For more information about the Asset Safety and Compliance end-to-end business process, which is served by SAP Enterprise Learning, please go to *www.sap.com/solutions/executiveview/manufacturing/asset-safety-and-compliance/index.epx*.

▶ For more information about Enhancement Packs and their content for various applications, please go to *https://websmp102.sap-ag.de/erp-ehp*.

1.9   Summary

Training employees in all levels of your organization is essential for business success. A learning management system enables you to manage learner information, deliver learning content, and track progress. SAP Enterprise Learning, the LMS of SAP, uses learner data stored in HR systems directly without the need for additional integration. It is also integrated with other applications in SAP's Talent Management Component. In this chapter we detailed the differences between SAP Learning Solution, SAP Enterprise Learning, and Training and Event Management, so that you can see how the solution began and where it is headed. In the next chapter we'll look at roles in SAP Enterprise Learning.

Despite all of the advanced technology, it is the people involved in the process who make learning happen. The objective of this chapter is to discuss the various people involved in a training organization, the roles they play, the tasks they perform, the way they collaborate with each other, and to identify the tools they use to accomplish their task.

2 Roles in SAP Enterprise Learning

There are several people involved in planning and executing a training event. These people fall into broad categories, including the training department, the resource providers, the consumers of training, the specialists who provide subject matter expertise and Course content, and the field organization that sells training to consumers. SAP Enterprise Learning recognizes the role played by people in all of these groups, and has tools such as the Learning Portal, the Instructor Portal, the Training Administrator Portal, the Online Content Player and the Offline Content Player, the Repository Explorer, and the Authoring Environment designed to help the specific roles accomplish their daily and ongoing tasks successfully (Figure 2.1).

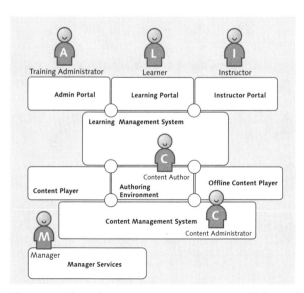

Figure 2.1 The Roles in SAP Enterprise Learning and the Tools They Use

Depending on the nature and size of an organization, these roles might be held by a single individual, a small group of people, or even large teams. In this chapter, we will discuss each key role in detail and have a look at the tools used in each. However, this chapter does not cover the detailed description and configuration of the tools, because such details are discussed in dedicated chapters later in the book.

2.1 The Learner

A *learner* is a person in an organization who benefits from the learning services provided by that organization. This person can be anyone in the organization, including a current employee, a customer, a partner, a supplier, or a distributor. A learner has access to several learning services, and most learners will take the following actions during the learning process:

- View the current qualifications
- View the profile match-up to compare current qualifications with required qualifications
- View a list of mandatory Courses
- View training history
- View notifications about missing or expiring qualifications
- View and search a Course catalog
- Book or pre-book a Course
- Cancel participation in a Course
- Request participation in the Course, if the Course requires approval
- Request cancellation of a booking, if necessary
- Take a Web-based Course
- Take a Web-based Course offline when not connected to the network
- Take an online test
- Confirm participation in a Course
- Evaluate a Course
- Provide an electronic signature to confirm participation in a Course

2.1.1 Learner Collaboration

In most cases, learners work with their training administrators before starting the Course and then work with the instructor during the Course (Figure 2.2). For instance, there could be some pre-work that may need to be completed prior to the actual session, and in some cases, the administrators can send information relevant to the session, such as directions, books required, etc.

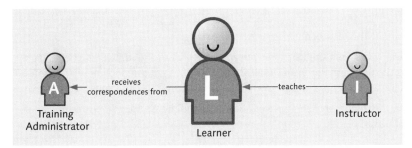

Figure 2.2 A Learner Collaborates with the Training Administrator and the Instructor

To manage their progress through the training process, learners have different tool options with SAP Enterprise Learning, so let's look at these now.

2.1.2 Tools Used by a Learner

There are two primary tools learners use in SAP Enterprise Learning: the *Learning Portal* and the *web-based Content Player*. The Learning Portal is an online application through which the learners perform training-related activities such as searching for a Course, booking a Course, and launching a Course. The Offline Content Player is an offline application that enables the learners to view Courses. They will also use the Offline Content Player to take Courses offline, when not connected to the office network.

> **Who Do Learners Call When They Need Help on the Day of Training?**
>
> In the case of classroom training, learners usually contact the training administrator to get info about training locations, hotels, and directions. On the day of the training, learners also call a facilities manager or the instructor for logistical information. In a Virtual Learning Room, learners work with an operator to deal with telephone issues or Internet connection issues using regular tools such as phone and email.

In addition, learner usually interacts with the manager, instructor, and training administrator. The learner can interact with the manager to discuss the development plan, and in some cases, the learner may need to request a manager's approval to enroll in Courses.

Learners in a Regulated Industry

Let's take the example of a machine operator who works in a medical devices company. This person may be required to read a procedure document before working on a machine. When such a document is created, the requirement will show up in the Learning Portal and prompt the learner that he needs to read it.

The learner can then open the document from the portal and read it. Once he reads it, he can access the Learning Portal and indicate that he has read the document. This information can be used to report in case there is an audit from the regulatory authorities.

In addition to the document, the worker could be required to take a classroom Course or an online Course.

We will look at these tools in greater depth later in the book, so for now let's take a look at the instructor's role.

2.2   The Instructor

As you would expect, an *instructor* is a teacher in charge of delivering Courses in a physical or virtual classroom. Some organizations have internal employees as instructors qualified to teach Courses. In some cases, organizations hire external instructors to teach particular Courses. Instructors support students who take Web-based Courses, especially when such Courses are prerequisites for classroom Courses. The goals of an instructor are to successfully deliver a Course in which learners can meet their learning goals and then gather Course appraisal information that provides feedback on the Course content, instructor, facilities, and general administration of the Course. However, an instructor performs a much broader task than just the delivery of the Course.

For an instructor-led learning event in a physical classroom, an instructor also performs the following tasks:

A few days before the Course, the instructor:

- Reviews the standard Course material
- Prepares additional material if required

▶ Contacts subject matter experts to clarify questions regarding material

▶ Contacts facilities to check on classroom supplies and equipment

▶ Contacts IT to ensure hardware and software availability for the class

---

Does an Instructor Create Course Content?

Content for corporate learning is usually created by a set of subject matter experts and is then delivered in classrooms by instructors. Instructors, in many cases, are content delivery agents, and are not usually subject matter experts, although there may be some exceptions.

On the day of the Course, the instructor:

▶ Reviews the participant list and completion of prerequisites

▶ Double-checks booked rooms and equipment

▶ Double-checks ordered supplies and Course material

Then, during the Course, the instructor:

▶ Takes attendance by passing around an attendance sheet

▶ Adds participants who arrived at the classroom without registration

▶ Replaces participants who came in place of a colleague

▶ Removes participants who did not show up

▶ Sends the attendance sheet to the training administrator via fax

▶ Contacts subject matter experts about questions that may arise on topics not covered in the Course

When the Course is over, the instructor:

▶ Confirms attendance

▶ Marks participants Pass or Fail based on their performance in class

▶ Collects feedback about the Course using a Course appraisal document

▶ Conveys feedback on Course content to Course developers

▶ Conveys key participant information and customer leads to sales

For a Course conducted in a virtual classroom, the instructor performs Course preparation in the virtual classroom before the Course. Instructors can create and edit virtual classrooms in SAP Enterprise Learning (EL), and they can enter the virtual learning room anytime and upload documents required for the Course.

Attendance information is captured automatically, and Course handouts are distributed electronically. Virtual classroom Courses are shorter in duration compared to classroom Courses and are generally used to deliver Course content of a different nature. We will cover virtual classrooms in depth in Chapter 7.

Preparing Content for a Virtual Learning Room

A Virtual Learning Room is an online classroom. Instructors upload existing content such as presentations and handouts to the room, and they can create simple text documents using tools available in the room. There are no sophisticated content creation tools in the Virtual Learning Room, however.

2.2.1 Instructor Collaboration

During the process of teaching a Course, the instructor will need to collaborate with multiple people in various roles within the company. For example, in the training department, he collaborates with several people (Figure 2.3):

- The training executive who provides training directives
- Course administrator who provides Course details and notifications
- Other instructors who may be teaching the Course

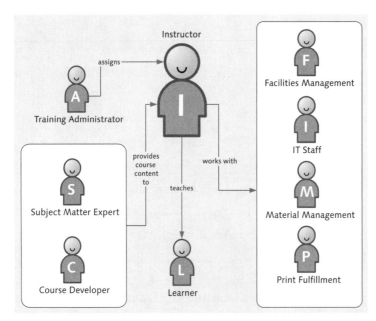

Figure 2.3 The Instructor Collaborates with Many Roles

In the resource provider area, the instructor interacts with:

- Print services for the Course material
- Materials management for classroom supplies such as flips charts and markers
- Facilities management for room reservation and equipment
- IT support organization for software and hardware

In addition, he'll work with those in the specialists' areas, including:

- The Course author to receive input and provide feedback on the Course material
- The subject matter expert to clarify doubts and answer questions not covered by the Course material. The subject matter expert is usually a person knowledgeable in the content being taught.

Instructors Differ from Company to Company

A large organization such as a big bank might have hundreds of instructors, while some organizations rely on external instructors to deliver their Courses. Organizations may also rely on subject matter experts within the company to deliver the training, especially when the topic is new. Such experts may not be expected to or may not be willing to perform the administrative activities associated with delivering a Course, so in such cases, an additional person can be assigned to a Course to perform administrative activities.

2.2.2 Tools Used by the Instructor

As with the learner, there are specific tools within SAP EL that the instructor will use. The Instructor Portal, provided by SAP EL, is a key tool in the daily work life of an instructor, along with email and phone, to communicate with the training administrator, materials management, subject matter experts, facilities management, and IT. The instructor may also use a fax to send attendance information and Course appraisal information to the training administrator, if such information is collected on paper. So, let's look at each of these tools for the instructor.

The Instructor Portal

The *Instructor Portal* will be covered in detail in later chapters, but as a quick overview, the Instructor Portal is different from the Learning Portal in that it will display the Courses a person is teaching, not the Courses a person is taking.

The instructor uses the Instructor Portal, before, during, and after the Course to perform instructor-related activities such as marking attendance.

Before the Course, the instructor uses the portal to display Course details and review participant information. After the Course is over, the instructor uses the portal to do follow-up activities such as summarizing attendance and participant evaluations.

The Instructor Portal enables all of these activities from the instructor work center with the following services:

▶ Display Course Details

▶ Manage Participation

▶ Manage Course Follow-Up

▶ Manage Virtual Learning Room

> **Inviting Guest Instructors**
>
> An instructor who teaches a Course may invite a subject matter expert from within the company or outside the company as a guest speaker. Even though this guest speaker also delivers training, such guest speakers usually do not perform any administrative activities associated with an instructor so that they do not need access to the Instructor Portal. They simply show up in a classroom or a Virtual Learning Room, deliver their presentations, and leave.

This covers the majority of who the instructor role collaborates with and which tools they will use, so let's move on to look at the training administrator.

2.3 The Training Administrator

The functions of a training department vary greatly from company to company, but they usually range from strategic activities, such as choosing the appropriate learning methodologies for the organization, controlling training expenditures, and designing the training catalog of the organization, etc. They also deal with tactical activities such as training demand assessment and management, planning and scheduling Courses, participation management, and the subsequent follow-up processes.

A training department might have several *training administrators* depending on the size of the organization. The role of such training administrators can range between any of the previously mentioned set of activities.

Typically, the role of a training administrator is characterized by the following:

▶ **Multiple responsibilities:** The role demands a varied set of responsibilities, including talking to unit and departmental heads to understand their training needs, consolidating training needs, planning Courses based on such demand, liaising with instructors, training providers and facilitators to organize the training event, managing related billing and accounting, on following up Courses, and managing certification processes.

▶ **Calendar-driven:** This involves planning Courses based on the availability of instructors and resources, and periodic activities such as drawing up the training calendar for the year or quarter. Also included is a definite set of activities that should precede and succeed a training Course.

▶ **Workflow-driven:** The work, which involves liaising with several different people and organizations, is time-driven and workflow driven. So, it's quite common that the training administrator spends a lot of time communicating with people via phone or email.

How Many Training Administrators Do Companies Need?

There are almost always two to three main training administrators who take care of critical activities such as designing and maintaining the Course catalog, handling exceptions, assigning costs, and sending invoices. Larger companies have a second set of training administrators who handle the day-to-day activities. Such administrators are sometimes referred to as field administrators.

2.3.1 Administrator Collaboration

A basic thread seen through all these characteristics is that the job of the training administrator is highly *collaborative*. The training administrator works with different sets of people and organizations on a day-to-day basis. He collaborates with his department members to work on training strategies and directives, deliver training plans, etc. He also works with line managers and individual learners to assess training needs, provide consulting, and offer support on appropriate training Courses (Figure 2.4).

A majority of his interactions also relate to managing resources for the Courses that are conducted — internal facilities management and IT departments, printing services, external venue providers, etc.

Apart from this, a training administrator also works closely with certain specialists, subject experts, and Courseware designers for preparing Course materials, external training providers, and content vendors.

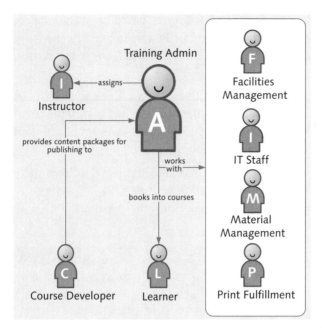

Figure 2.4 The Training Administrator Collaborates with Various Other Roles Every Day

Outsourcing the Training Administrator Function

Some companies outsource the day-to-day training administration function to a *business process outsourcing* (BPO) company. In such cases, the main administrators may be employees of the customer and the administrators who handle day-to-day activities may be employees of the outsourcing company. A training administrator of the outsourcing company may work out of a shared services center in another city or country, and he may work in shifts and share tasks. SAP Enterprise Learning and SAP Learning Solution are designed to handle such situations.

Now let's look at the role of the manager.

2.4   The Manager

Optimizing internal talent is increasingly becoming a prime focus area for organizations worldwide. Managers have a bigger role in planning and executing talent optimization programs, and they are responsible for assessing the talent potential in their teams. They are also responsible for identifying appropriate development programs and learning opportunities for improving their teams' capabilities.

The spectrum of activities that managers engage in covers strategic activities such as identifying key competencies needed for their team, planning ways of improving them, and performing tactical activities such as booking individuals to Courses.

Managers perform the following learning-related tasks with the help of tools provided by SAP Enterprise Learning (Figure 2.5).

▶ Review employees' training information such as current qualifications and training history

▶ Perform profile match-ups to see the gaps in the qualifications of employees

▶ Assign Courses as mandatory for employees

▶ Book employees directly in Courses

▶ Pre-book employees in unscheduled Courses

▶ Approve Course participation requests from employees

▶ Approve Course cancellation requests from employees

▶ Analyze employee training using business intelligence software

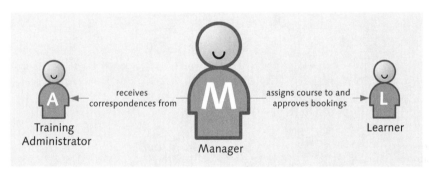

Figure 2.5 The Manager Interacts with the Training Administrator and the Learner

2.4.1 Tools Used by a Manager

A manager uses the *Manager Self-Service Portal* to perform all the learning-related tasks. Analysis is done using *Business Intelligence* software displayed within the Manager Self-Service Portal. We will talk about these tools in Chapter 5.

In addition, the manager usually interacts with the learner while performing learning-related tasks.

Next we need to look at the role of the content author.

2.5　The Content Author

Web-based Courses are created by an experienced team of people comprised of instructional designers, visual designers, HTML programmers, and content integrators. In most cases, such Web-based Courses are created by an external team working with the content development tools of their choice and then such Courses are imported into the SAP Enterprise Learning Authoring Environment for minor modifications or updates. If the online Course is a test, it is created using the Authoring Environment without the help of any other external tools. (The details of content and Authoring Environment are covered in Chapter 8.)

The content author creates online tests and modifies existing Course content in the Content Management System. In most cases, he is more of a content integrator than an instructional designer or subject matter expert. However, in rare cases, the instructional designer or the subject matter expert directly uses the Authoring Environment to create the Course content and thus may take on the role of a content author (Figure 2.6).

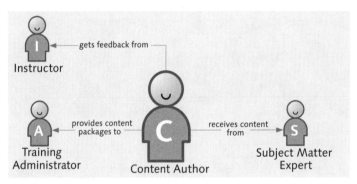

Figure 2.6　The Content Author Works with the Subject Matter Expert, Training Administrator, and Instructor

2.5.1　Tools Used by the Content Author

The content author uses the Authoring Environment to import, modify, and publish content to the Content Management System. We will talk about this tool in more detail in Chapter 8.

The Authoring Environment

The Authoring Environment (AE) was built for Course authors to create e-learning Courses. We have observed that content authors from companies that do not have an established content creation team use the AE to create content. However, companies that already have an established content creation team use third-party content creation tools, but they still use the AE to publish the content to the Content Management System.

In addition to the AE content authors use the *Repository Explorer* to check in and check out content packages from the Content Management System. The content author obviously collaborates with instructional designers, subject matter experts, and content administrators.

So now let's review the role of the content administrator

2.6   The Content Administrator

In a typical organization, hundreds of Web-based Courses are delivered from the Learning Management System. The content files associated with these Courses are called *content packages*. These content packages need to be acquired from internal authors and external vendors; they need to be published in the Content Management System and made available for training administrators, so they can deliver them as Web-based Courses. When there are updated versions of these online Courses, the updated content needs to be published in the appropriate location in the Content Management System and the training administrator needs to be informed about the updates. Such important tasks are carried out by the content administrator. The content administrator publishes and manages online Course content in the Content Management System (Figure 2.7).

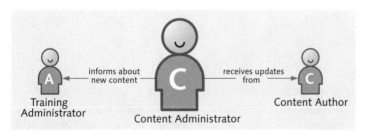

Figure 2.7   The Content Administrator Works with the Content Author and the Training Administrator

Almost all organizations have employees who are connected from an office with a low-bandwidth network connection. Such employees may not be able to download large Web-based Courses via the network. So, administrators create a content package and send the package to the employee via a CD or other removable media. The content administrator prepares such content packages for offline distribution to users connected via a low bandwidth network connection. For better control, it is recommended that the number of content administrators should be minimal.

2.6.1 Tools Used by the Content Administrator

Content administrators use the Authoring Environment, the Repository Explorer, and the *Publish Course Content* feature in the Training Administrator Portal, which we will discuss in Chapter 8.

In addition to using the appropriate tools content administrators also collaborate with content authors and third-party vendors to acquire Course content. They work with content developers and product teams to troubleshoot problems, and work with training administrators to update the necessary Courses with the latest version of the content.

This concludes the overview of the major roles in SAP Enterprise Learning, the tools they use, and the primary groups they collaborate with. As mentioned, all of these tools will be covered in more detail in later chapters.

2.7 More Resources on This Topic

More information on roles can be found at *http://help.sap.com*. SAP Enterprise Learning product teams maintain training material to explain roles and their configurations, so reach out to your SAP consultants to access such in-depth training material.

2.8 Summary

As you learned in this chapter, the main roles in planning and executing a training event are the learner, the instructor, the training administrator, the content author, the content administrator, and the manager. It is important that people in these roles interact with each other and with other people in the organization to get things done, and that they use the appropriate tools in SAP Enterprise Learning to support the tasks. In the next chapter we'll talk about the SAP Enterprise Learning architecture.

SAP Enterprise Learning is much more than a learning management system. It has components to create learning content, manage learning, and help users of the system perform their tasks efficiently. It also has enterprise services to integrate with other learning systems such as Questionmark Perception and SkillSoft. The technical architecture enables multiple deployment options serving small and large learner populations.

3   SAP Enterprise Learning Architecture

The SAP Enterprise Learning architecture is based on the architecture of SAP ERP HCM, which is the SAP solution for managing people working for an organization. SAP ERP HCM is part of SAP ERP but it can be deployed separately from the other ERP applications to protect sensitive employee data.

SAP ERP HCM is split into three layers of applications. The HCM core applications make up the foundation, which implement the core HR processes such as organizational management, personnel administration, payroll, personal development, and time management. They provide data and functions, which are reused by HCM extension applications to support additional processes like *e-Recruiting* and *Enterprise Learning*. HCM service delivery applications enable users to interact with the HCM applications.

3.1   SAP Enterprise Learning Product Architecture

The Learning Management System (LMS) provides the capability to administer, deliver, and track training activities of an organization. The LMS is the heart of SAP Enterprise Learning. The LMS stores information about Course Types, Courses schedules, learner enrollments, and training history. The LMS is accessed by administrators using the Administrator Portal, by learners using the Learning Portal, and by instructors using the Instructor Portal (Figure 3.1).

Online content is created using the *Authoring Environment* (LSOAE) and stored in a Content Management System. A learner launches online Courses using a *Content Player*, or when a learner is not connected to the network, the Courses can be viewed offline using the *Offline Player* component.

When a Course is conducted in a Virtual Learning Room, the Adobe Connect component is used. SAP Enterprise Learning includes SAP Learning Solution 6.04 and Adobe Connect. We'll talk about this in detail in Chapter 7.

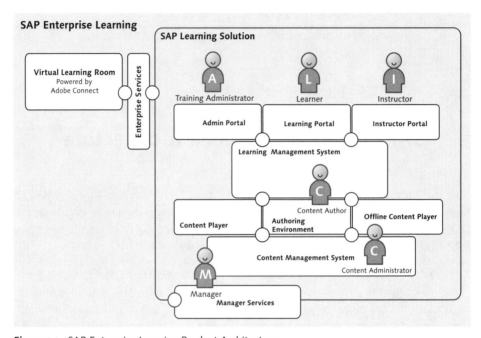

Figure 3.1 SAP Enterprise Learning Product Architecture

3.2 SAP Enterprise Learning Technical Architecture

SAP Enterprise Learning provides flexible installation and integration options. The distributed system architecture is designed for and enables a scalable solution. Knowledge of the communication channels and an understanding of the relationships between the individual components are important to select the optimum system landscape for your organization. Figure 3.2 provides an overview of the technical system architecture of SAP Enterprise Learning.

RFC and HTTP handle the communication between the individual components, which enables you to distribute the components on multiple servers and thus safeguard individual communication channels and servers specifically.

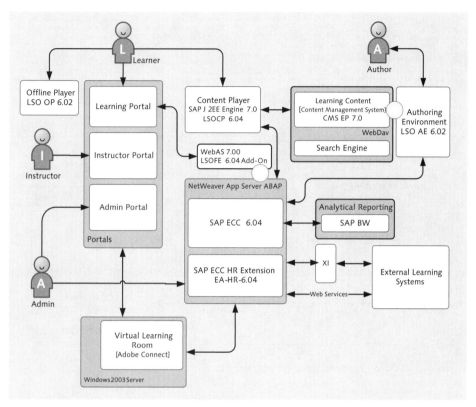

Figure 3.2 Technical System Architecture of SAP Enterprise Learning

If there are no critical security requirements, you can combine all components on one server. The advantage of using a distributed system landscape is that it enables you to maximize security for individual components. The advantage of using a single server is that it enables you to reduce costs.

3.2.1 Learning Portal (LSOFE)

The *Learning Portal* (LSOFE) is the entry point for learners in SAP Learning Solution. The Learning Portal can be called directly by the SAP Web AS or it can be integrated as an iView in SAP Enterprise Portal. Figure 3.3 provides an overview of the technical system landscape for the Learning Portal.

The learner requires a user ID in SAP Web AS. No special authorizations are required for the user because the frontend does not contain a persistence layer. All data is stored in the ERP system.

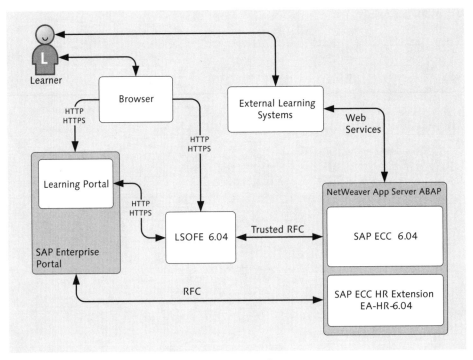

Figure 3.3 Technical Architecture of the Learning Portal

Configuration Settings

▶ **Browser**

  ▶ JavaScript must be active.

  ▶ SAP Web AS requires cookies for session handling.

  ▶ HTTP 1.1 is strongly recommended.

▶ **SAP Enterprise Portal**

  ▶ It may be necessary to map users between the user in the SAP Enterprise Portal and the Web AS user.

  ▶ You must maintain the RFC connection with the ERP system.

▶ **SAP ERP**

  ▶ Trusted relationship is required between SAP Web AS and the ERP system.

  ▶ If you want to implement the Objective Setting and Appraisals component, an HTTP/HTTPS channel is also required.

3.2.2 Instructor Role in the SAP Enterprise Portal

The *Business Package for Instructor* provides a work set for instructors in SAP Enterprise Learning. The following graphic provides an overview of the technical system landscape for the business package in the SAP Enterprise Portal (Figure 3.4).

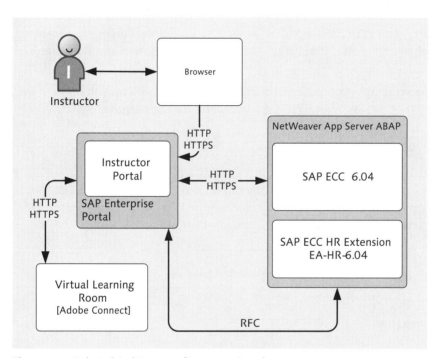

Figure 3.4 Technical Architecture of Instructor Portal

An instructor requires a user ID in the SAP Enterprise Portal and a user ID in the ERP system. The portal user must be assigned to the user in the ERP system. The role com.sap.pct.erp.instructor.instructor must be assigned to the portal user. The user in the ERP system must have the authorizations as described in the SAP_HR_LSO_INSTRUCTOR role template. All data is stored in the ERP system.

Configuration Settings

▶ **Browser**

  ▶ Java script must be active.

  ▶ SAP Web AS requires cookies for session handling.

  ▶ HTTP 1.1 is strongly recommended.

▶ **SAP Enterprise Portal**

- ▶ It is necessary to map users between the user in the SAP Enterprise Portal and the SAP Web AS user.

- ▶ You must maintain the RFC connection with the ERP system.

▶ **SAP ERP**

- ▶ If you want to use collaboration in the SAP Enterprise Portal, you must have configured the RFC connection between the ERP system and the Enterprise Portal.

- ▶ If you want to use an external collaboration server, you must set up the *Simple Object Access Protocol* (SOAP) connection for the purpose.

3.2.3 Content Player (LSOCP)

The *Content Player* (LSOCP) is called using a URL from the Learning Portal to play *Web-based training* (WBT) Courses. The Content Player does not have a persistence layer. It reads data from and writes all data to the ERP system. Figure 3.5 provides an overview of the technical system landscape for the Content Player.

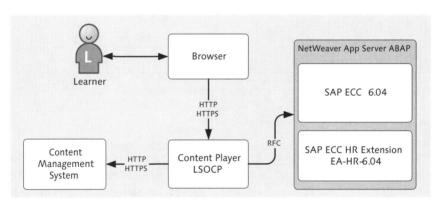

Figure 3.5 Technical Architecture of the Content Player

Configuration Settings

▶ **Browser**

- ▶ JavaScript must be active.

- ▶ Java Virtual Machine (VM) must be active.

- ▶ SUN Java Plug-In 1.4.2 must be installed (but only if you want to use tests created with LSO Test Author).

- HTTP 1.1 is strongly recommended.
- Cookies are required for Session Handling.

3.3 Offline Player (LSOOP)

The *Offline Player* (LSOOP) enables you to play instructional content offline without network access. It reads the instructional content and synchronizes the learner's progress using the Content Player. Instructional content and learning progress are stored in the local file system. In the standard system, this is the learner's home directory.

Figure 3.6 provides an overview of the technical system landscape for the Offline Player.

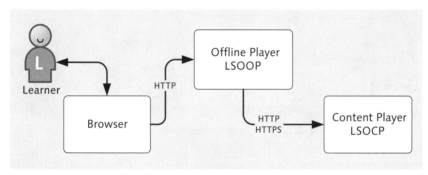

Figure 3.6 Technical Architecture of the Offline Player

Configuration Settings

- **Browser**
    - JavaScript must be active.
    - Java Virtual Machine (VM) must be active.
    - SUN Java Plug-In 1.4.2 must be installed (but only if you want to use tests created with LSO Test Author).
    - HTTP 1.1 is strongly recommended.
    - Cookies are required for session handling.
    - LSOOP
    - Java 2 SDK 1.4.2 must be installed

3.3.1 Authoring Environment (LSOAE)

The *Authoring Environment* (LSOAE) must be installed locally on the author's PC. The Authoring Environment can be used online or offline. In online mode, a connection is required to the ERP system and the Content Management System. If you use it in offline mode, all data is stored in the local file system. You can choose the directory in which to store data. The data comprises Course content and configuration data. You can protect this data at the operating system level. Figure 3.7 provides an overview of the technical system landscape for the Authoring Environment.

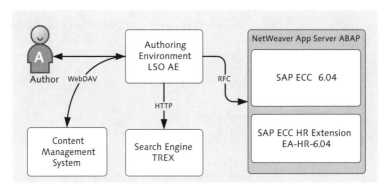

Figure 3.7 Technical Architecture of the Authoring Environment

The Authoring Environment contains a special version of the Content Player, which plays Course content locally. Similar to the Offline Player, you cannot use this local Content Player remotely. You can only call it from the computer on which it is installed.

Configuration Settings

▶ **Browser**

  ▶ Internal ArchiveX objects must be activated.

  ▶ JavaScript must be active.

  ▶ Java Virtual Machine (VM) must be active.

  ▶ SUN Java Plug-In from version 1.4.2 must be installed (but only if you want to use tests created with LSO Test Author).

  ▶ HTTP 1.1 is strongly recommended.

  ▶ Cookies are required for session handling.

▸ **LSOAE**

  ▸ Java JRE 1.4.2 or JRE 1.5.0 must be installed.

3.3.2 Environment for the Training Administrator

The SAP GUI transactions required for the training administrator role are available in the ERP system. The *Business Package for Course Administrator* contains multiple work sets that Course administrators can use to access the relevant SAP GUI transactions in ERP systems. Figure 3.8 provides an overview of the technical system landscape for the business package in the Enterprise Portal.

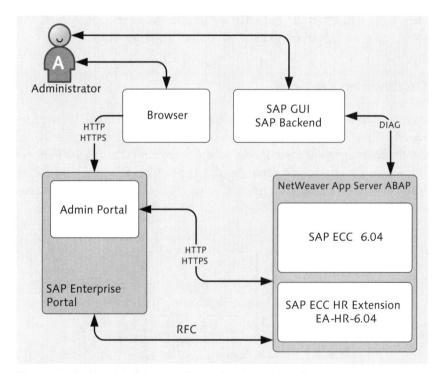

Figure 3.8 Technical Architecture of the Administrator Portal

A Course administrator requires a user in the SAP Enterprise Portal and a user in the ERP system. The portal user must be assigned to the user in the ERP system.

The role `com.sap.pct.erp.tradmin.training_administrator` must be assigned to the portal user.

3.3.3   Content Management

Learning content needs to be stored and managed; therefore, a content management system is mandatory. The following options are available.

▶ Part of the standard delivery of the SAP Learning Solution is the Content Management System from the Knowledge Management platform of Enterprise Portal.

▶ Due to the open architecture, WebDAV Level 2-compliant Server can be seamlessly integrated as a Content Management System.

3.3.4   TREX Text Retrieval and Information Extraction

TREX is the search engine to find Courses in the Content Management System. SAP Learning Solution 6.04 requires SAP NetWeaver 04S (includes TREX 6.1).

3.4   Deployment Options

SAP Learning Solution allows a user to set up a system landscape to suit his requirements. Generally, SAP recommends that a customer installs the Enterprise Portal and the Content Management System on a separate machine. The Adobe Connect software is installed in a separate server, which is not included in the following discussions. Please see Chapter 7, Virtual Learning Room, for system landscape details on Adobe Connect (Figure 3.9).

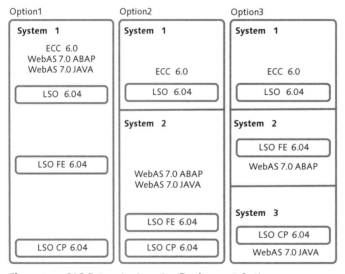

Figure 3.9   SAP Enterprise Learning Deployment Options

▶ **Option 1**

With Option 1, all components are installed on one machine, which reduces initial costs. Such a system landscape is particularly suitable for test systems or smaller installations. This option is less secure than the other options.

▶ **Option 2**

Option 2 installs the Content Player and the LSO frontend component on a separate *Web Application Server* (WAS) on a separate machine. The LSO backend system is installed separately. Two machines carry the burden, which improves system performance. This type of installation lets you set up a firewall between the two systems for increased security.

▶ **Option 3**

With Option 3, the Content Player, the LSO frontend component and the LSO backend are each installed on separate machines. Security aspects play a role here and, more importantly, improved performance thanks to the system distribution. Ultimately, however, each administrator will have to optimize for the three major aspects of security, performance, and costs. The final decision will depend on the enterprise's specific requirements.

3.5 Deployment Best Practices and Recommendations

The choice of the deployment option depends on the following factors:

▶ Purpose of the system

▶ Number of concurrent users expected

▶ Expected content size

▶ Required uptime

Once these parameters are known, the deployment options can be decided. There are no real rules for the deployment; however, here are some recommendations.

3.5.1 Purpose of the System: Development Box

Deployment Option: Option 1

Reason: Development box is primarily used by functional analysts and development team members. This number of concurrent users is usually low and the required uptime for this server is not high.

3.5.2 Purpose of the System: Quality Assurance

Deployment Option: Option 2

Reason: This box is primarily used by quality assurance (QA) team to ensure that the configurations and the custom development work function as expected. Typically, these boxes are also used to perform stress testing by simulating the expected number of concurrent users.

3.5.3 Purpose of the System: User Acceptance

Deployment Option: Option 2

Reason: This box is primarily used by the end users to perform User Acceptance Testing. For the system to have reasonable performance during the User Acceptance Testing, utilize deployment option 2.

3.5.4 Purpose of the System: Production

Deployment Option: Option 3

Reason: Production environment requires the best possible deployment configuration. Due to the performance requirements and the uptime requirements, utilize deployment option 3.

3.5.5 Purpose of the System: Disaster Recovery

Deployment Option: Option 3

Reason: Disaster Recovery environment typically mirrors the production environment. The performance must be on par with the production environment if the Disaster Recovery environment must be used.

As previously mentioned, the final deployment option depends on the exact requirements and the budget allocated for the system.

3.6 More Resources

More information about the technical architecture of SAP Enterprise Learning can be found in the following documents and locations.

References

SAP Architecture Blue Book – SAP ERP HCM authored by Sagar Joshi and edited by Jochen Boeder.

Online help for SAP Enterprise Learning: *http://help.sap.com*. Click Search Documentation and then search for SAP Enterprise Learning Technical Architecture.

SAP Notes

SAP Notes on sizing Notes 1136880, 746917, and 1063932

3.7 Summary

As we learned in this chapter, the SAP Enterprise Learning application supports three main use cases: creation, publication, and delivery of e-learning content; organization of training Courses; and learner activities. Within each scenario, different components of SAP Enterprise Learning are involved. The LMS handles the organization of Courses and management of training activities of users. The portals and the Virtual Learning Room provide interfaces for all users to interact with the system and with each other. The Authoring Environment, the Content Management System, and the Content Player handle the creation, storage, and delivery of e-learning content. There are three deployment options for SAP Enterprise Learning system landscape, depending on your needs: number of concurrent users, desired level of security and content size, and required uptime. In the next chapter we'll look at how SAP Enterprise Learning integrates with other SAP applications.

3.8 Contributors

Seshatalpasai 'Sesh' Madala and Jason Ichen contributed to this chapter. Sesh is with the SAP Enterprise Learning development team. Jason is an SAP Enterprise Learning consultant. Jason can be reached at *Jason.Ichen@learn2perform.com*.

Learning is essential for employee development, and the management of personnel planning and development is done using applications that reside within SAP ERP HCM. SAP Enterprise Learning has several integration points with such applications, but deploying the integrations is not essential. However, putting such integrations to use will help you derive more value from SAP Enterprise Learning.

4   Integration of SAP Enterprise Learning

SAP Enterprise Learning is fully integrated with SAP ERP HCM and other relevant SAP applications, facilitating end-to-end learning management processes. You can integrate and use Enterprise Learning effectively with these HCM applications:

- **Organizational Management**: Organizational units can be directly booked as attendees to Courses and can also serve as organizers of Courses.

- **Personnel Administration**: People or employees from the SAP HR master data record can be booked as attendees or they can serve as instructors or tutors to Courses.

- **Time Management**: Attendance records can be automatically created for learners' participation in Courses. Compatibility and time-availability checks can be carried out for employees and instructors.

- **Personnel Development**: Qualifications can be defined and checked as prerequisites to Courses and can be transferred to attendees as end results of successful participation in Courses. Learners can also use the appraisal functions of the Personnel Development component for appraising Courses through the Learning Portal.

In addition, EL can be integrated with other SAP components, including:

- **Cost Accounting:** Attendance and instructor fees can be settled using Internal Activity Allocation. The cost center of learners and instructors can be directly used for allocating Course and instructor fees.

- **Sales and Distribution**: Attendance fees can be billed and customers and contact persons can be booked as attendee types.

▶ **Materials Management**: Materials from the *Material Master* can be reserved as resources for Courses; purchase requisitions and material reservations can be generated.

▶ **SAP Knowledge Warehouse**: Training materials and documentation can be attached directly as supplementary materials to Courses and can be accessed from the Learning Portal.

▶ **SAP Appointment Calendar**: When employees are booked as attendees or instructors for events, these appointments can be automatically generated in the SAP Appointment Calendar.

Integration with these components is optional, because you can easily use SAP Enterprise Learning as a standalone option without availing of the advantages offered by such integration. These additional integration points, including talent management, will be discussed in Chapter 6, Training Administration.

4.1 Integration of SAP Enterprise Learning with HCM Application Components

From an SAP Enterprise Learning and backend HCM perspective, there are three key integration areas that you can use: *Personnel Administration* (PA), *Organizational Management* (OM), and *Personnel Development* (PD), including *Qualifications*, *Appraisals*, and *Development Plans*. So, let's begin by looking at integration with Personnel Administration. Within SAP ERP HCM, Personnel Administration supports the management of employee-specific data, such as the employee's name, date of hire, location within an enterprise, work assignment, benefits eligibility, Social Security number, educational and previous work experience, and much more. From an SAP Enterprise Learning perspective, not all of this data is required, but a few data elements are mandatory to support an implementation. These elements create a "mini-master" of data surrounding the employee that SAP Enterprise Learning uses.

In the next section, we will look at the required elements and discuss their importance from an implementation perspective. We will also examine a few other areas of data stored in PA that customers often use but that are not required from an implementation perspective. Let's begin with *Infotypes*.

4.1.1 Infotypes

All data within PA is stored on an infotype or screen containing similar data elements. Infotypes have both a name and an assigned number that is used for reference in backend tables. All infotypes consist of header data, which identifies the employee whose data is being viewed, and the main body of data, which contains the elements that are being tracked on a particular infotype. The header data is determined by your company during configuration, so it will vary in layout and content, while the main body of data generally consists of similar fields across companies. Again, this data may vary based on an employee's country assignment and the fields your organization deems necessary.

What is an Infotype?

If you are an SAP ERP HCM user, you are already familiar with infotypes, but for those of you new to SAP, a simple example of an infotype within SAP is an Address Infotype (Infotype 0006 or IT0006), because it contains data that is familiar to everyone, regardless of your level of SAP experience. The Address Infotype is not a required infotype to support an Enterprise Learning implementation, but administrative access is sometimes requested, so training coordinators can mail information to employees, such as CDs or welcome packages. The infotype specifically consists of a header and the main body of data.

Action Infotype

The first infotype that is required for an Enterprise Learning implementation is the *Action Infotype* (IT0000). This infotype is required for the existence of an employee within the HR database, because it assigns the employee ID or the personnel assignment number (PERNR). An Action Infotype must always exist for an active employee, because it indicates that they are viable in the system. In the standard system, only active employees may be booked to a Course. Upon termination, an employee's status changes in IT0000 and he is automatically removed from any Courses in which he has future bookings. From a data perspective, the Action Infotype consists of all organizational changes that impact an employee, such as hire and rehire actions, organizational reassignments, and termination actions. Unlike the Action Infotype, there is no specific data required on the Organizational Assignment Infotype for an employee to be able to use SAP Enterprise Learning. However, this infotype must exist for all active employees.

Organizational Assignment Infotype

A second required infotype is the *Organizational Assignment Infotype* (IT0001). This infotype indicates an employee's location within the organization both from an *Enterprise Structure* perspective and from an *Organizational Structure* perspective.

Enterprise Structure

Enterprise Structure data typically places your employee in a hierarchy based on personnel administration requirements, time management requirements, and payroll requirements. Generally, Enterprise Structure data does not drive training processes, but this is not always the case. For example, an organization may have decided to represent bargaining units within its Enterprise Structure and this could lead to training requirements for the members of a bargaining unit.

Organizational Structure

Organizational Structure data typically represents your organizational breakdowns within a company. The organizational unit an employee is assigned to generally represents departmental or budget unit breakdowns; the job an employee is assigned to generally represents classification from a legal and compensation perspective; and the position an employee is assigned to represents a budgeted post from a headcount perspective. These elements often drive training as all employees within a particular department or job may require similar training. Organizational Structure data also represents reporting relationships within SAP and thus drives workflow approvals. Finally, it is generally used to track cost center information and so it is used for charging or allocating Course fees. This is addressed in more detail in the training administration chapter.

Personal Data Infotype

A third required Infotype is the *Personal Data Infotype* (IT0002). This infotype stores an employee's name, his date of birth, his identification number (e.g., Social Security number), and possibly other data such as marital status. From an SAP Enterprise Learning perspective, this information is required for identification purposes on a roster (employee name) and this infotype must also exist for all active employees.

Communications Infotype

The final required infotype is the *Communications Infotype* (IT0105). Unlike the previously listed infotypes, IT0105 is not required for all active employees. However, it is required if an employee wishes to access the Learning Portal. Infotype 0105 links an employee to his User ID information, so when he accesses the Learning Portal, the training activities and progress he makes as a learner are associated with his personnel identification number within SAP. The email address is also maintained on IT0105, which is useful if you use the system to send automatic email notifications, such as booking confirmations, to attendees.

4.1.2 Additional Infotypes

Other infotypes that may be used by SAP Enterprise Learning are identified in Table 4.1, along with their typical usage. Please note that these infotypes are not absolutely essential for learning but may provide useful information to your administrator.

Note
Qualifications Profile data (IT0024) is not listed because it is discussed in detail later in this chapter.

Name	Number	Data Elements	Usage
Address	IT0006	Home address Emergency Address Mailing Address	Training Coordinators may require view access to this infotype to access mailing address information to send Course-related materials.
Education	IT0022	Name of previous educational institutions, years attended, degrees, graduation date	Organizations may require this information for educational reporting (e.g., for output in a CV).
Date Specifications	IT0041	Key dates in an employee's lifecycle — date types will vary by company. Examples include most recent hire date, last pay date, benefits eligibility date.	Dates may be used to trigger required training (e.g., book all new hires).

Table 4.1 Additional Infotypes

4.2 Organizational Management

As mentioned in the previous section, the Organizational Structure data typically represents your organizational breakdowns within a company, including organizational unit, job, and position, as well as reporting relationships and cost center assignments (Figure 4.1). All of this data is managed within *Organizational Management* (OM).

Elements such as organizational units, jobs, positions, and cost centers are known as *objects*. Each Organizational object has its own assigned letter abbreviation as shown in Table 4.2, as well as specific infotypes. The infotypes contain groupings of related data elements, just as infotypes in Personnel Administration do.

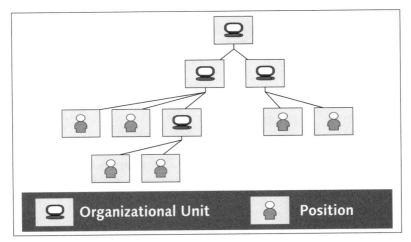

Figure 4.1 Organizational Structure

Object	Abbreviation
Organizational Unit	O
Job	C
Position	S
Cost Center	K

Table 4.2 Each Organizational Entity is Represented by a One-Letter Code in SAP ERP HCM

From an OM perspective, all OM objects are managed in one of the following two ways:

▶ Expert Mode Detailed Maintenance (Transaction PP01)

▶ Organization and Staffing Interface (Transaction PPOME)

The detailed maintenance mode allows you to view all objects and their related infotypes on a one-at-a-time basis, while the Organization and Staffing interface allows you to create and maintain objects via a hierarchical and tab-based interface. Because the Organization and Staffing interface is highly customizable and has good usability, you should use it whenever possible.

4.2.1   Organizational Management and Enterprise Learning

From an SAP Enterprise Learning perspective, OM is not required, but it does provide multiple benefits to the functionality of the solution. Specifically, organizational data in SAP Enterprise Learning supports workflow for Course bookings/cancellations, reporting requirements, cost and activity allocation functions for Course fees, and the ability to personalize training based on Organizational Assignment, so mandatory training appears for an employee based on his role and location in the company.

All of these functions can be managed without OM, but this would require that you perform nonstandard enhancements to the system. For example, you can support workflow using custom tables, rather than the organizational structure. Cost and Activity allocation functionality has several function modules that can be used to derive cost center information without using the Organizational Structure, and a BAdI can be used to arrive at the Mandatory Training for a learner. However, these customizations will extend the time of your implementation and require additional enhancements as you work to grow your solution. So, it is always recommended that you implement OM and use it for your SAP Enterprise Learning implementation.

Let's look at how the basic OM objects are generally used from an Enterprise Learning perspective. We will cover how these objects will relate to qualifications in Section 4.3, Personnel Development.

4.2.2   Organizational Units

Organizational Units represent departments or budget units within an organization. They are structured hierarchically in the system to illustrate your company's organizational reporting structure. Organizational units may represent budgeted units or cost centers. However, this is not required, because a separate, cost center–based structure is maintained in SAP ERP Financials application.

The cost centers from the SAP ERP Financials structure may be linked to one or many organizational units, or they may be linked at the position level, as discussed later. As mentioned earlier, an Organizational Unit is often used to manage charge-back processes.

Using standard functionality, when a learner books a class that has a fee attached, the system checks for his cost center (to charge) first at the position level and then at the organizational unit level. It continues up the organizational unit structure until it finds a valid cost center to charge. An Organizational Unit also provides reporting and administrative functionality.

> **Example**
>
> To book all persons within an Organizational Unit, you may use the *Book List* function-
> ality and select the option *Employee List*. Then you can book all attendees within a
> selected organizational unit.

An Organizational Unit also provides reporting and administrative functionality. You may generate reports that contain organizational unit data, such as the delivered roster report. You may also run some reports by organizational unit. One particular report many companies request is a report on all employees within an organizational unit who have not taken a specified Course. Although not delivered, this report may be created using SAP Query leveraging the organizational structure.

One of the biggest advantages the organizational unit provides is the ability to create mandatory training assignments for all members of an organizational unit. Mandatory Courses may also be specified for jobs, positions, and directly to individuals. An individual in your company have mandatory Courses assigned to each of these elements. When this Learner logs onto the Learning Portal, he will be alerted to his mandatory Courses via the Messages and Notes section. The alerts will stop when he takes appropriate action – that is, when he books the mandatory Courses or when he transfers out of the organizational elements that are pushing the Courses to him. If the Learner cancels a mandatory Course without completing it, the Course continues to show as mandatory in the Learning Portal (Figure 4.2).

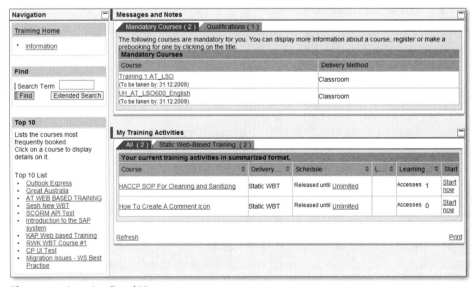

Figure 4.2 Learning Portal View

For example, a sales employee may have "Code of Conduct" pushed to him as mandatory in the Learning Portal through his organizational unit. Because of his sales role, he may also see "Selling Skills" pushed to him as mandatory by his job. He may also see a product specific Course in Messages and Notes based on his position assignment and a development class that his manager pushed to him directly. If this employee were to transfer to a new role, with a new job classification and departmental assignment, all of the mandatory classes would disappear from the Messages and Notes section of the Learning Portal except for the developmental class his manager pushed to him directly.

To create a mandatory assignment to an organizational unit (or a job or position), the administrator can indicate, via the Relationships Infotype (IT1001), that the Course Type is *Mandatory for* (relationship A/B 0615) the organizational unit. Figure 4.3 illustrates this process for a Job. Note that the start and end validity periods of this relationship are taken as the period of the mandatory assignment – the period in which the learner should act on the mandatory assignment.

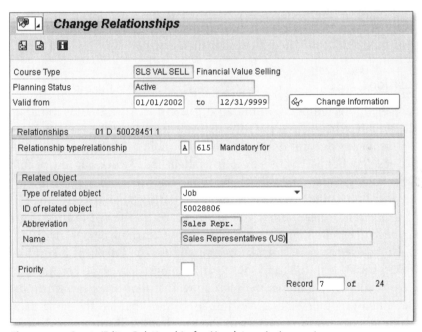

Figure 4.3 Create/Edit a Relationship for Mandatory Assignment

> **Note**
>
> It is important to note that, as delivered, if you make training mandatory for all persons within an organizational unit, the mandatory relationship does not flow down to subordinate organizational units. In other words, heredity is not a delivered function of the mandatory relationship.

Now we will look at two other types of OM objects — *Jobs* and *Positions*.

4.2.3 Jobs

Jobs are often described as classifications of positions. In SAP ERP HCM, Jobs are used to default pay scales or grades to employees and to provide Equal Employment Opportunity (EEO) or other classification information, as required in some countries. They are also used extensively from a Qualifications Management perspective, as we will discuss in the next section. From an Enterprise Learning perspective, Jobs may be used to mark mandatory training for everyone assigned to a particular Job. However, because Jobs are often defined during an initial SAP implementation, they are rarely defined with training requirements in mind. For that reason, very few companies are able to use them to push mandatory training.

4.2.4 Positions

Positions are the budgeted posts within an organization. As a rule of thumb, a Position should never have more than the equivalent of one full-time employee holding it. This means one full-time employee may hold a Position or two part-time employees may hold a Position as long as their hours work out to one full-time employee. But generally a Position should not have more than one full-time employee holder assigned to it. When an employee transfers out of a Position, this should create a vacancy that another employee can be transferred into or that a new employee may be hired into. From an Enterprise Learning perspective, Positions may also be used to mark mandatory training for the holder of a Position. Just as with Organizational Units and Jobs, if an employee leaves the Position that was marked as mandatory training, the training will no longer appear as mandatory for that employee, unless he moves into a position that has the same mandatory training. Using this functionality at the position level can be very useful when you have a position that requires specific skills, regardless of who holds the Position. However, if there are multiple training requirements that are required by a group of related Positions, it can be difficult to maintain these requirements, because you must keep the many relationships current.

The next integration point with SAP Enterprise Learning and SAP ERP HCM is Personnel Development.

4.3 Personnel Development

The Personnel Development component of SAP ERP HCM is used to view and maintain details related to a staff member's development history. This application includes many different functions, which we will review in this section.

4.3.1 Personnel Planning

The Personnel Planning functionality in SAP ERP HCM supports employee development functions used by SAP Enterprise Learning through:

▶ The tracking of competencies and certifications (Qualification Management)

▶ The ability to use sophisticated level one evaluations (Performance Management)

▶ The ability to include training requirements as an element of employee growth in either development plans or in employee appraisals (Development Plans and Performance Management).

Although none of these elements are required to implement SAP Enterprise Learning, each enhances the delivered functionality significantly.

4.3.2 Qualifications

Qualifications within SAP represent both the requirements of the position an employee holds and the skills or competencies the employee possesses. When discussing qualifications at the position level, they are called *Requirements*. When discussing qualifications as attained by an employee, they are referred to as *Qualifications*. Requirements and Qualifications are both represented by a single element, the *qualification* object (object type 'Q'), which is maintained within the *Qualifications Catalog*, accessed via Transaction OOQA.

The Qualifications Catalog is a structure that allows you to categorize qualifications within major groupings known as Qualifications Groups (object type 'QK'). Generally, similar qualifications are found within the same Qualifications Group. Within each Qualifications Group, there may be multiple sub-groupings, also represented by Qualifications Groups (Figure 4.4).

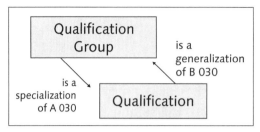

Figure 4.4 Relationship Between Qualifications and Qualifications Groups

4.3.3 Proficiency

Each Qualifications Group has a *Proficiency Scale* assigned to it, which is inherited by subordinate Qualifications Groups and by subordinate Qualifications. At the subordinate Qualifications Group level, the inherited proficiency scale may be overridden. However, at the subordinate Qualifications level, the standard system does not allow you to override the inherited proficiency scale, so all Qualifications within a single Qualifications Group will have the same Proficiency Scale. Proficiency Scales as used by Qualifications are always quantity scales. This means they are subjective evaluation scales, as opposed to point-driven or percentage-driven scales. A straightforward illustration of a section of the Qualifications Catalog with an associated proficiency is the example of Languages. In this model, the superordinate Qualifications Group is *Languages*. Subordinate to Languages are three Qualifications: English, Chinese, and German. The proficiency scale associated with Languages is illustrated in Table 4.3.

Proficiency	Proficiency Text
1	Ability to understand
2	Ability to speak
3	Ability to speak and read
4	Fluent

Table 4.3 Proficiency Levels Used for Qualifications Associated with Language Proficiency

Proficiency Scale

The scale starts at the level *Ability to understand*. From a business perspective, an organization would not be interested in noting an employee's skill at a lower level than this. From a systems perspective, an employee who does not have the ability to understand a language qualification would not have the qualification associated with his profile.

Another typical scale is the *"Yes/No"* scale. This scale is often used when tracking position requirements that are critical to a job to ensure employees have the required skills. An example of this type of skill is Forklift — the requirement to safely operate and maintain a forklift. An employee whose position requires this skill must be appropriately certified in Forklift with a scale evaluation of *"Yes."* An employee would never have the scale evaluation *"No"* — the employee would simply not have the skill. For this reason, the "Yes/No" scale is defined for a qualification as a "Yes" scale. There is never a need to track a "No" proficiency. If an employee's pre-existing certification expires, it simply drops off the employee's profile or is manually end-dated or delimited.

4.3.4 Depreciation Meters and Validity Periods

In addition to Proficiencies, Qualifications may also have *Depreciation Meters* and *Validity Periods*. These attributes are associated directly with the Qualification and only one may be used per Qualification. The Depreciation Meter allows you to define a *half-life* for a Qualification (Figure 4.5). For example, if a Depreciation Meter value of 2 Years is associated with a Qualification, when that Qualification is attained by an employee, the proficiency level will be halved every two years. This functionality is not commonly used, unlike the *Validity Period* functionality (Figure 4.6).

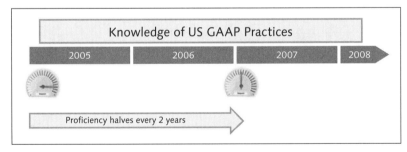

Figure 4.5 Depreciation Meter

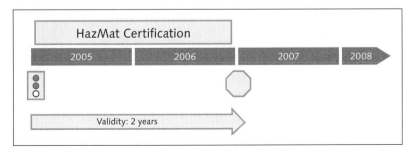

Figure 4.6 Validity Period

Validity Period allows an organization to assign a monthly or yearly period to the Qualification, which indicates when the skill will expire. For example, if an employee's position requires HazMat certification and the employee must be recertified every four years, a validity of four years is assigned to the qualification HazMat. If the employee attains the HazMat qualification on July 1, 2009, it will be placed on his record with a validity period of four years from the assignment date (i.e., the Qualification will be valid from July 1, 2009, to June 30, 2013). On June 30, 2013, the Qualification will automatically expire and the employee will be flagged as having a Qualifications deficit.

4.3.5 Maintaining Requirements and Qualifications

Now that we have an understanding of the elements of the Qualifications Catalog, let's discuss how requirements are maintained for positions and how qualifications are maintained for employees. The *Profile Maintenance* function (transaction PPPM) supports the maintenance of both *Requirements Profiles* (at the Position level) and *Qualifications Profiles* (at the Employee level). The Profile Maintenance function provides a simple interface to add qualifications and the associated proficiency to either a requirements profile or a Qualifications Profile (Figure 4.7).

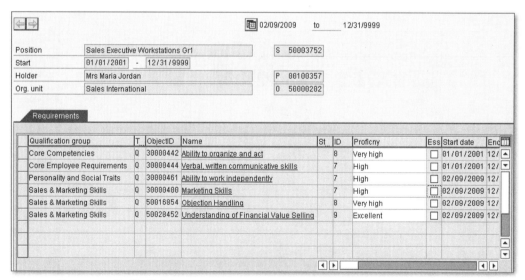

Figure 4.7 Profile Maintenance

When an organization uses qualifications, the requirements profile at the Position level is compared to the employee's Qualifications Profile to determine proficiency or skill gaps. However, requirements are not always maintained directly at the position level. Indeed, they are usually maintained a level higher, at the Job level. Requirements that are maintained at the Job level are inherited by all related positions. To help clarify this, imagine that your organization has 500 Operator positions. Each of these operators must be HazMat certified and able to Work in Confined Spaces. Both of these skills are represented as Qualifications in your Qualifications Catalog and the proficiency scale is a "Yes" scale.

Rather than creating 500 profiles for each of these operator positions with these two qualifications and the associated proficiency "Yes," plus any other relevant skills and their required proficiency, you can create a single requirements profile at the Operator Job level and these requirements and their proficiency will be inherited by all 500 positions. If a new requirement is identified for all operator positions, it can be associated with the Job as well, and the requirement will be inherited by all 500 Jobs. If one of the requirements becomes obsolete, it can be end-dated or delimited at the Job level and this action will also be inherited by all 500 positions. If you have position-specific skills, such as the ability to operate a forklift, these can be maintained at the position level and will show up in addition to any requirements that are required by the associated Job.

In addition to the Job and Position level, a requirements profile may also be tied to the object Task (object type 'T'). Tasks can be associated with Jobs or Positions and their requirements profile will be inherited by the associated entity and become part of the Position's *Requirements Profile* (Figure 4.8).

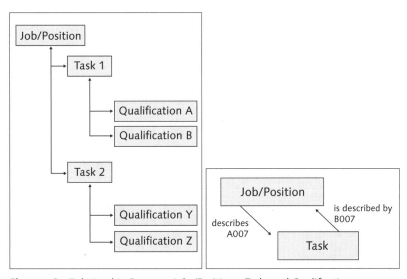

Figure 4.8   Relationship Between Jobs/Positions, Tasks and Qualifications

> **Note**
>
> In the standard system, a Requirement Profile may not be associated with an Organizational Unit.

At the Employee level, the Qualifications Profile may be maintained in the same way — via the Profile Maintenance transaction. An administrator is able to enter the Qualification the employee has attained and the appropriate proficiency. However, the Qualifications Profile may also be updated manually by the employee, via Employee Self-Service (ESS), or automatically by the system, from appraisal elements or via completion of training.

From an SAP Enterprise Learning perspective, a Qualification and an associated Proficiency may be associated with one or many Course Types. Upon successful (passing) completion of a classroom Course or a Web-based Course, the learner's profile is automatically updated. Proficiency may be passed as well, or it may be manually updated by an administrator at a later point.

4.3.6 The Profile Match-Up Report

The Profile Match-up Report (RHPEPLWR) supports the ability for an administrator to check for missing required qualifications or required qualifications on an employee's profile that are not sufficiently proficient (see Figure 4.9). Versions of this report are also available via MSS and ESS. From SAP Enterprise Learning, the learner has the ability to perform a Profile Match-up, which provides the same information. The learner then has the ability to drill down on a qualification to find and register for a Course that will impart the required qualification at the appropriate proficiency.

Display Profile Matchup

Person	Mrs Maria Jordan (00100357)
Position	Sales Executive Workstations Gr1
Key Date	02/09/2009
More Settings	Alternative qualifications were not included
	Depreciation meter was not included

Qualification group	Qualification	Essential Reqt	Required	Existing	Difference	Training
Core Competencies	Ability to organize and act	☐	Very high	Rudimentary	5-	
Core Employee Requirements	Verbal, written communicative skills	☐	High	Rudimentary	4-	
Personality and Social Traits	Ability to work independently	☐	High	Do(es) Not Exist	7-	
Sales & Marketing Skills	Marketing Skills	☐	High	Do(es) Not Exist	7-	
Sales & Marketing Skills	Objection Handling	☐	Very high	Do(es) Not Exist	8-	
Sales & Marketing Skills	Understanding of Financial Value Selling	☐	Excellent	Do(es) Not Exist	9-	

Figure 4.9 Profile Match-Up Report

4.3.7 Essential Qualification

A qualification may be flagged as *Essential* when associated with a Requirements Profile. When this is done, the Qualification appears on the front page of the Learning Portal when there is a deficit. If a Qualification is missing, does not have the appropriate proficiency level, or is expiring, it will appear in the top Messages and Notes section, on the Qualifications tab. Again, the learner then has the ability to drill down on a Qualification to find and register for a Course that will impart the required Qualification at the appropriate proficiency.

4.3.8 Development Plans

Development Plan functionality in SAP supports the ability to plan and track development activities for employees within an organization. Typically, development plans are designed to support employee growth and provide experience required to advance within a role (e.g., a Managerial Development Plan) as seen in Figure 4.10.

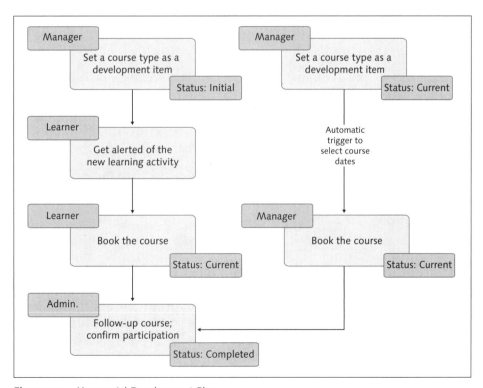

Figure 4.10 Managerial Development Plan

4.3.9 Structure of Development Plans

Development Plans are managed in a catalog structure and similar Development Plans may belong to Development Plan Groups within this catalog. Development Plans consist of a series of items, including *Location* (spending time in a specific location), *Position* (holding a specified position), *Organizational Unit* (holding a position belonging to the specified Organizational Unit), and *Course Type* (attending a class or e-learning.). Each of these items may be sequenced, associated with time frames, and/or marked as mandatory items indicating that they must be completed before the *Individual Development Plan* may be marked as completed.

Development Plans are then leveraged as *templates* when creating Individual Development Plans for employees. For this reason, customers often decide not to use development plans when attempting to track required or mandatory training, such as On-the-Job Training elements. As soon as a Development Plan's items are associated with a person, these items become part of a new object, an Individual Development Plan. As such, the Individual Development Plan can be modified (elements may be added or removed, including items from other Development Plans) and changes made to the original Development Plan will not flow down, because there is no relationship between the original Development Plan and the Individual Development Plan.

From an SAP Enterprise Learning perspective, any item within an Individual Development Plan that is training related (e.g., Course Types) will appear as Mandatory items within the Messages and Notes section of the Learning Portal. These elements will remain in this section until the learner books an associated Course or e-learning, or until the Individual Development Plan is modified.

> **Note**
>
> With the release of enhancement pack 4, a new development plan object is available with enhanced functionality

4.4 Performance Management Integration

SAP Performance Management is one of the main components of SAP's Talent Management suite of applications. It supports performance appraisal functionality as well as other types of employee evaluations.

4.4.1 Integration Points

SAP Performance Management has two key integration points with SAP Enterprise Learning. Since the initial release of the product, *Objectives Settings and Appraisals* forms may be used to create *Course Evaluations,* often referred to as *Kirkpatrick Level 1 Evaluations* or *Happy Sheets* (Figure 4.11). And with later releases, integration to Talent Management processes has been enhanced.

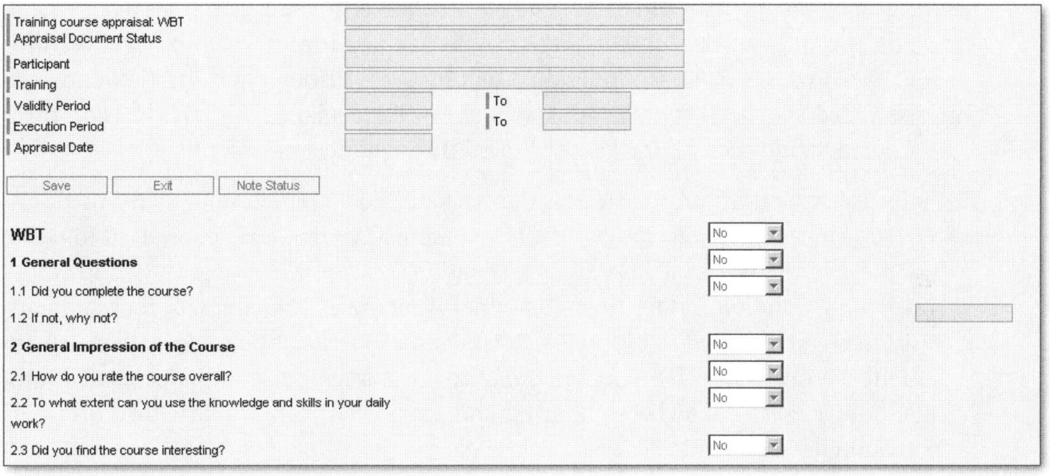

Figure 4.11 Course Evaluation Appraisals

SAP Performance Management provides a flexible framework in the Appraisal tool that helps organizations develop different appraisal templates suited for different processes, such as regular appraisal processes or other processes such as for employee potential assessment, performance improvement plans. The templates used for each of these processes govern the content of the appraisal/assessment and the process flow and control. SAP Enterprise Learning leverages a simple form of these templates to create Course Appraisals.

You can make use of SAP Enterprise Learning in several ways with SAP Performance Management to design templates that are suited for a variety of purposes.

Additionally, Courses can be added as evaluation criteria to an appraisal document. For example, an assessment sheet can be prepared for a batch of new recruits. Critical Courses that each individual will go through during induction can be added as criteria to this assessment sheet. Performance of individuals on these Courses could be tracked and rated through the assessment sheet.

As you may know, SAP Performance Management provides a flexible framework in the Appraisal tool that helps organizations develop different appraisal templates suited for different processes such as regular appraisal processes, employee potential assessments, or performance improvement plans. The templates used for each process govern the content of the appraisal/assessment as well as the process flow and control. SAP Enterprise Learning leverages a simple form of these templates to create Course Appraisals.

Additionally, Courses can be added as evaluation criteria to an appraisal document. For example, an assessment sheet can be prepared for a batch of new recruits. Critical Courses that each individual will progress through during orientation can be added as criteria to this assessment sheet. Performance of individuals on these Courses could then be tracked and rated through the assessment sheet.

Course Appraisals are created in the backend via Transaction LSO_EVAL_CATA-LOG. This takes you to a view that is very similar to the transaction used to create Objectives Setting and Appraisals evaluations, except the Category Group is SAP Learning Solution, rather than Personnel Appraisals. As delivered, these appraisals may only be used to evaluate Courses and elements of Courses (e.g., instructor delivery and materials). The functionality does not support attendee evaluations, although these could be configured and supported in the Instructor Portal, via custom development.

If you choose to use Course Evaluations for the SAP Enterprise Learning, you must turn off the old appraisal functionality. To do this, you must configure the entry *Switch on Performance Management*, entry HAP00 REPLA, in T77S0. Although the documentation indicates you can choose to switch on the new appraisal functionality for SAP Enterprise Learning alone, this is not the case. Entry values 'T' — Replace only Course Appraisal and 'A' Replace Old Appraisal System, both replace the entire system. This means you may not use old appraisal functionality if you wish to leverage Course Evaluations in the SAP Enterprise Learning. (See SAP Note 728542 for more information.)

4.4.2 Features in Enhancement Pack 4

With the release of SAP Enterprise Learning enhancement pack 4, there is enhanced integration with Performance Management. When a manager or other appraiser creates an Appraisal form, the appraiser may include Course catalog elements (Course Types) as appraisal criterion within the appraisal document. This requires that the free enhancement BAdI *Add Course from LSO* is included as an option at the Category level and assigned to the appraisal template. Once these elements are assigned as mandatory within the appraisal document, the Courses will be displayed in the Mandatory Courses tab in the Messages and Notes section of the Learning Portal.

> **Technical Requirements**
>
> To leverage this functionality, the technical requirements are: SAP ECC 6.0, SAP Enterprise Learning 6.0 enhancement pack 4, Business Function 'HCM, Performance Management 01' (HCM_OSA_CI_1), Business Function 'CA, Appraisals, Evaluations and Surveys 01' (CA_HAP_CI_1), SAP NetWeaver 04s Portal 7.0, Employee Self-Service Business Package 1.41, and Manager Self-Service Business Package 1.41.

4.5 More Resources on This Topic

Books on This Topic

HR Personnel Planning and Development Using SAP by Christian Krämer, Christian Lübke, and Sven Ringling. SAP PRESS.

SAP Help

http://help.sap.com/erp2005_ehp_04/helpdata/EN/cd/dae8a24ab011d18a0f0000e-816ae6e/frameset.htm.

4.6 Summary

As you have seen throughout this chapter, SAP Enterprise Learning is tightly integrated with Personnel Administration, Organization Management, Personnel Development, and SAP Performance Management. Such integration allows you to effectively align learning with your other talent management processes.

In the next chapter, we will take a detailed look at the Learning and Instructor Portals.

Learners, instructors, and managers use Web-based tools extensively to perform their day-to-day learning management tasks. This chapter talks about the tools, their capabilities, and what users can do with these tools.

5   Tools for Learners, Instructors, and Managers

In this chapter, we will look at the tools available to three main roles in SAP Enterprise Learning. As we discussed in Chapter 3, each group has different tools available, but the user experience provided by these tools is the same, so it is easy to transition between the tools.

The first group of tools we will look at are those for learners. A learner accesses the solution through the Learning Portal, where he can request and book his classroom Courses. If he chooses to take Web-based Courses, then he'll use the Online Player to run those Courses. Next we will look at the tools for an instructor. The solution provides the Instructor Portal, a Web-based interface that lets him manage his work, the Courses, and the learners. And we will conclude with the tools for a manager. The Manager Self-Service (MSS) Portal provides everything he needs for managing the training for his team members.

Let's begin with the Learning Portal.

5.1   The Learning Portal

The *Learning Portal* is the Web-based interface used by learners to manage their qualification profiles and learning activities. The Learning Portal serves as the gateway for managing many learning activities.

5.1.1   Employees Can Use the Portal to Plan Their Careers

The portal allows an employee to get started with his training by:

▶ Viewing his personal Qualification Profile (Figure 5.1)

▶ Comparing his qualifications with his position's requirements

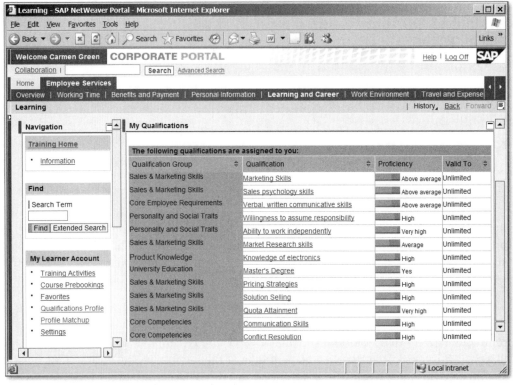

Figure 5.1 The Qualifications Profile of a Learner

Learners can also use the portal to:

▶ Identify qualification gaps

▶ Identify qualifications and certifications that are about to expire

5.1.2 Learners Can Take Appropriate Action to Address Skill Gaps

Once an employee becomes aware of his qualifications and the status of such qualification, he can use the Learning Portal to:

- Find system-recommended training Courses that could fill these gaps
- Find mandatory Courses that are essential for his job role
- Browse through Course catalogs or search for appropriate Courses
- Book or cancel Courses
- Request specific Courses through pre-bookings

Example

Once your learners become aware of the qualifications required for their jobs and they understand their gaps, they can use the Learning Portal to identify the Courses provided by your company to address their qualification gaps. They can also book themselves in these Courses right from the Learning Portal. The Learning Portal empowers your learners to take charge of their training and significantly reduces the administration overhead for the training team.

5.1.3 Learning Portal Delivers Training and Collects Feedback

The Learning Portal is not just for Course bookings: it's also a place where learners can complete training (see Figure 5.2) by launching e-learning Courses or joining Virtual Learning Room sessions. They can also do the following:

- Confirm Course participations and complete online Course feedback forms
- Track their training histories

Example

Let's say most of your Courses are delivered over the Web and you do business in a country or state that requires you to train all managers in your company on sexual harassment. The Learning Portal is the place where learners complete Web-based training. Learners also enter Courses conducted in Virtual Learning Rooms from the Learning Portal. Once they are done with their Courses, they can provide feedback about the Courses from the Learning Portal. In certain countries and states, it is necessary to collect employee signatures after they complete their training. The Learning Portal accepts an electronic signature from an employee after he completes his training.

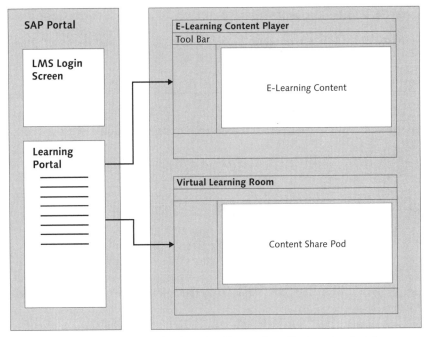

Figure 5.2 A Learner Can Launch e-Learning Courses from the Learning Portal

5.1.4 Structure of the Learning Portal

The Learning Portal has two main areas:

► A navigation pane on the left allows learners to access different activities. The navigation panel also allows quick searching and browsing of Course catalogs.

► Content frame on the right. The content pane displays details of activities selected on the navigation panel (see Figure 5.3).

There are three main areas in the Learning Portal that learners work with to manage their qualifications and coordinate their learning activities:

► Training Home page

► Course catalog and search

► My Learning Account

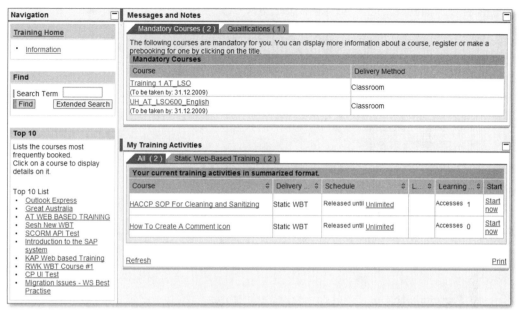

Figure 5.3 The Structure of the Learning Portal

5.1.5 Training Home

The *Training Home* page provides a snapshot of the most important information that learners should know and would need to access frequently and quickly.

The Training Home page contains two main areas: *Messages and Notes* and *Training Activities* (see Figure 5.4).

Messages and Notes

This area is designed to alert learners of missing and expiring qualifications. It is also designed to inform learners of mandatory Courses that have been set for their job roles, either by their managers through the Manager Self-Service Portals, or by any of their appraisers through Performance Management documents.

(Mandatory Course assignments and qualifications were discussed in detail in Chapter 4.)

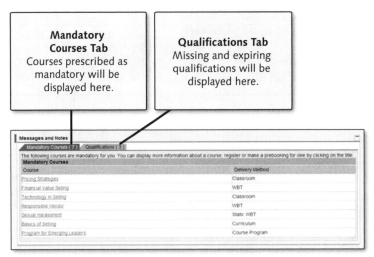

Figure 5.4 Messages and Notes Area

Prerequisites for Using Messages and Notes

The following information needs to be defined in SAP ERP HCM for using the Messages and Notes functions:

▶ Qualification catalogs should be defined.

▶ Qualification requirements for jobs or positions should be defined in organization management.

▶ Qualification profile of employees should be defined in Personnel Management.

My Training Activities

This area displays the current training activities of learner's information about currently booked Courses and requests for participation in Courses (Figure 5.5).

In case of e-learning Courses, learners can start Courses directly from the My Training Activities area. Similarly, in the case of Virtual Learning Room Courses, learners can also directly join such sessions directly from this area.

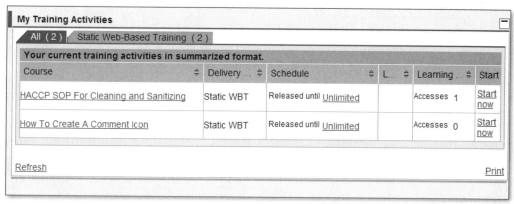

Figure 5.5 My Training Activities Area

5.1.6   Course Catalog and Keyword Search

Learners can find Courses either by browsing through the Course catalog or through keyword searches.

Course Catalog

The Course catalog is, by default, always visible on the navigation bar. This Course catalog is arranged by subject areas. Subject areas represent specific areas of knowledge and contain Courses that belong to certain areas of knowledge.

Flagging Course Groups as Subject Areas

Course groups can be specifically flagged as subject areas in the SAP Enterprise Learning Backend System, through the Course Group Info (1063) Infotype. Such Course Groups are displayed as the top-level subject areas in the Course catalog. The Course Group Info Infotype (1063) enables structuring Course offerings thematically and thus present a clearer structure to learners. If this infotype is not set, the highest hierarchy level of the Course catalog is automatically displayed as the highest-level subject area.

Learners have two different option of browsing the Course catalog:

► A top-level list where Courses are structured according to their subject areas
► A hierarchical display, where the Courses are displayed in a tree structure, grouped again by subject areas

Controlling Catalog Access

The subject areas and the Course Types that can be seen by a learner can be controlled through the Structural Authorization technique. This is explained in Chapter 9, Enhancing the SAP Learning Solution.

Keyword Search

Keyword searches are used when browsing and searching through the Course catalog is too time-consuming, especially when the catalog is long.

The Learning Portal allows both a basic search and an extended search that allows learners to do a quick search or a more focused search for Courses.

The *Find* function in the navigation area helps learners find Courses quickly and easily. A hit list displays a list of the Courses found that match the search criteria. Detailed information about Courses can be obtained by clicking on any of the Course hyperlinks.

> **Note**
>
> The keyword specified is matched with the Course title and various descriptions (Description Infotype) of the Course.

Extended Search

The Extended Search feature allows a more focused search by providing further search criteria:

- Subject area
- Delivery method
- Prerequisite
- Aspired qualification
- Target group
- Jobs or positions participating

5.1.7 My Learning Account

My Learning Account is an important area that allows a learner to manage his qualifications as well as take stock of his learning activities. It also allows a learner to set his preferences for accessing the Learning Portal.

Qualification Management

In this area, a learner can view his qualifications and compare them with his position's requirements to understand qualification gaps and deficits. SAP Enterprise Learning makes learning relevant, by automatically suggesting Courses that could fill these qualification gaps. Learners can also quickly find and choose one of the Courses at his convenience.

Learning Activities Management

My Learning Account area helps learners track the following activities:

- **Training Activities** — A list of a learner's training activities includes past Courses and cancelled Courses, as well as a current list of Courses. A subset of this list, the current list of Courses, is shown in My Training Activities.

- **Course Pre-bookings** — List of Courses that learners have requested for and have not booked, possibly because suitable Course dates were not available.

- **My Favorites** — Learners can also set some training Courses (Course Types as well as Course dates) as favorites for quick access. Such Courses are displayed here.

Settings

Settings allow a learner to set his preferred way of accessing the Learning Portal. To an extent, the behavior of the Learning Portal can be controlled by the settings that are made here. Some of the important settings that can be done in this page are listed below.

- **Catalog Settings** — This allows a learner to specify his preferred view of the Course catalog: top-level list view or hierarchical display.

- **Search Options** — The preferred Course language and location and the length of the time period (for viewing Course dates) can be set here. This can be then used to augment the Course search functions for more appropriate search results.

- **Preferred Learning Strategy** — This allows a learner to specify his preferred learning strategy for e-learning content. If this preferred strategy is one of the allowed strategies for the content, then the system presents the content according to the learner's preferred strategy.

5.1.8 Course Booking and Participation

Through the Learning Portal, learners can book Courses of any delivery method. The booking can be either automatic or can be routed via workflow for approval.

Standard workflow templates delivered with SAP Enterprise Learning provide for one-level authorization, where the booking request is sent for the immediate manager's approval. When a booking is pending approval, the status is shown as Participation Requested in My Training Activities.

If no convenient dates are available for a Course Type, or if a Course Type is not scheduled, a learner can request the Course by pre-booking. Later, when planning the Course calendar, training administrators can use the number of pre-bookings for a Course Type to determine the demand for a Course. And because, at the time of pre-booking, learners are just requesting a specific Course, no specific approval workflow is triggered.

System Checks in Course Booking and Participation

Several checks can be made when a learner books a Course. It can also be configured if the system should issue a warning or an error or simply display a message for information. The system can check if the learner has the prerequisite qualifications or has attended prerequisite Courses to be able to book a Course.

> **Note**
>
> Prerequisite qualifications are specified via the relationship *Has Prerequisite* (A 029) for a Course Type.

The system can check if the learner is participating in another schedule (Course) of the same Course Type via IMG menu path CUSTOMIZING • TRAINING AND EVENT MANAGEMENT • SAP LEARNING SOLUTION • TRAINING MANAGEMENT • DAY-TO-DAY ACTIVITIES • BOOKING • PARTICIPANT CHECKS.

The system can then check if the learner is participating in another Course during the same period, either as a learner or as an instructor via IMG menu path CUSTOMIZING • TRAINING AND EVENT MANAGEMENT • SAP LEARNING SOLUTION • TRAINING MANAGEMENT • DAY-TO-DAY ACTIVITIES • BOOKING • CONFLICT REACTION.

The system can check if the learner has other absence or attendance records during the period of the Course via IMG menu path CUSTOMIZING • TRAINING AND EVENT MANAGEMENT • SAP LEARNING SOLUTION • TRAINING MANAGEMENT • INTEGRATION • TIME MANAGEMENT • INTEGRATION YES OR NO?

5.1.9   Web-Based Learning

Through the Learning Portal, a learner can book Web-based Courses and also start e-learning Courses immediately. E-Learning content is played through the Content Player, an inherent component of SAP Enterprise Learning. The Content Player understands the preferred learning strategies of the learner and adapts the content and navigation dynamically. It communicates essential information on the learning progress and pass or fail information to the core LMS. It also communicates Shareable Content Object Reference Model (SCORM) and Aviation Industry CBT Committee (AICC) data elements for Courses that are compliant with these standards. In addition, the learning progress is shown in the Learning Portal for a learner to view (Figure 5.6).

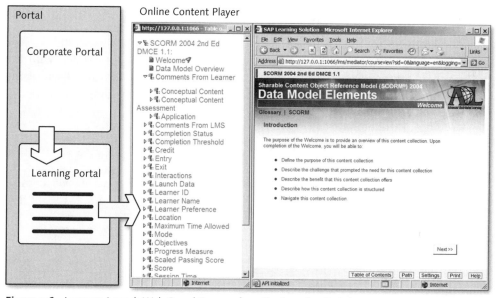

Figure 5.6   Learners Launch Web-Based Courses from the Learning Portal

Administrators can also selectively allow specific Courses to be downloaded for offline learning. The Offline Content Player is the tool through which such offline learning is accomplished. This tool should be installed in a learner's computer. In case of offline learning, a learner can download the e-learning content after registering to the Course. He can learn the content completely offline, and later synchronize his progress online. Offline learning is a good way of conserving network bandwidth.

(The content Player and Offline Content Player are explained in detail in the subsequent sections.)

5.1.10 Technical Settings for the Learning Portal

The Learning Portal is a Business Server Pages (BSP)–based solution. To install the Learning Portal, the SAP Enterprise Learning/SAP Learning Solution add-on LSOFE 600 or above (with enhancement packs) should be imported in the Web Application Server with J2EE. To play e-learning content, the Content Player should be installed and configured in the J2EE engine with the LSOFE 600 add-on. The administration functions are part of SAP ERP 6.0 core components ECC 6.0. You configure the settings for the Learning Portal via IMG menu path CUSTOMIZING • TRAINING AND EVENT MANAGEMENT • SAP LEARNING SOLUTION • LEARNING PORTAL.

5.1.11 Enhancing the Learning Portal

The Learning Portal provides a generic structure meant for all customers. Your needs may be different from the features and configurations provided with the standard solution. Most customers customize and extend the Learning Portal using tools called *BAdIs* provided by SAP Enterprise Learning or by doing custom development work.

> **BAdI**
>
> BAdI stands for *Business Add-Ins*. Business Add-Ins are enhancements to the standard version of the system. They can be inserted into the SAP System to accommodate user requirements too specific to be included in the standard delivery. Because specific industries often require special functions, SAP allows you to predefine these points in your software.

Customer-Specific Training Proposals

The Messages and Notes section can be personalized to display customer-specific training proposals. For instance, customers might want to display Courses that are added to the individual development plans of employees. In such cases, the customers can implement the Business Add-In LSO_LEARNER and use the method GET_ALERTS.

To implement the BAdIs follow IMG menu path CUSTOMIZING • TRAINING AND EVENT MANAGEMENT • SAP LEARNING SOLUTION • LEARNING PORTAL • EDITING OPTIONS • BUSINESS ADD-IN: DEFINE CUSTOMER-SPECIFIC PERSONALIZED TRAINING PROPOSALS.

This Business Add-In allows you to replace or augment the standard training proposals delivered with SAP Enterprise Learning.

Top 10 Courses

Apart from the Course catalog, the standard SAP Enterprise Learning facilitates displaying a list of top 10 Courses in the Learning Portal (in the left-hand side navigation panel). This listing is based on Courses that have the most frequent booking. This is done through a sample implementation of the Business Add-In TRAINING-TYPE_ADV, delivered with the standard solution (Figure 5.7).

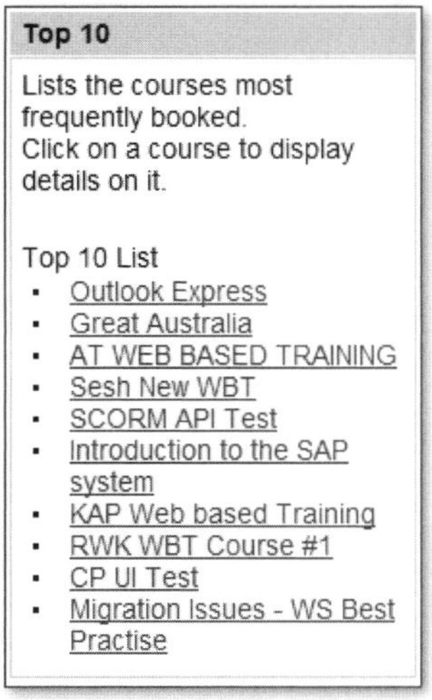

Figure 5.7 The Top 10 Most Frequently Booked Courses

It is possible for a customer to create his own version of a Course listing. For example, this listing can be used to publicize specific Courses to specific learners. To do so, the Business Add-In TRAININGTYPE_ADV_C needs to be implemented. Follow IMG menu path CUSTOMIZING • TRAINING AND EVENT MANAGEMENT • SAP LEARNING SOLUTION • LEARNING PORTAL • FORMATTING OPTIONS • BADI: DEFINE CUSTOMER-SPECIFIC COURSE OFFERING.

Information Page

The *Information Page* in the Learning Portal offers useful information and tips to learners for using the Learning Portal. You can configure this page to display any other useful information such as training and development policies and opportunities provided by your organization.

To do so, you need to manage the required settings in the frontend system in View Maintenance, by editing the view LSPAGE_ALIAS_C. Under the alias "Information," you can enter your own BSP page, which should be displayed in the Learning Portal under Information.

Identifying Learners Based on User ID

Usually, when an individual logs into the Learning Portal, the system identifies the Person (object type P) (through the Communication Infotype (0105), subtype System user name (0001)), which will then represent the learner. If such identification is not possible, the user object itself is considered the learner.

There is also a customer-specific way of identifying a learner by implementing the Business Add-In LSO_LEARNER, and using the method GET_LEARNER. For example, you can identify customers or other business partners corresponding to a User ID by following the IMG menu path CUSTOMIZING • TRAINING AND EVENT MANAGEMENT • SAP LEARNING SOLUTION • LEARNING PORTAL • FORMATTING OPTIONS • BADI: DEFINE ASSIGNMENT USER ID TO LEARNER.

5.2 Content Player

The Online Content Player plays e-learning content from the Learning Portal. Learners launch online content such as Web-based Courses and online tests from the Learning Portal using the Online Content Player.

> **Keywords Used in This Section: SCO, SCORM, API**
>
> ► SCO stands for Sharable Content Object. For the purposes of this section, think of the SCO as a logical collection of content pages. Conceptually, it is similar to a chapter in a book. Ideally, an SCO should cover content that can be completed in about 12 minutes; however, this guideline is often violated. It is not uncommon to see an SCO that lasts for 60 minutes. Some content designers build the entire Course in an SCO for better control of content display.
>
> ► SCORM stands for Sharable Content Object Reference Model, the most popular e-Learning content standard.
>
> ► API stands for Application Programming Interface. These are standard messaging protocols used by the content to interact with LMS. For example, when the content has to tell the LMS that a learner has completed a Course, it uses the appropriate API call to inform the LMS. These calls are usually made during the launch and completion of each SCO.

Launching the Online Player

Before a learner can launch an online Course using the content player, he needs to book the online Course or test. Once the learner books the Course or test, the Course is displayed in the My Training Activities area of the Learning Portal and a link to launch the Course is enabled. A learner clicks Start Now to launch the Course or test in the content player.

The content player has the following main screen elements: the Back and Continue buttons, the Table of Contents, the Help button, Path, and the Log Off button (see Figure 5.8). Let's look at each of these elements.

Tip: The Content Player Can Display Documents

Although the content player is designed to display standards-compliant e-learning Courses, the content player can also display files of all types, as long as the programs required to display those file types are installed in the learner's computer. For example, the Content Player can display a PDF file if Adobe Acrobat Reader is installed in the learner's computer.

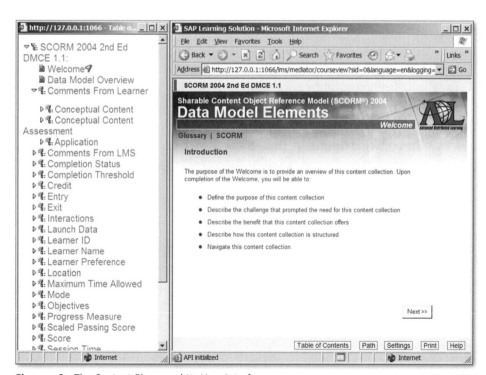

Figure 5.8 The Content Player and Its User Interface

▶ **The Back and Continue buttons**

Back and Continue buttons take the learner to the logical next page. This is determined by the design of the content. For example, if the learner has already met the objectives associated with the next SCO, the Content Player will skip that SCO and go to the next logical page. This concept is described in detail in Chapter 8, which covers content development and SCORM standards.

▶ **Table of Contents**

The *Table of Contents* provides the learner with the organization of the Course. The learner can see all the SCOs in the Course, the SCOs that have been completed already, and the current SCO the learner is in. Usually, the learner can click on the name of the SCO and jump directly to the SCO.

> **Note**
>
> The behavior of the Table of Contents is determined by the content design. For example, the content can determine if the learner should be allowed to click on the Table of Contents to jump directly to a SCO. The content designer does this by choosing the appropriate SCORM navigation strategy.

▶ **Log Off button**

When a learner completes a Course, it is important that the learner logs off by clicking the *Log Off* button in the content player. This enables the content player to write all progress and performance information about the Course back to LMS. The learner should not close the content player by simply closing the browser.

Once the learner closes the content player using the Log Off button, the learner's progress and performance information is displayed in the Learning Portal. This information includes the number of times the learner has accessed the Course, the progress made by the learner, and the total time spent by the learner in the Course.

> **Progress and Performance Information**
>
> Progress information is determined and sent to the LMS by the content. The Course content determines the progress and informs the LMS by sending the progress information to the LMS. The LMS merely receives and displays this information. Configuration settings and content design affect the progress information displayed in the learning portal.

▶ **Help**

The learner can call the content player *Help* function. A help window explains all the functions described in this section.

► **Path**

The learning *path* gives a preview of the content yet to be completed in the correct sequence. The learning path is determined by the chosen learning strategy and the learning objectives achieved to date.

Tip: Learning Strategies

The learning strategies concept of SAP Enterprise Learning was designed and built before the release of SCORM 2004, the industry standard for e-learning content navigation strategy. SAP Enterprise Learning is certified for SCORM 2004 by ADL, the governing body of SCORM. The authors of this book have learned that customers are relying increasingly on SCORM 2004 for their content learning strategies. In such cases, the Path button in the Content Player may not be relevant. The Table of Contents becomes a more appropriate and relevant tool for learners to understand the path they need to take. Because SAP Enterprise Learning is certified for SCORM 2004, the authors recommend that all customers follow SCORM 2004 strategies to design and build their learning content.

Book Marking

The Content Player supports *book marking*. If a learner logs off the content player while he is in the middle of a Course, the content will inform LMS using the appropriate API calls.

Note

In case of SCORM 1.2, the data element `cmi.core.lesson_location` is used to store the last visited SCO. The player by default takes the user to the first page of the SCO (in case of multi-SCO content). There are no visual elements to depict this feature in the content player.

Playing Online Tests in the Content Player

An online test is a standalone test created in the SAP Enterprise Learning Authoring Environment. Once a learner chooses a test, the test can be launched from the Learning Portal using the Start Now button.

Browser Configuration and Plug-In Requirements

To play Course content in the content player, JavaScript should be active in the learner's browser, which is usually enabled for cookies. The JavaScript version of SCORM API should be enabled. To play tests created in the Authoring Environment, Sun Java Plug-In 1.4.2 is required.

This concludes our review of the Learning Portal, so let's move on to the Instructor Portal.

5.3 Instructor Portal

The *Instructor Portal* is the Web-based interface used by an instructor to interact with SAP Enterprise Learning. An instructor sees information about the Courses he is teaching in the portal. He can also perform his day-to-day tasks from the portal.

An instructor performs several tasks while preparing for Courses, teaching Courses, and after teaching Courses. The Instructor Portal helps an instructor in all these stages.

5.3.1 User Experience and Structure of the Instructor Portal

When an instructor logs into the Instructor Portal using his username and password, he is presented with a personalized view of the portal. The Work Overview in the Instructor Portal displays the Courses he is going to teach in the future, the Courses he is teaching now, and the Courses he has taught in the past (see Figure 5.9).

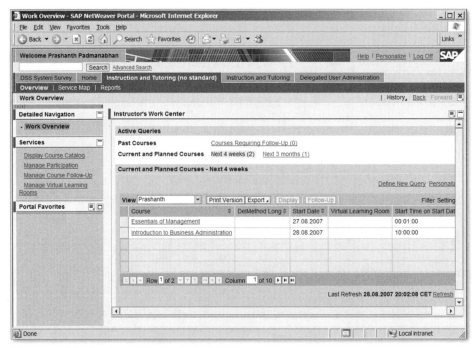

Figure 5.9 The Structure of the Instructor Portal

5.3.2 Stages of Instruction and Features Used

There are three distinct stages of a Course for an instructor: *Course preparation*, *Course delivery*, and *Course follow-up*.

Course Preparation

In the Course preparation stage, the instructor uses the *Display Course Details* feature to perform the following tasks:

- ▶ Review participant list
- ▶ View information about Course contacts
- ▶ View information about classroom equipment
- ▶ View location and schedule information
- ▶ View documents attached to the Course
- ▶ Check status of equipment and material
- ▶ See the Course description

> **Example: Preparing For a Course**
>
> Preparing and delivering a Course conducted in a classroom involves wearing multiple hats, keeping track of many things, and staying flexible. Even though the training administrator is responsible for organizing the classroom, the material, and the equipment, the administrator is rarely on-site. It is up to the instructor to verify that everything is in place and set to go. The Web-based Instructor Portal empowers your instructors to stay on top of all the things they need to track.
>
> The Curriculum for a classroom Course is designed for a particular set of audience and the instructor is trained to deliver the content. In reality, the nature of a target audience is never the same. Let's say an energy company has a generic technical class to train English-speaking gas turbine operators. When the Course is scheduled, an instructor may find out that some of the registered participants are from the sales team and some learners are not native English speakers. The instructor can use the Instructor Portal to research the participant list and understand the nature of audience to plan the delivery of Course content to suit the needs of that particular audience.

If the instructor teaches the Course in a Virtual Learning Room, the instructor shall use the Manage Virtual Learning Room feature to do the following tasks:

- ▶ Create a new virtual learning room
- ▶ Change the details of an existing virtual learning room

▸ Change the virtual learning room assigned to a Course

▸ Enter a virtual learning room to prepare the room for the Course

Conducting the Course

While conducting the Course, the instructor uses the Manage Participation feature to perform the following tasks:

▸ Add or replace a learner

▸ Handle cancellation

The Day of the Course

The training administrator is responsible for managing participations in a Course. However, on the day of a classroom Course, there are several things that could happen. A confirmed participant may not arrive due to a cancelled flight. A company or department may send a different person instead of the person who booked the Course. A new participant may arrive at the location and request for participation. In such situations, the instructor manages Course participation tasks on his own. The instructor can book new learners in a Course, replace a learner, and cancel a booking for a learner. The Instructor Portal enables an instructor to perform all these tasks.

Course Follow Up

After the Course is completed, the instructor uses the *Manage Course Follow-Up* feature to do the following tasks:

▸ Confirm attendance

▸ Evaluate participants

▸ Transfer qualifications

5.3.3   Provide Access to the Instructor Portal to All Instructors

It is important that you provide all instructors with access to the portal, so they can confirm attendance for learners who attended the Course and mark them passed or failed. Although a paper-based attendance sheet may be used, which is mailed or faxed to the training administrator who then makes the necessary entries in the system, the Instructor Portal eliminates the need for such offline activities. The instructor can confirm attendance, evaluate participants, and transfer qualifications from the Instructor Portal.

Administrators can then decide which of the follow-up activities are to be performed by instructors for each Course Type. Such settings can be specified at a global level in SAP Enterprise Learning for all Courses or can be specified in the Follow-up Control Options Infotype for a Course Type. Instructors will be permitted to perform only such allowed activities.

It is also important to ensure that your configuration setup is correct, because your company may have tens or hundreds of instructors teaching various topics. Some Courses may be taught by employees of your company and some Courses may be delivered by contract instructors who do not have a say over the final evaluation of a learner. Some instructors may be qualified to mark attendance and evaluate a learner but may not be legally allowed to transfer qualifications to a learner. In such situations, there is a need for different authorizations at the Course-type level, and the Instructor Portal can be configured to meet such needs.

5.4   Managing Learning Activities of a Team

SAP Enterprise Learning helps managers and business unit heads manage their teams' learning activities in alignment with the overall talent management initiatives of their organizations.

Through the SAP Manager Self-Services portal, managers see the complete personnel development profile of their reporting employees. The personnel development profile summarizes key employee information that helps managers assess and take appropriate action to improve the talent in their teams. These include:

▶ Qualification profile and qualification gaps of an individual

▶ Courses recommended by SAP Enterprise Learning to fill these qualification gaps

▶ Other mandatory or essential Courses for the individual

▶ History of the individual's learning activities and past performances

> **Example: Your Managers Can Get a Bird's Eye View of Their Teams Qualifications**
>
> Let's say one of your managers is preparing for a key project to be started in a couple of months, which is to be staffed by his team members. Apart from his team's availability, one of the things he worries about is the specific skills required by the team to execute the project well. If you are in a regulated industry, the manager will also need to determine if his team members have the necessary qualifications to perform the job and their qualifications will not expire before the project is completed. The Manager Self-Services Portal enables a manager to view the necessary information and make a decision about the team composition.

Based on the information in the example, a manager can also take specific action to manage his team's learning activities. Through SAP Manager Self-Services, a manager can:

▶ Manage mandatory Course assignments of his team members — specify new mandatory Courses, change/delete existing mandatory Course assignments

▶ Track an individual's progress on assigned mandatory Courses

▶ Book team members directly to Courses

A manager can also drive people development and training adoption. For instance, a manager, having viewed the talent profile of one of the new entrants in his team and his qualification gaps, can decide to specify a few Courses as essential for the new entrant. He might also intend to book the new entrant to a few preparatory Courses before starting his job. He can perform all of these activities through his Manager Self-Services Portal.

5.4.1 Managing Mandatory Course Assignments

Managers are responsible for defining the Courses that are essential or mandatory for their reporting employees. These essential Courses are those that help individuals meet their current job demands, and possibly augment them to move higher up in their career ladder.

The Manage Mandatory Assignments activity helps managers to specify such mandatory assignments. Through this activity, managers can assign new mandatory Courses to any of their direct or indirect reporting employees. Managers can select one or more individuals reporting to them and assign new mandatory Courses to them.

Managers can also view and track existing mandatory assignments of individuals and change or delete them. The system displays not just the mandatory Courses directly assigned to the individuals but also those that are derived by virtue of their positions in the organization.

> **Note: The Booking Exists Flag**
>
> The Booking Exists flag is ticked whenever a booking is made by the learner for that mandatory Course. However, it is not an indicator for the manager to know if the individual has completed the Course or not.

A manager also takes a big role in defining organizational entities that report to them. For instance, a manager is better qualified to specify what competencies are essential for a new organizational unit or position under his organization. On the same note, managers also are aware of those essential Courses that make up a role or a position definition.

Through the Manage Mandatory Assignments activity, managers can not only specify new mandatory Courses for reporting individuals but also to their reporting organizational units and positions. The initial selection screen in this activity allows managers to select such organizational entities other than individuals.

5.4.2 Tracking Progress on Mandatory Course Assignments

The Mandatory Assignments report lets managers see if individuals have acted on their mandatory Courses. Managers can report on specific Courses that they have set as mandatory for their reporting entities. The report gives information on the overall status at the organizational unit level (number of individuals who have completed ÷ total number of individuals), as well as the individual status.

The Manage Mandatory Assignments activity and Mandatory Assignments Report are also available in the Course Administrator Portal for training administrators to manage mandatory assignments at the organizational level. Unlike managers who can only influence the training activities of their reporting organizations and members, training administrators can manage mandatory Course assignments for any organizational entity or individual in the organization.

5.4.3 Booking Team Members to Courses

Managers can also book direct and indirect reporting members to Courses, through the Manage Participation activity. This activity is similar in its interface to the Manage Mandatory Assignments activity. In this case, the manager would be selecting a specific Course schedule to book his team members, whereas in the latter, the manager would be selecting a Course Type and assign it as mandatory to his team members. While assigning mandatory Courses is guiding an individual to take a Course, direct booking to Courses is a definitive action that directs an individual to attend the Course.

Through this activity, managers can also view the training history of individuals. If needed, managers can change these details. For example, managers can cancel existing Course participations or change cancellation reasons. Managers can also pre-book their reporting employees to Courses if there are no suitable Course schedules available for booking. This concludes our review of the tools available to learners, instructors, and managers.

5.5　More Information

Installing the Learning Portal and Instructor Portal

More detailed information on installation of the Learning Portal and Instructor Portal can be obtained from the installation guides at *http://service.sap.com/instguides*.

Content Player and Web Based Courses

▶ SCORM Navigation Strategies: *http://www.adlnet.gov/scorm/20043ED/examples/MSCE.aspx*

▶ The Multiple Sequencing with API Content Example (MSCE) builds foundational knowledge on the key concepts that apply to sequencing and the application programming interface (API) and the SCORM 2004 3rd Edition. Sequencing allows the learner to navigate through the content in a predetermined or sequenced manner. API provides a standardized way for the Sharable Content Objects (SCOs) to communicate with LMSs. Each content package listed in the website provided above demonstrates a different sequencing strategy.

▶ SAP Enterprise Learning online help on the Online Player: *http://help.sap.com/erp2005_ehp_03/helpdata/EN/75/b4b341800e3231e10000000a155106/frameset.htm*

5.6　Summary

In this chapter, we looked at the tools used by the learner, the instructor, and the manager to learn, teach, and manage, respectively. We first looked at the Learning Portal and reviewed the tasks performed by the learner in the portal. We also looked at how an SAP Enterprise Learning consultant configures the Learning Portal to alter its structure and behavior. We had a look at the Content Player, the program that enables learners to view Web-based Courses and looked at the Offline Player, a program that enables learners to view Courses when they are not connected to their office networks. We then looked at the Instructor Portal and reviewed the tasks an instructor can perform in the Instructor Portal. Finally, we looked at the learning services available for managers and how they can use them to drive training adoption within their teams.

In the next chapter we will discuss training administration.

Training administration functionality is the heart of a learning management system. Every transaction that happens in a learning system depends directly or indirectly on training administration functionality. A healthy learning organization depends on a well-oiled training administration team supported by robust training administration software.

6 Training Administration

Training Management is an integral and essential component of SAP Enterprise Learning, and is required for any implementation. Customers who have already implemented SAP Training and Event Management will be familiar with most of the functionality of Training Management in SAP Enterprise Learning, but not all of it. New objects, infotypes, and reports, as well as new functions, have been added to enhance the old Training and Event Management functionality. We will discuss all of these elements in Chapter 7.

6.1 Training Management Process

As we discovered in Chapter 2, a training administrator interacts with the system, from both a backend and a portal perspective. The core of training administration activities is carried out in the SAP backend system, but with the advent of EhP4 on Learning Solution release 6.0, many of the regular activities may also be handled through the Training Administrator Portal. When we talk about these activities from a Training Management perspective, we discuss them in major phases that relate to the typical training management processes in most organizations (see Figure 6.1).

The training management process typically consists of four different process stages:

▶ **Course Preparation** — This stage consists of initial setup activities, such as defining the necessary master data for learning management (e.g., structuring the Course catalog, defining the Course master data, defining supporting master data such as venues resources needed for training, and time schedules).

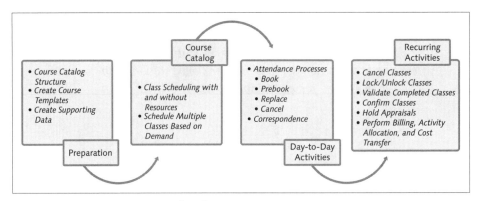

Figure 6.1 Training Management Lifecycle

Once the initial set-up is complete, Training preparation activities become maintenance activities that may be performed on an ongoing basis. For example, new Courses may be created, qualified instructors may be added to existing Courses, obsolete Courses can be end-dated, or the Course catalog might be restructured.

▶ **Course Catalog** — This phase consists of activities related to scheduling Courses, such as assessing demand for Courses, planning and scheduling Course dates, and assigning resources for Course dates.

▶ **Day-to-Day Activities** — Activities in this phase include everyday administrative activities such as managing participation and managing the communications to be sent to learners and other people involved in the training process, such as instructors or an attendee's supervisor or manager.

▶ **Recurring Activities** — This final phase is made up of regular activities that may not occur on a daily basis (depending on the size of your catalog and the number of offerings, as well as your business processes). The activities include following-up (or closing out) Courses, recording pass/fail results, imparting and evaluating competencies and certifications, recording Course evaluation results, billing Course fees, and allocating training costs through a charge-back process.

Because the Implementation Guide (IMG) is arranged based on these phases, we have chosen to arrange this chapter into sections based on these phases as well. This should make it simpler for you to reference activities you are interested in from a process and a configuration perspective.

6.2   Key Transactions in Training Management

The processes previously outlined take place within three main transactions:

▶ **The Master Data Catalog**, where the Course Catalog is designed and maintained (Preparation)

▶ **The Dynamic Course Menu**, where classes are scheduled and maintained (Course Catalog and Recurring Activities)

▶ **The Dynamic Participation Menu**, where participation activities are managed (Day-to-Day Activities and Recurring Activities)

These transactions allow administrators to work with one single view of the organization's training offering — the Course catalog. In all these transactions, administrators can select a specific catalog item, such as a Course and perform appropriate activities. For example, in the *Dynamic Participation Menu*, administrators can select a Course and book participants to that Course (see Figure 6.2).

Access to these transactions may be restricted by authorizations, so you may choose to create a Training Coordinator role that will support catalog creation and maintenance and a Training Administration role that will support Course scheduling and booking functions.

We'll see more about these transactions later in this chapter.

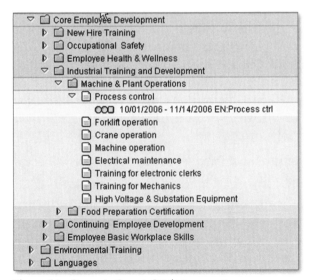

Figure 6.2 Dynamic Course Catalog

Transactions such as the Dynamic Course Menu present the Course catalog view, thus allowing administrators to work with a familiar interface to manage their activities.

6.3 Course Preparation

Course preparation activities are important because the training catalog and the training offerings (Courses) are defined here. They also constitute the first set of activities that any customer would perform when he starts using SAP Enterprise Learning.

6.3.1 Designing the Course Catalog

The Course catalog is a structured list of the organization's training offerings (see Figure 6.3). Designing the Course catalog in a logical and easily understandable manner is important because it simplifies searching for appropriate Courses as a learner and eases the administrator's job of managing training activities.

> **Tip**
>
> Because the administrator is using the same view that the learner sees in the Learning Portal when managing the training catalog, this ensures that the catalog view remains orderly from a Portal perspective.

When creating a Course catalog using using SAP Enterprise Learning, a simple interface, the *Master Data Catalog* (LSO_PVCT), creates a well-structured catalog. The Master Data Catalog allows the user to view the catalog structure and add existing or new elements with a simple right-click of the mouse. To an extent, the view of the catalog is customizable. The user may indicate the range of dates in which he would like to view the catalog in, and the starting point from which he typically works in the catalog. Additional information may be added to the catalog view of some or all users using a BAdI, which is discussed in more detail in Chapter 9, Enhancing the SAP Learning Solution.

The catalog itself is comprised of several different elements, which we will detail for you in this section, beginning with Course Groups.

Course Groups (Object Type L) — As the name indicates, Course Groups are used to logically group a set of Courses that belong to the same subject area. For example, all Courses meant for managers can be grouped under a Course Group called "Managerial Training." If appropriate, subgroups may be used within a Course Group to further enhance the grouping. For example, under "Managerial Training," Courses might be further grouped into the subgroups: "Leadership Training," "Management Techniques," "Project Management," and so on. Because of this, Course Groups enable learners to narrow down their searches to easily find their selected Courses in the catalog. For instance, a manager looking for leadership training should be able to easily navigate the structure above to find the subject area "Leadership Training."

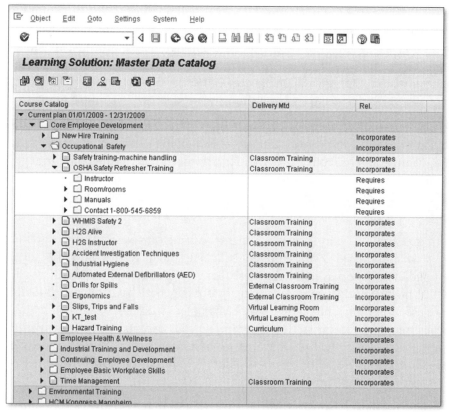

Figure 6.3 Structure of a Course Catalog

There is no limit to the level or depth of the Course catalog – Courses can be structured under multiple levels of Course Groups and sub groups. However, it should be noted that an optimum level should be chosen — too few Course Groups would make it difficult for everyone to find Courses, whereas too many Course Groups can make it cumbersome to manage and administer Courses.

> **Tip**
>
> From a system response time perspective, you should never have more than 50 subordinate Course Groups within a Course Group or 50 Course Types within a Course Group. From a usability perspective, you may decide to make this number even smaller (e.g., 30 Course Types within a Course Group).

Course Groups are also useful if you need to offer a selective view of the Course catalog to different learners (often referred to as *Domains* and discussed in detail in

Chapter 9, section 9.2.1, Configuring Structural Authorizations). You may limit the learner's or the administrator's view of the Course catalog based on these domains. Course Groups may also facilitate easy reporting if they are set up with this requirement in mind. For example, you may want to show all training history records for your organization's "Ethics and Compliance" Courses over the past year. If "Ethics and Compliance" is equivalent to a Course Group, your report will be simple to run.

Often, an organization spends a large amount of time determining its Course catalog structure. The biggest conversation point is, should the catalog be arranged in a global manner, to reflect our global training organization, or should it be arranged by function or location. If you have been involved in this discussion in the past, your consultant probably told you, "It depends," which probably isn't what you wanted to hear. But this response is, in fact, a valid answer.

If your organization is, for example, a manufacturing organization, with different products manufactured at your different plant sites, then creating a Course catalog structured by subject may not make sense. For example, even though your peanut butter plant and your peanut butter cracker plant may both have training about the proper use of peanuts, the training may be completely different and should probably be arranged by location. In the same way, your organization may only offer global Courses that should be delivered in the same way, by the same qualified instructors (if instructor-led) regardless of location. In this case, it probably makes sense to structure your catalog by subject.

Most organizations, however, fall in between these two extremes. For example, two plants may manufacture the same thing slightly differently because one plant was acquired from another company and has legacy training materials. In this case, you may have decided that one of the goals of your implementation is to align Courses globally, where it makes sense. If this is the case, you need to allocate extra time to your project to accomplish this alignment. This project step is a *data clean-up* step. If you can incorporate it during your implementation, it will positively impact your Course maintenance processes on a go-forward basis, improve your analytics, and probably reduce your bottom line in terms of your training budget, because you won't be maintaining duplicate Course Types and materials.

However, during project preparation, not all organizations plan for such a large data clean-up process. If this is the case for your project, you may decide to go-live with a Course catalog that reflects your current training catalog structure and then slowly reorganize it after go-live, as part of an organizational training initiative. Because all Course elements in Training Management are date driven, it is a simple process to plan your Course alignment on spreadsheets or in an alternate database, all the while maintaining your current catalog structure. As soon as your planned catalog is complete and approved by all stakeholders, you can easily load the new catalog with a future effective date, end date your current catalog one day prior to the selected effective date, and, on the cutover date, the catalog view will switch to the new view and still maintain an accurate picture of your historical catalog.

Course Types (Object Type D) — Course Types, also called Course templates, denote the training offered and all the supporting master data required for the training offering. They act as the master templates based on which new scheduled offerings of that Course Type can be created. For example, "Shop Floor Safety Training" may be a Course Type within a manufacturing organization. The master data for this Course Type will indicate delivery method (e.g., is this Web-based or instructor-led?); the typical schedule and qualified instructors, if instructor-led; the Course content and completion requirements if Web-based; etc. As mentioned, a main characteristic of a Course Type is its delivery method — whether it's classroom training, or virtual classroom training, or an e-learning Course, for example. Additional attributes that characterize a Course are also maintained at the Course Type level, such as the time schedule (e.g., one-day Course for eight hours, starting at 8 am, ending at 5 pm, with a one-hour break), the resources needed for the Course (rooms, instructors, manuals, etc.), the expected Course capacity, and any Course fees associated with the Course from an expenses perspective or a charge-back perspective. We will talk more about Course Types and delivery methods in the next section.

Courses (Object Type E) — Courses are the specific scheduled instances of Course Types created with a delivery method that requires a time and location. Outside of SAP Enterprise Learning, most organizations would consider Courses as *scheduled classes*. Courses are created based on the Course Type templates and data from these templates defaults to the Course level. Almost all Course Type data that defaults may be overridden at the Course level, so the functionality does not replicate the inheritance functionality you may be familiar with from organizational management. For example, at the Course Type level for the "Shop Floor Safety Training" Course Type discussed earlier, there may be four qualified instructors and a suggested schedule of eight hours, starting at 8 am and ending at 5 pm. When scheduling a Course based on this Course Type, the administrator may allow the title "Shop Floor Safety Training," to default in from the Course Type and choose one of the suggested instructors provided by the Course Type. However, the administrator may know that in the specific instance of the Course he is scheduling, the room that is typically used won't be available until 8:30. In this case, the administrator may select a schedule that starts at 8:30 and ends at 5:30 or the administrator may choose a schedule that starts at 8:30 and only provides a half-hour break, so the class may still conclude at 5 pm. This illustrates the *default* functionality provided by the Course Type. The more data that is maintained at the Course Type level, the fewer decisions your administrator must make on a day-to-day basis when scheduling Courses.

> **Warning**
>
> Delivery Method should never be overridden at the Course level. SAP Enterprise Learning is designed to expect that the delivery method at the Course level will reflect the delivery method at the related Course Type level. Changing delivery method for either Course Type or Course may cause data inconsistencies.

Learners book themselves to specific Course dates, so booking is an activity done at the Course level. When a Course Type is not scheduled, learners can indicate interest for that Course Type by *pre-booking* that Course Type. Pre-booking only occurs at the Course Type level. Both the number of bookings and the number of pre-bookings may later be used to assess demand for a specific Course Type from a reporting perspective. This information may also be used to plan out multiple Courses at once, using the *Dynamic Planning Menu*.

> **Note**
>
> A Course with a Web-based delivery method does not have a scheduled Course. Instead, when the Course is published to the Course catalog in the Portal, the first time a learner looks at the Course in the catalog, an *e-learning* (object type ET) is generated. If that learner or any subsequent learner chooses to book to that Course, a relationship between the e-learning and the learner is created.

6.3.2 Course Types and Delivery Methods

As mentioned earlier, the Course Types are the master templates on which actual scheduled Courses (classes) are based. A Course Type is characterized by several attributes, the most important of which is the *delivery method*.

The delivery method represents the channel or mode of delivery of the Course. For instance, a Course can be offered as instructor-led classroom training or as a self-paced Web-based Course. The delivery method of a Course Type is selected based on several factors such as the nature of content and the type of skill or knowledge that the Course will impart. Delivery method is actually determined well before a Course Type is entered in the Master Data Catalog — it is one of the drivers that determines the design of the content.

For instance, consider a Course such as "Fluency in English." The Course content for this class would most likely be designed with instructor facilitation in mind and the Course Type would be created with a delivery method *Classroom Training*. The effectiveness of this Course depends on an instructor *talking* to the participants. However, a Course on employee workplace ethics may be designed and delivered as e-learning instead of an instructor-led or classroom-based training. The organization delivering this training probably considered consistent and rapid delivery of content as well as the learner's ability to easily review key sections of content when determining the best way to provide the Course to its employees.

Delivery methods, by their very nature, determine whether a Course Type is time dependent. For example, a classroom Course is time dependent — the Course is scheduled on specific date. An e-learning Course is time independent; so a learner can take the Course whenever needed and he can choose his own pace of progressing through the Course content.

Delivery methods also determine if a Course Type is location dependent or not. Again, a classroom Course is location dependent whereas a virtual classroom Course or Web-based training is not (although the virtual classroom delivery method drives the need for a virtual location [i.e., the virtual classroom]).

Table 6.1 lists 11 standard delivery methods provided by SAP Enterprise Learning as of Learning Solution 6.0, EhP4:

Delivery Method	Definition	Time dependent	Location dependent
Classroom Training	Training held by an instructor, in a reserved room, with a set schedule.	Yes	Yes
Virtual Classroom Training	Training held via virtual classroom tool, such as WebEx, Interwise, etc. Connections to such virtual room environments need to be set up.	Yes	No
Virtual Learning Room	In-built virtual classroom training in SAP Enterprise Learning using Adobe Connect solution.	Yes	No
External Classroom Training	Training held by an external training vendor, most probably in his premise	Yes	Yes

Table 6.1 Standard Delivery Methods

Delivery Method	Definition	Time dependent	Location dependent
External Virtual Classroom Training	Training held via a Virtual Classroom tool hosted externally.	Yes	No
Web-Based Training	e-Learning content for self-paced learning; the content is typically managed in an internal Content Management System. Content can be dynamic.	No	No
Online Test	A test designed and maintained in an internal Content Management System.	No	No
Static Web-Based Training	A static URL that directs the learner to a web page or other such source for learning. For example, a static URL to safety guidelines can be provided.	No	No
External Web-Based Training	e-Learning hosted by an external training provided and accessed from SAP Enterprise Learning using XI, SOAP, or some other interface.	No	No
External Online Test	An online test hosted by an external content provider and accessed from SAP Enterprise Learning using XI, SOAP, or some other interface.	No	No
WBT in Classroom	e-Learning that is delivered to a set of learners in a classroom environment.	Yes	Yes

Table 6.1 Standard Delivery Methods (Cont.)

SAP Enterprise Learning supports different channels for delivering learning, and as you can see in Table 6.1, this includes blended learning methodologies.

Apart from these delivery methods, SAP Enterprise Learning also groups Course Types of different delivery methods to form Course packages in which learners can enroll. Course Types can be grouped together to form a *Curriculum Type* (object type DC) or a *Course Program* (object type EK), each of which represents a single, logical unit of learning.

A Curriculum Type is a group of related Courses that can be scheduled together and offered to learners. Curriculum Types are best described as a method to blend multiple delivery methods together to create a blended learning object unique to your organization.

A *Course Program* is another way of grouping Courses in a more flexible manner that needs no further scheduling. Course Programs are often called *Learning Paths* by organizations. We will talk about Curricula and Course Programs later in this chapter.

Grouping Course Types into a Curriculum Type or a Course Program is different from grouping them into Course Groups. Course Groups are purely structural elements to design the Course catalog, whereas Curriculum types and Course Programs represent training offerings that can be booked by learners.

Customers may also copy the standard delivery methods to create their own custom delivery methods. For example, a blog that talks on a specific subject area can be converted into a Course. In this case, the delivery method *static Web-based training* can be used to create a new delivery method called "Blog"; the URL of the blog site can be provided as the static link.

6.3.3 Course Type Attributes

Each delivery method determines the type of data required to support a scheduled class, a series of classes, or e-learning Course. And as we already discussed, delivery methods can drive the need for a location or a schedule at the Course level.

For a Course Type of delivery method WBT, the delivery method drives the need for the e-learning content, as well as criteria for Course completion and success (e.g., number of chapters or units that must be completed before the system will allow a learner to indicate completion).

Attributes are defined in the form of infotypes or as relationships to a Course Type. Table 6.2 lists some of the common attributes usually specified for a Course Type. Keep in mind that some of these attributes might not be applicable to a Course Type, depending on its delivery method.

Attribute	Description
Description	Different types of descriptive text about the Course Type, such as general description, target audience profile, Course objectives and goals, etc. Customers can also create their own categories of description.
	Descriptions can also be maintained in different languages.

Table 6.2 Common Attributes Usually Specified for a Course Type

Attribute	Description
Time Schedule	Applicable for time-dependent Course Types; schedules can be specified in terms of the number of days or hours for a Course Type. Detailed schedule models can also be defined and associated with the Course Type.
Capacity	Applicable usually for time and location dependent Courses; capacity can be specified in terms of minimum, optimum and maximum number of participants allowed for the Course. Minimum capacity indicates the least number of participants to make a schedule of this Course Type viable; maximum capacity indicates the maximum number of participants that are allowed for the Course. (Participants who book over the maximum will be automatically put on a waitlist.)
	It is to be noted that the capacity of a room associated with a Course will also influence the capacity considerations of a Course (e.g., if the room assigned to a scheduled Course has a smaller capacity than the Course, the room's capacity will drive the waitlist functionality).
Price and Cost information	Course fee can be maintained differently for external participants and internal participants. Cost for a Course Type can be defined in terms of different cost items, such as cost of Course materials, cost of equipments, etc. The total cost of the Course can also be used to simulate and propose a price for the Course that will cover the basic cost.
Resource Requirements	The resources needed for a Course are specified through the relationship "Requires (A/B 022)". Resources include rooms, instructors, materials, and other elements needed to schedule a Course, such as computer equipment.
Prerequisites	A Course Type may have prerequisite qualifications and prerequisite other Course Types. For example, the Course Type "Advanced Electronics" may have a qualification prerequisite "Basic knowledge of electronics" or a Course Type prerequisite "Basic Electronics."
	Prerequisites are specified as relationships to a Course Type ("Has Prerequisite" A/B 029).
Imparted Qualifications	A Course Type may impart qualifications (i.e., competencies or certifications) to learners who have successfully completed a Course associated with that type. The qualifications imparted are specified as relationship ("Imparts" A/B 028). Qualifications imparted by a Course can be added to a learner's qualification profile during follow-up.
Mandatory for	A Course Type can be made as essential or as mandatory for different organizational entities such as organizational units, job, position, or individuals.
	As seen earlier, this is specified by the relationship "Is Mandatory For" (A/B 615).

Table 6.2 Common Attributes Usually Specified for a Course Type (Cont.)

Attribute	Description
Knowledge & Web links	Supplementary materials to a Course and sources of additional information can be specified for a Course Type in the form of knowledge and Web links. For instance, the knowledge links can link the Course manuals stored in the knowledge warehouse — Course manuals can then be directly downloaded by learners from the Learning Portal. Additional information from other websites can be linked as Web links.
Collaboration Rooms	A virtual community that is related to the subject of the Course Type can also be linked to the Course Type, in the form of Collaboration Rooms. Learners enrolled to a Course can automatically join such collaboration rooms for extended learning. (We will discuss Collaboration rooms in detail later in this chapter.)
Workflow and Correspondence control options	Workflows can be used for Course approval and cancellation process. The workflow process can be different for different Course Types.
	Correspondences denote the communications sent to different parties involved in learning — such as booking confirmation mails to learners, Course participation confirmation to managers, etc.
	(These topics are discussed in detail later in this chapter.)

Table 6.2 Common Attributes Usually Specified for a Course Type (Cont.)

Apart from these attributes, there might be specific attributes for a Course Type, depending on its delivery method. For example, Web-based training Courses need the e-learning content to be specified, which is done through the Course Type Content Infotype. The criteria for completion and other parameters governing access for such Course Types can be specified through the Course Completion Specification Infotype.

Some of the attributes of a Course Type can also be specified at a higher level, so such settings become applicable for all Course Types. Typically, the workflow procedures for Course booking approval and cancellation are common for all Courses and hence can be defined generically in the implementation guide, instead of defining this for each Course Type level. The same can be said about other settings, such as correspondence control options and completion specifications.

6.4   Course Offering

The *Course Catalog* phase of training administration consists of scheduling a single Course and also of scheduling multiple Courses, a process called *Planning* in Training Management.

One of the primary inputs for such assessment is the demand for the Course Type. The demand is usually assessed by the number of pre-bookings for a Course Type. A learner pre-books a Course Type when he finds that a Course Type is not scheduled in the near future or when the dates scheduled are not convenient for him. By comparing the number of pre-bookings and the Course capacity, the system can determine the number of times a Course Type needs to be scheduled. Another way of planning Course dates is by estimating a fixed percentage increase or decrease to the total number of participants for a Course Type in the past planning periods. Such a planning option may not be sufficient for an organization's planning.

When scheduling individually or en masse, Courses can be scheduled either in *Planned* or *Firmly Booked* status. The Planned status indicates that the Course date is planned to ensure enough attendees book the class, whereas the Firmly Booked status indicates the schedule is confirmed, regardless of the number of attendees.

A learner can still book a Course that is in Planned status. The administrator can confirm the Course and change its status to Firmly Booked, once there are sufficient participants to the Course. So, system-wise, the behavior of both planned and firmly booked Courses is almost the same, except that it would not be possible to follow up Courses in Planned status.

While scheduling a Course, the system checks for the resource types specified as needed for the parent Course Type and prompts the administrator to fulfill such requirements. For example, for a Course that needs a room and an instructor, the administrator might be prompted to specify the actual room (e.g., Training Room 1, Main Building) and instructor (e.g., Carmen Green from Marketing).

Course scheduling is mostly done through the *Dynamic Course Menu*. Administrators can also cancel or change Course schedules through the Dynamic Course Menu, and Courses can be locked for valid reasons to prevent learners from booking the Course.

6.5   Day-To-Day Activities

On a day-to-day basis, an administrator might manage participation for Courses and send correspondences to different parties involved in learning. Most of these participation management activities are carried out through the Dynamic Participation Menu (see Table 6.3). Both internal and external learners can be booked to a Course — for instance, you may just as easily enroll a customer contact person from Sales and Distribution as enroll an employee hired into SAP ERP HCM. We will talk about the configurations governing participation management later in the chapter.

Dynamic Participation Menu Functions	Definition	Dynamic Course Menu Functions	Definition
Book attendee	*Enroll attendee in Course, with fee recorded if appropriate. All delivery methods supported.*	Cancel Course	*Cancel a Course (track cancelation reason and history).*
Book multiple attendees (Book List)	*Enroll more than one attendee at a time in a Course. Selection may be from a list, a query, or by department.*	Firmly booking a Course	*Move Course from a planned to an active status (validate minimum participation/generate confirmation emails).*
Cancel attendee	*Cancel an attendance (track cancellation reason and associated fee)*	Locking/ unlocking Course	*Temporarily remove a Course from enrollment by flagging as "locked."*
Prebook attendee	*Track interest in or demand for a Course Type*	Appraisal management	*Enter appraisal results for those attendees who completed paper forms, rather than online forms for Course evaluation.*
Rebook attendee	*Cancel an attendance for a Course date and book the same attendee in a new Course date in one step.*	Follow-up Course	*Mark attendance, indicate Pass/Fail/Completion status for all attendees, impart and evaluate qualifications, and flag Course completion.*
Replace attendee	*Cancel an attendance and book a different attendee to the same Course date in one step.*		
Correspondence Generation	*Correspondence not generated automatically may be managed manually.*		
Cost Allocation	*Manage charge-backs (Course fee) and instructor activity functions and generate a document to transfer costs to SAP Controlling application.*		

Table 6.3 Dynamic Participation Menu Functions

Note

Later in this chapter, we will also see how many of these functions are replicated in Section 6.19, Training Administrator Portal.

6.6 Follow-up Activities

Recurring Activities are activities that don't occur as regularly as those listed in the 'Day-to-Day' activities section, such as closing out a class (Course follow-up) or Course evaluation processes. Of these processes, it is important to understand Course follow-up because the process is extremely flexible and has enhanced functionality as of LSO600.

Following up a Course is an important post-training activity that consists of the following steps:

▶ Confirming Course participation (marking learner as present or absent for the class)

▶ Evaluating participation (marking learner as passed or failed)

▶ Transferring qualifications imparted by the Course to the learner's profile (with or without changing the qualification proficiency)

▶ Marking the Course as "followed-up," indicating that the Course is finished

The different steps of a follow-up process can be carried out by different parties, such as learners, instructors, or administrators. For example, learners can confirm their participation and administrators can do the rest. Instructors can confirm and evaluate participation, and the final stages can be carried out by administrators. It's also possible that some of the follow-up steps are automatically performed by the system. For instance, for Web-based training, learners can confirm their participation in the Course. The system can then perform the rest of activities.

6.7 Configuring Enterprise Learning

As with many SAP solutions, the configuration of SAP Enterprise Learning takes place within the Implementation Guide (IMG) of the backend ERP system, under TRAINING AND EVENT MANAGEMENT • SAP ENTERPRISE LEARNING • TRAINING MANAGEMENT. The IMG consists of multiple entries that direct you to tables that allow you to drive the functionality of SAP Enterprise Learning. There is additional setup that takes place outside the IMG in the installation of the Portal views and the setup of the Content Management System and the Authoring Environment. We discussed this in Chapter 3, SAP Enterprise Learning Architecture.

In addition to the four sections of the IMG we discussed in the previous section that parallel the Training Management process, two additional configuration areas exist in Training Management.

▸ **Basic Settings** contains tables that are replicated in many of the SAP HR modules.

▸ **Integration** contains the table entries that allow Enterprise Learning to integrate with other SAP functional areas such as Sales and Distribution or Financials.

Although Basic Settings and Integration appear at the front of the IMG, we will discuss these at the end of the configuration section, after we have addressed the configuration specific to the training administration phases discussed previously.

If you implemented Training and Event Management at your organization in the past, much of the configuration from the previous implementation will transfer over to your Enterprise Learning implementation. This is an automatic process that occurs as soon as Enterprise Learning is activated. Even if you did implement Training and Events Management in the past, you should definitely review all existing configuration, because some functions and table entries from Training and Event Management have been replaced with new functions in Training Management. Three examples include the *Correspondence Functionality*, *Follow-up Functions*, and *Course Appraisals*.

6.7.1 Activate Business Functions

Before you begin any implementation of SAP Enterprise Learning, ensure that Enterprise Extension EA-HR is implemented. To activate this, you must go to the IMG via Transaction SPRO and select the first entry, located directly under SAP Customizing Implementation Guide: ACTIVATE BUSINESS FUNCTIONS (Transaction SFW5). In the Enterprise Business Functions folder, select EA-HR and then ACTIVATE CHANGES.

Once this is complete, open the subordinate folder ENTERPRISE BUSINESS FUNCTIONS and ensure HCM_LSO_CI_1 and HCM_LSO_CI_2 are activated. These provide enhancement package 2 and enhancement package 4 functionality, respectively. A third business function, HCM_LSO_VLR, provides additional functionality with Enterprise Learning, specifically the Adobe Connect functionality, which we will cover in detail in Chapter 7.

6.7.2 SAP Learning Solution

Three entries fall immediately under the SAP Enterprise Learning section of the IMG ACTIVATE/DEACTIVATE SAP ENTERPRISE LEARNING • EXECUTE BOOKING RELATIONSHIP HARMONIZATION • MIGRATE SCORM ELEMENTS FROM SCORM 1.2 TO SCORM 2004.

The first entry, ACTIVATE/DEACTIVATE SAP ENTERPRISE LEARNING, is key when using Enterprise Learning functionality. Upon execution of this IMG entry, you will see a report interface. Execute the report and all old Training and Event Management data will be converted to the new Enterprise Learning format. Table 6.4 lists key elements that will change.

Element	Change Description
Object Names	Old Training and Event Management object names (e.g., Business Event Group or Business Event Type) are replaced with Enterprise Learning Names (e.g., Course Group and Course Type).
Infotype Texts	Old Training and Event Management infotypes (e.g., Business Event Info) are replaced with Enterprise Learning infotypes (e.g., Course Info).
Relationship Texts	Old Training and Event Management relationships (e.g., "is location of") are replaced with Enterprise Learning relationships (e.g., "is Course location of").
Customizing Settings in Tables	The HRLSO-HRLSO value in table T77S0 is set to "X" to indicate Enterprise Learning is activated. Function modules are updated in many tables to reflect Enterprise Learning functionality (e.g., the SEMIN CCDCT value in table T77S0 is updated to LSO_PRICES from RH_PRICES).
Screen Adjustments	New screen views are added to table to support the Enterprise Learning delivery methods.

Table 6.4 Key Elements

Configuring the entry EXECUTE BOOKING RELATIONSHIP HARMONIZATION is only necessary if you have legacy Training and Event Management data in your system or if you have SAP Enterprise Learning data from a release earlier than release SAP Learning Solution 600 version. This entry is another report interface and executes the program RHSETPADBOOK_LSO. Execution of this program causes the system changes included in Table 6.5.

Element	Change Description
Document Number	A booking document number is created for all legacy booking relationships between a person and an instructor-led Course. Ensure that the Document Numbers are configured prior to executing this report (see Basic Settings for a discussion of Document Numbers).
Follow-up Information	All employees with training history will have the values "Confirmed," "Passed," and "Followed-Up" added to their training records.

Table 6.5 System Changes

The final entry, Migrate SCORM Elements from SCORM 1.2 to SCORM 2004, is the supporting feature of SCORM 2004 compliance, a feature delivered with enhancement pack 2 for SAP ERP. This step is only necessary if you have SCORM 1.2 data in your LSO* tables, which is the related learning progress information of learners prior to implementing the SCORM 2004 compliance feature. This IMG report moves data from the backend table that supported SCORM 1.2 values (LSOLEARNSCORM_C) to new SCORM 2004 tables (LSOCPSCOMRSSTR, LSOCPSCORMLSTR, LOCPSCOR-MINT, and LSOCPSCORMREAL). The documentation for this IMG entry provides in-depth information about legacy values and how they will be supported with the new table structure.

6.7.3   Course Preparation

The Course Preparation IMG section allows you to create and maintain master data and supports some minor configuration settings as well. This master data is generally created in the *Current Settings* section of Training Management, via the Master Data Catalog, because transactional data is rarely created in the IMG and transported. Examples of this data include Course Catalog data (e.g., Course Groups, Course Types, Curriculum Types, and Course Programs) and supporting elements such as rooms and equipment, schedules, and training providers. Because the tables that store this data are considered customizing tables, this information can also be set up initially in the IMG and transported to the Production client. Transports take place using the RHMOVE30 and RHMOVE50 programs and are driven by the setting TRSP CORR in Table T77SO. As noted earlier, this rarely happens because most companies create this data during their initial Training Management implementation via a conversion and then training coordinators maintain it as needed in the production system.

Integrating with Externally Hosted Content

In addition to the Current Settings data discussed previously, the Course Preparation section also supports the setup of external training providers who host learning content or who manage Virtual Classrooms (VCs) and the creation and maintenance of Delivery Methods. The External Training Providers configuration allows your learners to access hosted third-party content and track progress data back to SAP Enterprise Learning. When third-party content is hosted, there is no need for it to adhere to the SCORM or AICC standards, as long as the required data can be mapped back to SAP leveraging XI Services. This information is maintained via the IMG menu path COURSE PREPARATION • TRAINING PROVIDER • EXTERNAL TRAINING PROVIDER. In this setting, you identify each Training Provider in a table, using a unique key. Once Training Providers are identified, you associate them with the appropriate services, based on what they support. SAP supports XI services that allow for the following functions: Course Enrollment; Course Access, Course Cancellation; and Read/Write Learning Data. You may also use XI services to Create, Change, and Delete External Courses.

Once the appropriate functions have been associated with each vendor ID, you associate the ID with an actual vendor or company as *Master Data*. If you use this functionality, work with an XI consultant or expert to manage the connections to and from the third-party providers. Your third-party provider will also need to support Web services and there may be development effort on their side as well. One additional switch, HRLSO TRACK, allows you to determine whether learning progress on a hosted site should be automatically synchronized or whether it should be updated in a batch. If you select the batch option, report RHWSTRACKING_LSO will need to be scheduled. This configuration may be overridden via Course Type Maintenance on the External Course Catalog Connection Infotype (IT5042.)

Configuring Course Delivery Methods

SAP delivers 13 Delivery Methods in Table V_LSOTFORM_C for use with SAP Enterprise Learning. You may access these via menu path COURSE PREPARATION • DELIVERY METHODS • DEFINE DELIVERY METHODS. You may review the SAP Standard Delivery methods and, if necessary, rename or copy them to create Custom Delivery methods (see Table 6.6).

When you create Custom Delivery methods, you are unable to change the properties of the Standard Delivery methods. For example, if you offer training that you identify as "Coaching," you might choose to copy the standard delivery method Classroom Training and rename it "Coaching." Because you chose this standard delivery method as your model for Coaching, all Courses with the Coaching delivery method must be scheduled with a specific time and a specific location.

Delivery Method	Object Type Created	Relationship Type Created	Time Specific?	Location Specific?	Backend Booking Supported?	Content Stored
Classroom Training	D/E	A 025	Yes	Yes	Yes	None
Virtual Classroom Training	D/E	A 025	Yes	No	Yes	Static link to the virtual classroom URL
Web-Based Training	D/ET	A 614	No	No	Yes	e-learning content
Online Test	D/ET	A 614	No	No	Yes	online test
Curriculum	DC/EC	A 614	Yes	No	Yes	None
Static Web-Based Training	D/ET	A 614	No	No	Yes	Static URL of the web page to be launched
External Web-Based Training	D/ET	A 614	No	No	Yes	Externally hosted content
External Classroom Training	D/E	A 025	Yes	Yes	Yes	None
External Virtual Classroom Training	D/E	A 025	Yes	No	Yes	External
External Online Test	D/ET	A 614	No	No	Yes	Externally hosted online test
WBT in Classroom	D/E	A 025	Yes	No	Yes	e-learning content

Table 6.6 Standard Delivery Methods and Their Properties

Delivery Method	Object Type Created	Relationship Type Created	Time Specific?	Location Specific?	Backend Booking Supported?	Content Stored
Course Program	EK/EK	A 614	Yes	No	Yes	None
Virtual Learning Room	D/E	A 025	Yes	No	Yes	None

Table 6.6 Standard Delivery Methods and Their Properties (Cont.)

Control Elements

The final entry in this section of the IMG, CONTROL ELEMENTS in table view LSO_ T77S0, controls system reactions for Curriculums and Web-based training. All entries configured here will default when a Course Type or Curriculum type is created but may be overridden by the Course administrator when working in Create or Change mode. Table 6.7 illustrates these entries and shows the possible values.

Definition	Table Key		Value	Table Description
Determine if Courses that must be sequential in a Curriculum may have dates that overlap.	HRLSO	ECOVL	"X" = Yes " " = No	Create Curriculum with Overlapping Participation
Determine what percentage of Learning Objectives must be attained as a learner progresses through a Course to achieve "Pass"	HRLSO	FPEBO	Any percentage up to 100.00 in the format "00.00"	Percentage Learning Objectives to Be Achieved
Determine what percentage of Learning Objects must be completed as a learner progresses through a Course to achieve "Pass"	HRLSO	FPLO	Any percentage up to 100.00 in the format "00.00"	Percentage Learning Objects to Be Completed
Indicate whether the default value for Learning Objectives configured in HRLSO FPEBO should be "Active" for all WBT Course Types.	HRLSO	FREBO	"X" = Active " " = Inactive	Achieved Learning Objectives as Success Criterion

Table 6.7 Control Elements

Definition	Table Key		Value	Table Description
Indicate whether the default value for Learning Objects configured in HRLSO FPLO should be "Active" for all WBT Course Types.	HRLSO	FRLO	"X" = Active " " = Inactive	Completed Learning Objects as Success Criterion

Table 6.7 Control Elements (Cont.)

6.8 Course Offering Section

The COURSE OFFERING section of the IMG corresponds to the training phase in which training coordinators plan Course offerings and set up Course dates with and without resources. There is no new configuration in this section in relation to the SAP Enterprise Learning, so if you have already configured it for a previous TEM implementation, you may skip the following configuration steps.

Course Offering has only one executable, CONTROL ELEMENTS, with three configuration entries:

▸ SEMIN FORCA

▸ SEMIN KAP

▸ SEMIN PFORC

SEMIN FORCA provides a default value for how many days in advance training coordinators may view the training catalog in the Dynamic Course and Dynamic Participation Menus. The delivered entry is 90 and this is generally acceptable, because administrators may override this value when they personalize their view of the catalog.

The entry *SEMIN KAP* indicates the default capacity for a Course if an administrator did not enter this information when he created the Course Type.

> **Note**
>
> In the delivered system, this field is required, so this value rarely comes into play.

Finally, the entry *SEMIN PFORC* shows the default date range an administrator will see the first time he schedules a class. The default value is 360, but this will be overridden at the administrator view when the user specific settings of the Course Catalogs are maintained.

6.9 Day-to-Day Activities

Many of the settings in this area are switches that control how the system should react in various situations related to bookings and cancellations or the day-to-day administrative steps of a training coordinator or administrator. This section also controls the settings related to correspondence and workflow. Again, you may already have configured much of this section in a previous TEM implementation.

6.9.1 Control Elements

The first section of Day-to-Day Activities is a Control Elements view of Table T77S0. Three switches and their functions and values are outlined in Table 6.8.

Definition	Table Key		Value	Table Description
Determine if Courses that have been historically followed up may have attendance changes made to them.	SEMIN	HISTO	"E" — Error (no changes possible) "W" — Warning (changes possible with warning) "I" — Information (changes possible with informational message) " " – Changes possible, no message.	Message type for changes to historical attendances
Determine if you need a maximum capacity for a class waiting list.	SEMIN	WKAPM	Enter a percentage value of the maximum number of attendees that may appear on the waiting list. A blank value means there is no maximum capacity.	Maximum waiting list capacity
If there is a maximum value entered in SEMIN WKAPM, you may issue a message when that value is exceeded.	SEMIN	WKAPT	"E" — Error (May not exceed maximum capacity) "W" — Warning (May exceed maximum capacity with warning message issued) "I" — Information (May exceed maximum capacity with informational message issued) " " — May exceed maximum capacity, no message.	Message Type When Waiting List Capacity Exceeded

Table 6.8 Control Elements

Definition	Table Key		Value	Table Description
Determine if the administrator should be notified if there is a Course scheduled when a prebooking transaction to a related Course Type is made.	SEMIN	OFFER	"1" — When a prebooking occurs, notify the administrator if there is a class scheduled in the future. " " – No notification is issued for future scheduled Courses.	Read Business Event Offer when Prebooking

Table 6.8 Control Elements (Cont.)

6.9.2 Booking

The Booking section of Day-to-Day Activities allows you to determine the types of attendees you will work with and how the system should treat each type of attendee. A series of entries in the IMG support the following decisions.

- What types of attendees will our implementation support?
- What types of checks should occur for different training activities surrounding each attendee type?
- If there are issues with attendances, how should these be handled?
- How should Course fees be determined?

The Attendee Types table is from Training Management, so not all Attendee Types in the table are valid or currently supported. The settings noted in Table 6.9 may be overridden if there is a business need to do so, but these settings are designed to meet the needs of most organizations.

The delivered Attendee Types and their properties are as follows in Table 6.9.

Attendee Type	Definition	Organizational Assignment	Course Fee Information
Applicant	This attendee type is related to the old recruitment module and is not valid for the SAP Enterprise Learning.	N/A	N/A

Table 6.9 Attendee Types and Properties

Attendee Type	Definition	Organizational Assignment	Course Fee Information
External person	This attendee type is an individual attendee type that is created in Training Management to store training history for persons who are not maintained in the HR Master Data.	External persons may belong to Companies.	Billing may occur based on SD integration configuration.
Prospect	This attendee type is created within Training Management and has no current functionality.	N/A	Free of Charge
Customer	The attendee type is a group attendee type maintained in SD.	N/A	Billing may occur based on SD integration configuration.
Candidate	This attendee type is an individual attendee type pulled from e-recruiting.	N/A	Free of Charge
Organizational unit	This attendee type represents organizational units as created in HR Organizational Management. It is a group attendee type and may be used to hold places for unknown participants from a particular organizational unit.	N/A	Activity allocation occurs as determined by cost center assignment. This is determined by evaluation path A011, which finds the cost center related to the Organizational Unit via the A011 relationship.
Person	This attendee type represents an individual employee and is pulled directly from the HR Master Database.	Person should belong to an Organizational Unit	Activity allocation occurs as determined by cost center assignment. This is determined by function module RH_GET_KOSTL_P, which checks cost center assignment at the person level, the position level and the organizational unit level to determine the appropriate cost center.

Table 6.9 Attendee Types and Properties (Cont.)

Attendee Type	Definition	Organizational Assignment	Course Fee Information
Contact person	This attendee type is an individual attendee type maintained in Sales and Distribution.	Contact person should belong to a Customer.	Billing is determined based on customer billing information.

Table 6.9 Attendee Types and Properties (Cont.)

For each Attendee type outlined in the table above, you must also determine a series of system checks.

▸ Should the attendee type receive qualifications?

▸ What type of message should the attendee receive if he books or is booked to a class where the attendee does not have the required prerequisite attendance or qualification?

▸ Should a qualification be imparted (when associated to the Course Type) for the specific attendee type?

The IMG entry DAY-TO-DAY ACTIVITIES • BOOKING • PARTICIPANT CHECKS (table V_T77KV_1) allows you to configure default values for each of these business processes. These values may be overridden by an administrator in the Procedure Infotype at the Course Type level (IT1030). Usually, organizations give access to the Procedure Infotype only to "super users" or users who are experts in their understanding of the system. This is because overriding these settings at the Course Type level may impact how the system records history or imparts qualifications for those specific Courses.

You can also determine what should happen (Error Message; Warning Message; Information Message; No system reaction) if an attendee attempts to attend two classes with overlapping time schedules or to attend a class while he is scheduled to instruct. This functionality does not require Time Management integration, because the system simply checks booking/instruction relationships and the associated Course schedules. It is configured in Table T77S0, found in the IMG under DAY-TO-DAY ACTIVITIES • BOOKING • CONFLICT REACTION and is a global setting, so it may not be overridden by an administrator.

6.9.3   Versioning

Versioning functionality is supported from SAP Learning Solution 600 version. This allows you to drive how bookings are managed when content is re-versioned. During requirements gathering, you identify the types of changes that may occur to content during its lifecycle (e.g., Major Changes, Minor Changes, Corrections). In the IMG, you record the change types in Table V_LSOCHANGECAT and then specify how the system should react to each type of change in table V_LSOCHANGEREAC. The reactions you may choose from are as follows:

▶ Does the learner have to start the content again or may he choose to start again with the updated content?

▶ Will the learner's progress remain or will it be deleted?

▶ If the learner chooses to start a Course again, will an additional fee be charged?

Both of these entries are found in the IMG under Day-to-Day Activities • Booking • Versioning. This configuration may be overridden at the Course Type level on the Version Control Options Infotype (IT5049).

6.9.4 Participation Cancellation

Cancellation functions for participants are also managed in the IMG, via path Day-to-Day Activities • Participation Cancellation. The first entry is another Control Options executable, which allows you to define the following:

The relationship that should be created between an attendee and a Course, when that attendee cancels or is canceled from a Course. The default relationship *is cancelled by* (A/B 040) and should not be changed.

▶ The default percentage of a Course fee that should be charged when the Course participation is cancelled and if such fees are set up to be automatically charged. The value may range from "0" (no fee) to "100" (full fee).

▶ The mode for attendees to move up from a waitlist when a booked attendee cancels from a full class. When using Enterprise Learning, it makes sense to configure this value as "D" for "Automatic Selection". This means the move-up will occur automatically, based on the prioritization of the waitlist. The other options are "I," which provides an administrator the facility to manually select from the waitlisted learners (this option cannot be utilized when the Course is cancelled by a learner from the Learning Portal) and "N," which indicates that nothing will happen to the attendees on the waitlist in such situations.

> **Note**
>
> Waitlist priority is determined as follows: priority of booking if (manually) entered by an administrator, date of booking, and then by attendee name (alphabetical).

The second entry in the Participation Cancellation section is GUIDELINES. In structure LSO_T77S0, you set up default values regarding self-cancellations for Curriculums and Web-based trainings via the Learning Portal. These settings may be overridden by an administrator at the Course Type or Curriculum type level, so it makes sense to determine what should generally happen and configure these entries appropriately with the understanding that these values may vary among Course Types and Curriculum types. In the first entry, HRLSO ECCAN, you indicate whether a learner can cancel himself from a Curriculum. At a global level, you indicate (a) whether a learner can cancel from a Curriculum and (b), if so, if the learner must cancel from every element in that Curriculum or only from those not already completed.

If you are using Curriculums to support attendees booking themselves easily into related Courses and have no need for completion of all the Curriculum elements, you would probably choose option (a). If you are using Curriculums to support blended learning, you are more likely to select option (b), because you will not want a learner getting partial credit for a blended learning offering. In the second entry, HRLSO ETCAN, you indicate whether a learner can self-cancel from a WBT that has already been started. If you disallow self-cancellation, an administrator can still cancel a learner on the backend.

The entry immediately below the Guidelines executable is "Reasons for Participant Cancellation" (Table T77CART). Here, you enter general attendance cancellation reasons such as "No Show," "Unplanned Leave," "Business Related Emergency," and "Manager requested Cancellation" (to support workflow). Each reason may also have a percentage associated with it for chargeback purposes. The percentage will be compared to the Course price and the calculated amount will be charged to the attendee, unless overridden.

If you choose to implement this functionality, you must have configured ACTIVITY ALLOCATION in the Integration section of the IMG. If you are allowing self-cancellation via the Portal, you will need to add a generic cancellation reason such as "Self-Cancellation via Portal" to this list of reasons. You then indicate this reason is the default reason used when someone self-cancels via the Portal in the entry Cancellation Reason for Cancellations in Learning Portal (entry SEMIN WEBST in structure LSO_T77S0). You may allow learners to choose their own cancellation reasons by implementing the BAdI Define Customer Specific Cancellation Reasons (LSO_CANCELREASONS_C).

6.9.5 Workflow and Correspondence

While the previous entries are simple configuration switches, the next two entries in Day-to-Day Activities are more complicated. Out of the box, SAP delivers standard Approval Workflow and Correspondence functions. This chapter will explain the standard processes, but you may want to consult technical resources to customize Workflow and Correspondence to fit your business requirements.

The delivered workflow functions in Enterprise Learning allow you to request approvals for booking and cancellations globally, by delivery method, and by attendee type. You may override these settings at the Course Type level. The delivered booking functionality has two sub-workflows: one related to time-dependent classes, such as ILT; and one related to time-independent classes, such as WBT. The Workflow checks for the attendee's manager via the chief (A/B 012) relationship and routes the appropriate request to the holder of the chief position.

If the request relates to booking to a time-based class, such as an ILT, a spot is held for the attendee until receiving an approval or rejection. In this subflow, you can set a time frame to indicate that the learner's booking should be automatically approved if the system receives no managerial approval until this time frame. For example, if the system does not receive approval five days before the class starts and the timing is five days, it automatically enrolls the attendee. The subflow that relates to a time independent class does not cause an enrollment spot to be held and there is no approval time frame, because time independent classes do not have a capacity or schedule. The cancellation request works similarly and also has two subflows. The following is a list defining the configuration entries for workflow in Table LSOWF_CUSTOMIZE.

- **For Booking:**
  - The delivered booking workflow ID is task 12000003.
  - The Object type is LSO_PARTIC.
  - The Event is "BOOKREQUEST."

- **For Cancellation:**
  - The delivered cancellation workflow ID is task 12000004.
  - The Object type is LSO_PARTIC.
  - The Event "CANCELREQUEST."

- **The options for Create Event include:**
  - **Always Generate Event:** Select this option if you want workflow called regardless of the Learner's authorization profile.
  - **Execute Action Without Event Generation:** Select this option if you wish to lock down cancellation or booking requests within a certain time frame but not invoke workflow approvals. As an example of this, as an organization

you may not wish to use workflow approvals, but you would like to disallow learners from cancelling five days before a Course is scheduled to begin. To do this, you would configure Workflow for the delivery method "Classroom Training" and indicate that you would like to execute the action "Lockdown the Course" at five days before the start date without generating a Workflow Event to a manager or supervisor for approval. Any learner who wishes to book a class five days or less before the begin date must contact an administrator to book to the class.

▶ **Only Generate Event if Authorization for Action is Missing:** Select this option if you wish to trigger workflow for certain users only. For example, you might decide that workflow should only trigger for employees in a certain organizational unit.

This configuration may be overridden by an administrator at the Course Type level on Infotype Workflow Settings (5041).

Enterprise Learning's Request-Based Correspondence function is an alternative to the SAPScript-based notifications used in SAP Learning Solution, and earlier in Training and Event Management. The new correspondence allows you to use Adobe PDF and SmartForm functionality via the Print Workbench. You still have the option to use SAPScript-based correspondence functions, if you prefer, but you will not be able to use the increased functionality of the new Correspondence. In addition to the new output format, the new functions allow you to determine:

▶ Which business process trigger which notifications

▶ Which roles should receive which notifications

▶ The exact notification per activity and role

▶ Where and when to send notifications (by activity, role, and notification type)

Additionally, the new correspondence supports Microsoft Outlook or Lotus appointments and short message service (SMS) notifications. Five Business Add-Ins (BAdIs) can further personalize the correspondence functions.

The BAdI "Specify Correspondence Control Options" allows you to fine tune the rules you have set up to control correspondence. For example, you may use this BAdI to identify specific attendees who should not receive correspondence when they attend specific classes.

The BAdIs "Specify Access to Communication Data" and "Specify Communication Parameters for Recipients" allow you to send correspondence to recipients via methods other than email, such as SMS/pagers.

The BAdI "Change Output Control Options" (LSO_CORRESPONDENCE43) allows you to change the delivered name of a notification (in the standard, the email title is the same as the form set up in the Print Workbench), while the BAdI "Determine Sender" provides the ability to specify who the sender of a mail should be (for example, a default email address for the Training Department).

An ABAP consultant familiar with the Correspondence Tool and Print Workbench functions is necessary as these tools are not LSO specific.

> **Tip**
>
> If you wish to send Lotus or Outlook attachments, the delivered documentation for Correspondence describes the process in detail, including code examples. Review chapter "Example: Adding Attachments" under Training Management • Day-to-Day Activities • Correspondence • Request Based Correspondence • Integration of SAP Tools • Examples for Changing Output Options via the following link: *http://help.sap.com/saphelp_erp2005/helpdata/en/30/e63a3c24b4a00ae10000000a11402f/frameset.htm*

6.10   Recurring Activities

As mentioned, recurring activities include activities that are performed regularly such as Course follow-ups, tracking Course participation and completion, tracking and analyzing Course feedbacks and billing and training cost allocation activities.

The following business decisions are considered when configuring the recurring activities:

▶ Upon Course completion, will you impart qualifications to attendees, when relevant?

▶ How will you track successful completion of online learning?

▶ How will you follow up on Curriculums (on a Course-by-Course basis or all at once when the Curriculum is complete)?

▶ Who/what should handle the follow-up process for different delivery methods (the system automatically, the learner, the instructor, the administrator, or a combination of these roles)?

▶ What types of appraisals (or Course/instructor/attendee evaluations) do you wish to support?

6.10.1 Completion Specifications for a Course

IMG entry FOLLOW UP • DEFINE LEARNING PROGRESS CONTROL allows you to enter default values in structure LSO_T77S0 to indicate how completion of online Courses should be managed. These entries may be overridden at the Course Type level by an administrator:

▸ Entry HRLSO FPEB0 indicates how many Learning Objectives or knowledge indicators a learner must achieve to pass an online Course. These are often attained by passing a pre-test or post-test associated with a Course.

▸ Entry HRLSO PPL0 indicates how many Learning Objects or SCOs a learner must progress through to pass an online Course.

The next two entries, HRLSO FREB0 and HRLSO FRL0, simply indicate whether the first two values should be taken into account as success criterion.

6.10.2 Course Follow-Up

New functionality with LSO600 allows you to configure more specific follow-up functions for all delivery methods. In this configuration, you will indicate per delivery method, the appropriate roles that will carry out a specific follow-up step (see Figure 6.4).

Table 6.10 summarizes the different follow-up options that are available to different roles.

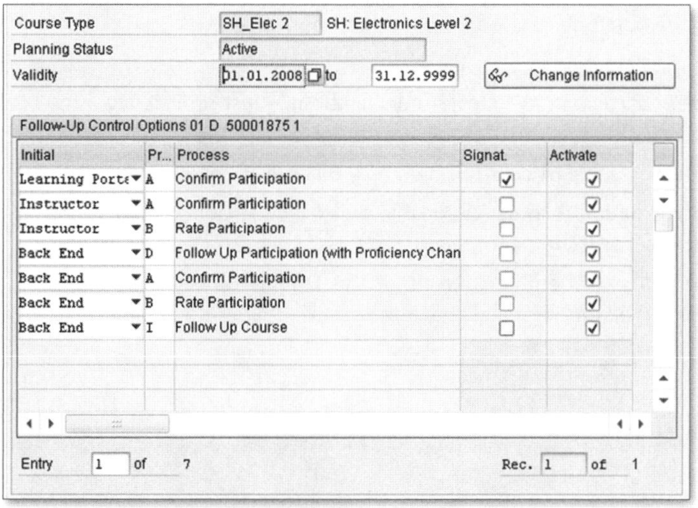

Figure 6.4 Follow-Up Control Options

Training Administrator	▸ Confirm Participation
	▸ Evaluate Participation (In the case of WBTs, the content player can determine whether a learner passed or failed the Course.)
	▸ Follow up participation:
	— Follow-up participation (transfer qualification, adjust proficiency or not, set participation to status "follow-up complete") or
	— Follow-up passed participation (i.e., only if status is "passed")
	▸ Follow-up Course (set entire Course to status "follow-up complete"; this is possible only if all participations have the status "follow-up complete")
	▸ Historically record Course (sets entire Course to status "historically recorded," which is equivalent to archiving the Course; this is possible only if all participations have the status "follow-up done").
Learner	▸ Confirm participation
	▸ Confirm passed participation (can only confirm a Course that the learner has passed; applicable only for WBTs)
Instructor	▸ Confirm Participation
	▸ Evaluate Participation (In the case of WBTs, the content player can determine whether a learner passed or failed the Course)
	▸ Follow up participation:
	— Follow-up participation (transfer qualification, adjust proficiency or not, set participation to status "follow-up complete") or
	— Follow-up *passed* participation (i.e., only if status is "passed")
System (Automatic Processing)	▸ Evaluate Participation (In the case of WBTs, the content player can determine whether a learner passed or failed the Course)
	▸ Follow up participation:
	— Follow-up participation (transfer qualification, adjust proficiency or not, set participation to status "follow-up complete") or
	— Follow-up *passed* participation (i.e., only if status is "passed")
	▸ Delimit participation records (applicable only for WBT Courses where the participation records are delimited)
	▸ Follow-up Course (set entire Course to status "follow-up complete"; this is possible only if all participations have the status "follow-up complete")

Table 6.10 Follow-Up Options

Table 6.11 gives several scenarios for following-up a Course.

Scenario	Description
Classroom Training	
Scenario 1	Administrator carries out all process steps
Scenario 2	Lerner confirms participation in Learning Portal; administrator carries out all subsequent steps
Scenario 3	Learner confirms participation in Learning Portal; all subsequent steps are done by system
Scenario 4	Instructor confirms and rates participation; administrator performs all other steps.
Scenario 5	Learner confirms participation in the Learning Portal; Instructor evaluates and follows-up participation; administrator does other activities.
WBT Course	
Scenario 1	Learner confirms passed participation; all subsequent steps are done by system
Scenario 2	Learner confirms participation for a passed Course; administrator carries out all subsequent steps

Table 6.11 Follow-Up Scenarios

Note

The follow-up functions discussed in the previous paragraph may be overwritten at the Course Type level using Infotype 5047 (Follow-up Control Options). If you have implemented a previous version, Infotype 5047 replaces the electronic signature functionality on Infotype 5044 (see Figure 6.4).

6.10.3 Course Appraisals

From an appraisals standpoint, SAP delivers a template for classroom Courses (in general, instructor-led Courses) and Web-based training Course evaluations that you can copy and use for Level 1 Appraisals (based on Kirkpatrick's Four Levels of Evaluation).

Via the IMG from Recurring Activities, open the Appraisals section. Here, you see the option to switch on Performance Management in Structure LSO_T77S0, Entry HAP00 REPLA. Although there appear to be multiple options for turning on appraisals, the only valid entries are "blank," which indicates that you are not using the appraisals functionality or "A," which indicates that you are replacing the old appraisals functions with the new. Be aware that selecting this entry also requires that you replace the old Performance Management functionality with the new Performance Management appraisal functionality, regardless of what the configuration options seem to indicate. The entries "T" (Replace Only Course Appraisal) and "X" (Replace only Personnel Appraisal) have the same functionality as entry "A."

> **Note**
>
> To access appraisals via SAP Enterprise Learning, you must complete this step. The appraisal functionality from older releases (R/3 4.6C and back) is not supported via the Portal.

Once you have indicated that you are using the new appraisals functions, you must create your appraisal templates via the IMG entry EDIT FORMS. Here, you use SAP's delivered templates as models to create your own, custom templates. Finally, in structure LSO_T77S0, entry HRLSO TEMPL, you indicate the default template that should be used for all Courses if a Course specific template has not been identified.

6.11 Basic Settings

As noted in the introduction to Section 6.2, Configuring Course Preparation Activities, the BASIC SETTINGS section of the IMG is replicated among many different SAP ERP HCM components. Configuration of many of the Basic Settings is required for Personnel Development, Performance Management, and Organizational Management functionality. Rather than touching on every switch within this section of the IMG, we will highlight only those that have Enterprise Learning specific functionality or that significantly impact Enterprise Learning functions.

Basic Settings is located under TRAINING MANAGEMENT in the SAP Enterprise Learning section of the IMG. The first entry that must be reviewed and possibly configured is DEFINE NUMBER RANGES FOR COURSE PARTICIPATION DOCUMENT within the IMG section NUMBER RANGE MAINTENANCE (Transaction LSP_TP_C) (see Figure 6.5). Your configuration should mirror that shown in Figure 6.5.

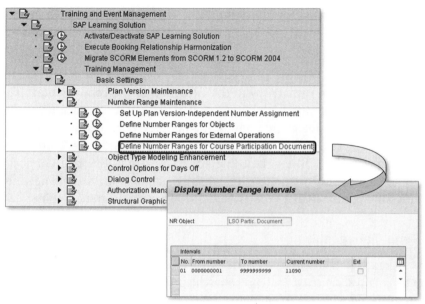

Figure 6.5 Number Range Maintenance

As mentioned previously, for each booking made within Enterprise Learning, whether to an Instructor-Led Class or to a Web-based Training, a number is generated by the system. This number acts as a reference to that particular booking throughout SAP Enterprise Learning backend tables. Thus, to book a person to a Course using Enterprise Learning, you must set up participant document number ranges. You will see the document numbers referenced in the Additional Data structure of every online learning enrollment record (field TPARTDOCNO in structures PAD25 and PAD614).

If you are interested, you can also review the new objects, infotypes, and relationships associated with SAP Enterprise Learning. These are located in the section of the IMG titled OBJECT TYPE MODELING ENHANCEMENT in Tables T777O, T778T, and T778V, respectively.

6.12 Integration

As you have progressed into the IMG, you have probably noticed that much of the configuration options follow a similar pattern — they are a series of switches, most of which are entries in Table T77S0, which you make selections on based on your business processes as determined during your Blueprint. The INTEGRA-

TION section of the IMG is no exception to this. It lists all the integration points between Training Management and other components and highlights their related configuration.

If you have worked with Training and Event Management, you will note there is little new functionality in this area with the exception of the configuration that relates to the Virtual Learning Room and Collaboration. However, we will outline each of the different integration points at a high level and discuss how they support Enterprise Learning. The one exception, the Virtual Learning Room, will be discussed in Chapter 7, Virtual Learning Room, powered by Adobe Connect. Please note that for the majority of the integration configuration, you will need to work with your cross-functional experts as you set up each integration point.

6.12.1 Time Management

The first integration point, Time Management, allows the system to check an attendee's attendance and absence types to prevent schedule conflicts with training bookings or instructor bookings. If an employee attempts to book to a class in this situation or if an administrator attempts to reserve an instructor in this situation, the system will issue an error indicating that Course attendance or Course instruction is not possible. When bookings or instruction are possible, this integration updates an attendee's or instructor's time records with training related attendance types. Specifically, the integration with Time Management allows administrators to:

1. **Prevent conflicts when booking a learner or an instructor's time for training.**

   For example, you might not want a learner who is on a vacation to be accidentally enrolled to a Course, or another employee who is on a business trip to be assigned as an instructor to a Course.

2. **Log time spent in training by employees, either as instructors or as learners, automatically.**

   For example, if an employee spent three days in training, then his time records can be updated for those three days as "In Training." These attendance records can be later used in payroll processing (if there are any special payments involved). It can also be used for analysis on total hours and amount spent on training.

   It is to be noted, however, that these integration settings are valid only for Course Types that are instructor led.

This integration is only valid for Course Types that are instructor led. Please note that regardless of whether integration to Time Management is activated, Enterprise Learning will check for attendance/attendance conflicts, attendance/instructor conflicts, and instructor/instructor conflicts. However, if integration is not turned on, this data is not tracked in Time Management for Time Evaluation purposes.

6.12.2 Materials Management

The integration point between Enterprise Learning and Materials Management (MM) allows your organization to track materials inventory. For instance, you can track Course manuals in your MM Material Master and ensure that each class has enough manuals to support an instructor led class. As a class is scheduled and the integration program is run, the inventory in the Material Master is depleted based on the number of attendees in the class. Training Administrators responsible for Courses can then be notified as the inventory level reaches a level that indicates more manuals need to be ordered.

6.12.3 Budget Management

The Budget Management (PM) component follows similar budgeting processes as Compensation Management (CM). A manager administers a training budget (object BU) at the Organizational Unit level. Using this process, a manager may track credits and debits to his training budget based on attendance and cancellation costs. There is no delivered MSS view or iView to access this data. In the delivered system, it is only available directly through the SAP ERP environment. Therefore, if you wish to use this functionality, you will probably need to develop access views via the Portal.

6.12.4 Billing and Activity Allocation

Course fees collected from learners can be realized in different ways depending on the type of learners:

▶ Joe, a sales executive, attends a Course on "Increasing Sales Effectiveness." The fee for this Course is debited from his department and credited to his organization's training department.

▶ Joe's organization, a maker of high-tech machinery, also provides training facilities to its customers. Sam, a member from one such customer organization is enrolled to such a Course. He has to pay the Course fee, which is also credited to the training organization but debited from Sam's employer via the Sales and Distribution functionality.

In the former case, the standard configurations in SAP Enterprise Learning allows charging Joe's cost center for the Course fees associated with bookings or cancellations and crediting the organizer of the Course — the organizer can be the training department or a different cost center. This is called *Activity Allocation*. A Course fee may also be charged to the learner's projects or specific internal orders.

Activity Allocation also supports charge-backs for instructor activity, so an instructor's cost center receives fees associated with instructing from the Course organizer's cost center.

In the case of Sam, SAP facilitates payments through billing documents or through payment cards. For example, Joe's organization can issue a purchase order. The training organizers can use this order number as the reference billing document and maintain the other relevant payment details, such as the bill-to-party, ship-to-party details. The payment details are subsequently transferred to the SAP Sales and Distribution (SD) application from where invoices can be generated and payment clearance activities can be triggered. In such cases of external learners, the details of the learner and his organization can be maintained in SAP Sales and Distribution application.

The cost transfer posting function allows for distributing/transferring and accounting Course setup and maintenance costs among departments within your organization. For example, you might have a training room equipped with desktops. Each time you hold a Course in that room, you can automatically transfer a charge of $10 per desktop from the Educational Services department to the IT department for maintenance costs.

The configuration to support Activity Allocation and Billing is contained in the IMG under TRAINING MANAGEMENT • INTEGRATION • BILLING AND ACTIVITY ALLOCATION. A series of Wizards walk you through the configuration requirements for these activities. They ensure that you enter the appropriate organizational elements from an SD and CO perspective, so the system knows how the integration should occur. You should work with a representative from SD or CO to determine the appropriate values for the Sales Area and Controlling Area/Activity Types when configuring these entries.

The Wizards also ensure that the appropriate documents are generated in SD. The Wizard also ensures that the number range for HRTEM reference documents is created. The number range interval "01" in the number range object "HRTEM_REFN" must be configured. You may do this outside the IMG via the transaction SNUM.

Additional configuration that supports this integration was discussed at a high level earlier, in the Day-To-Day Activities section. As noted, in the section DAY-TO-DAY ACTIVITIES • BOOKING • SPECIFY PARTICIPANT TYPE CONTROL OPTIONS, you indicate how the system determines individuals' cost centers for charge-backs (Course fee and cancellation charges). This section of the IMG also provides access to the function module that drives activity allocations and billing functions. The IMG entry Day-to-Day Activities • Booking • Fee Handling (Table T77S0 entry SEMIN CCDCT) contains the function module LSO_PRICES. You may copy this function module and enhance the copy to meet your organization's specific requirements from a billing or activity allocation perspective and then replace LSO_PRICES with the new function module.

6.12.5 Appointment Calendar and SAP Knowledge Provider

The Appointment Calendar and the SAP Knowledge Provider integration points are obsolete, for the most part. The Appointment Calendar entry supports integration to the ERP backend appointment calendar, but because most clients use Outlook or Lotus Notes, they prefer to create a VCAL attachment when they set up their request-based correspondences. The SAP Knowledge Provider entry supports the integration of Training Management and the SAP Knowledge Warehouse (KW). However, the KW may not be used to store online content for e-learning because it is not WebDav compliant.

6.12.6 Collaboration

Learning that happens in a classroom forms one aspect of a bigger learning environment that an organization intends to establish and maintain for its employees. Much of learning happens through collaboration between organization members and through informal learning techniques.

SAP Enterprise Learning helps to facilitate such an extended environment that supports such collaborative learning.

For instance, consider Maria, who wants to improve her knowledge on a new computer technology, such as cloud computing. She finds a Course on this topic and enrolls herself. She also wants to find out other experts and teams in her organization who are working on this area and who could help her learn further on this topic.

Training administrators who know this need for community-based learning can help Maria. They can:

▶ Establish a virtual collaboration room that would include members who are experts on the topic

▶ Associate this collaboration room with appropriate Course Types in the training catalog

All learners, including Maria, who have enrolled to the Course can be automatically added as members of such a collaboration room. This gives them the chance to attend the Course as well as learn further by interacting with the members of the *collaboration room* (see Figure 6.6).

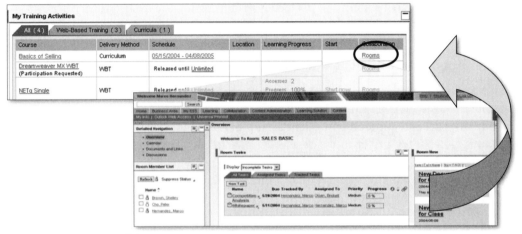

Figure 6.6 Collaboration Rooms

A collaboration room is a feature of SAP NetWeaver Enterprise Portal's people integration functionalities. A collaboration room can have its own template that determines the behavior of the room, such as whether the rooms are open to everyone or open only to those who are registered for a class or specifically invited to a room. Room templates also determine the collaboration options that are available within a specific room — the options include synchronous collaboration methods such as messaging, contact list, and application/desktop sharing, as well as asynchronous collaboration options such as document sharing, team calendar, and team tasks

A collaboration room can be associated with a Course Group, Course Type, or Course (as of SAP Enterprise Portal 6.0 SP4 and Learning Solution 2.0 SP8), through the Collaboration Infotype. This means you can have collaboration functions (e.g., Discussion Boards; Document Sharing) for all Course Types within a subject area, for a specific Course Type, or simply for a scheduled Course.

You also determine who can access collaboration rooms by setting up the appropriate roles. These might include learners, instructors, and tutors. Roles help in defining access to different functions within a collaboration room. For example, an instructor might be allowed to invite an individual to a room while a learner may not be allowed to do this.

6.13   Curriculum Types and Course Programs

In this section, we will discuss the Curriculum Type and Course Program delivery methods. Both of these methods allow administrators to bundle Courses together, but they provide very different capabilities from the learner's perspective.

6.13.1   Curriculum Types

Usually, when you think of the word "Curriculum," you think of the Curriculum offered at a university: a group of related Courses that you progress your way through. The Curriculum Type (object type DC) offered by Enterprise Learning, a method of grouping related Course Types, provides a single blended learning experience rather than a path of learning experiences. Because of the expectation the word "Curriculum" brings to the table, the Curriculum Type functionality has often been disregarded because it doesn't meet this expectation. However, while the Curriculum functionality doesn't provide a university Curriculum experience, it does provide strong capabilities in terms of blended learning and rapid booking.

Specifically, grouping Course Types into Curriculum types has several advantages:

▸ For the learners, a Curriculum represents a logically structured group of Courses that are booked together, taken together, and completed within a specified time frame.

▸ The Curriculum functionality enables learners to book all Courses together, instead of booking individually (see Figure 6.7).

▸ Grouping Courses together simplifies the way Course booking is managed by training administrators — instead of booking learners to each of the Courses separately, administrators can book learners directly to the group of Courses.

Course Types related by a Curriculum type are referred to as Curriculum elements. These elements may be of any delivery method. A Curriculum may consist of all Web-based trainings or a mix of instructor-led, Web-based, VC, and static classes. For every Course Type element included, it is also possible to specify one or more alternative Course Types. This means an administrator might set up a Curriculum type that offers the opportunity to take a Course in its Web-based format or its instructor-led format.

> **Note**
>
> It is important to understand that while the Curriculum type offers the opportunities to create alternatives, the scheduled Curriculum does not. Therefore, a learner may never choose from alternatives while completing a Curriculum.

In addition to supporting the use of any delivery method for elements, the Curriculum functionality also allows you to sequence the elements, if you chose. In fact, a Curriculum type might have a combination of sequenced elements as well as elements without sequence order.

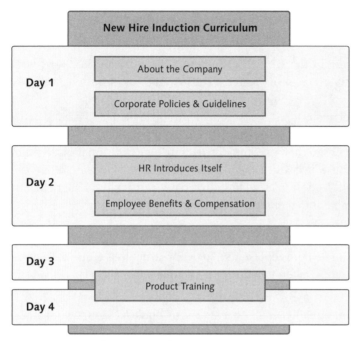

Figure 6.7 Curriculum Functionality

The Curriculum functionality allows you to group logically related Courses. For example, your new hire orientation training might be structured as a Curriculum.

6.13.2 Creating a Curriculum Type

As we've mentioned, a Curriculum type is a grouping of Course Types, which you may chose to sequence. The Curriculum type is created in the master data catalog and may fall in the same Course Group as its elements or it may fall in a different Course Group. This will depend on how you've decided to structure your catalog.

When you create a Curriculum type, you have some decisions to make. Some of these items were discussed earlier, in Section 6.2, Configuring Course Preparation Activities, but it is good to review them now that you are more familiar with the

Curriculum functionality. First, you must decide if the elements of the Curriculum type may be booked outside of the Curriculum — in other words, if a Course Type belongs to a Curriculum type, can a learner book it individually or must the learner book it as part of the Curriculum? The next factor you must consider is how follow-up should be handled: Will you allow the learner or administrator to follow up each element individually or must the learner complete the entire Curriculum before follow-up can be performed (and credit achieved for each element as well as for the entire Curriculum)? Another related decision is how cancellations will be managed. Will you allow the learner to cancel out of the Curriculum? If so, what should happen to the bookings of the individual elements? Should they remain or should they be cancelled along with the Curriculum cancellation?

Each of the decisions you make regarding these questions will relate to how you are using the Curriculum. If you are using it as a tool to make it easy to enroll in a lot of related Courses at once and to give guidance to the learner in terms of the order the Courses should be attended, then you might chose to allow learners to book a class either within or outside a Curriculum, to follow up each element individually (so they receive completion credit for the element even if they don't complete the Curriculum), and to cancel out of a Curriculum whenever they like but keep all related Course bookings.

If, instead, you have created Curriculums of required training to ensure that your learners complete the entire training Course exactly as prescribed and within a set time frame, you may decide to disallow booking to Curriculum elements (Course Types) outside of the Curriculum; you will probably allow follow-up (and Course credit) upon completion of the entire Curriculum; and you will not allow cancellation unless the learner cancels out of every element. This is a much more restrictive use of Curriculum and is much closer to the concept of *blended learning* that many of you are familiar with.

Note
The infotype setup for each of these decision points is discussed in detail in the next section.

Once you have created your Curriculum type and added the Curriculum elements (with or without sequence order) to the Curriculum type, you may decide you are ready to schedule an actual Curriculum (object EC) that a learner may book to (and an administrator may book a learner to in the backend).

6.13.3 Course Types and Courses Exclusive to Curriculum

As mentioned, it's possible to specify that a Course Type or a Course is exclusively meant for booking only through a Curriculum.

To do this at the Course Type level, the field Booking Option in the Infotype Course Type Info, can be set appropriately to specify if the Course Type is bookable only as a part of Curriculum or if individual Course bookings should also be allowed (see Figure 6.8).

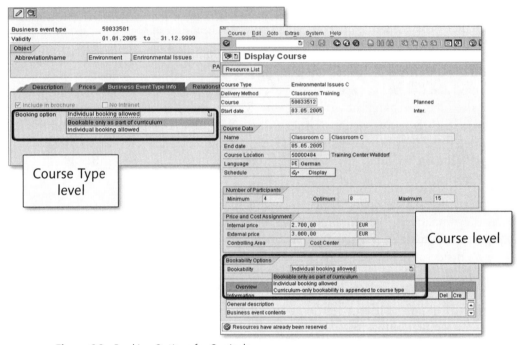

Figure 6.8 Booking Options for Curricula

The same information can also be specified at the Course level for a specific schedule of the Course Type. When a Course is meant for exclusive booking through a Curriculum, the system displays an error message when booking is attempted on the Course schedule directly, either by learners or training administrators.

Cancellation Options for a Curriculum

The Curriculum Type infotype controls the way cancellation and follow-up are handled for a Curriculum (see Figure 6.9).

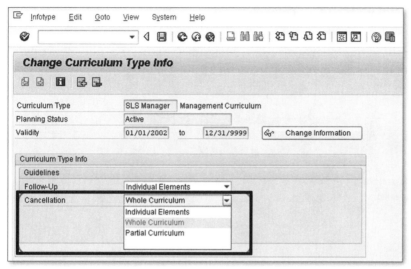

Figure 6.9 Curriculum Cancellation

There are three options available for cancelling a Curriculum:

▶ Cancelling a whole Curriculum

▶ Cancelling a Curriculum in part

▶ Cancelling individual Curriculum elements

In this case, the learner can cancel a Curriculum only as a whole. There are no options to cancel a part of the Curriculum or the individual Curriculum elements.

In this case, the learner can cancel part of the Curriculum. When a learner decides to cancel a specific element in the Curriculum, all the remaining part of the Curriculum, that is, all the elements that succeed the selected element are also considered as cancelled. The Course bookings before the selected element are retained.

In this case, if a learner wants to cancel selectively, say two Courses out of five Courses in a Curriculum, he can do so. The bookings made for the remaining three Courses hold good, but are converted as direct Course bookings. The relationship between the learner and Curriculum is severed.

If the cancellation options are not maintained for a Curriculum type, the default value for the cancellation guideline stored in table T77SO, under group HRLSO - ECCAN is taken.

Follow-up Options for a Curriculum

The Curriculum Type Info also allows specifying the follow-up guidelines. It is possible to specify if the follow-up process would be done at the individual Course (elements in the Curriculum) level or would be done at the Curriculum level itself (see Figure 6.10).

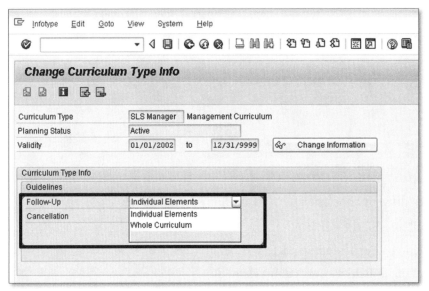

Figure 6.10   Curriculum Follow-Up

If you choose the option Follow-Up Individual Courses, learners are followed up, as it is done for a usual Course. These individual Course follow-ups have no effect on the Curriculum. The Curriculum might impart some qualifications to its participants. So, in many cases, it makes sense to follow up the Curriculum also, so such qualifications can be transferred.

> **Note**
>
> If the some or all of the qualifications imparted by the Curriculum are also imparted by individual Courses, the participant's qualification profiles are updated with the qualification records with earliest validity end dates.

In the second case, Follow-Up Whole Curriculum, the follow-up is done fully at the Curriculum level — in this case, the follow-up activities such as confirming attendance for the Curriculum elements are done as a part of the Curriculum follow-up.

When one of the individual Courses (Curriculum element) is followed up, the Course bookings that were made as a part of Curriculum (for that Course) are not displayed and thus are removed from the individual Course follow-up. An appropriate warning message is shown to this effect.

When follow-up is done for a Course, a system indicator is set beside the A614 (Is Participated in by) to indicate that the follow-up is completed. Participations that are so flagged are skipped when following up the Curriculum as a whole. This ensures that participations are followed up just once. If the follow-up options are not maintained for a Curriculum type, the default value stored for follow-up guidelines in table T77S0, under group HRLSO - ECFUP is taken.

6.13.4 Scheduling a Curriculum

A Curriculum is scheduled in the Dynamic Course Menu, just as a Course is scheduled. To schedule a Curriculum, training administrators need to follow these steps:

1. Schedule individual Courses for each of the time/location dependent elements in the Curriculum type or ensure that appropriate scheduled dates already exist.

2. Select the appropriate Curriculum type in the menu and select Create.

3. On the creation screen, specify the overall start and end dates of the Curriculum. Specify the location and the delivery language of the Curriculum.

> **Note**
>
> Location and language information are optional, because they can be derived from the individual Courses included in the Curriculum.

4. Select the appropriate dates for each element in the Curriculum. You may select multiple dates for each element.

5. If there are alternatives, select one of the alternative you wish to present for the Curriculum you are creating. Both alternatives may not be included in the final, scheduled Curriculum.

> **Note**
>
> The system will display the Course schedules that fall between the overall start and end dates of the Curriculum.

6. If some of these elements are sequenced, then the screen displays the Course schedules in the order specified in the Curriculum definition.

> **Important Concept**
>
> In the configuration section, we discussed entries in the Control Elements folder of the Course Preparation section of the IMG menu path CUSTOMIZING • TRAINING AND EVENT MANAGEMENT • SAP ENTERPRISE LEARNING • TRAINING MANAGEMENT • COURSE PREPARATION • CONTROL ELEMENTS • TURN ON THE SWITCH "CREATE CURRICULUM WITH OVERLAPPING PARTICIPATION."

The first entry in this section, entry HRLSO ECOVL from table T77S0, plays a very important role in how Curriculums work from a sequencing perspective. If this entry is set to [Blank], then an administrator may schedule a Curriculum with sequenced elements that overlap. If this occurs, a learner will not be able to book to the elements out of sequence. However, if the entry is set to [X], the administrator is not able to select dates that do not fall in the sequence. In other words, when the value for HRLSO ECOVL is set to "X," an administrator scheduling a Curriculum with sequenced elements is forced to select Course dates that enforce the order.

Let's consider this in practical terms, with an example of a Management Curriculum containing the following three sequenced Courses in Table 6.12:

1. Principles of Management

2. Organizational Behavior

3. Finance for Non-Finance Managers

	Course	Available Course Schedules
1	Principles of Management	01 Jan - 02 Jan
		10 Jan - 11 Jan
2	Organizational Behavior	03 Jan - 05 Jan
		13 Jan - 15 Jan
3	Finance for Non-Finance Managers	06 Jan - 08 Jan

Table 6.12 Possible Curriculum Course Dates

Let's consider the following two cases of scheduling the management Curriculum with these Course dates in Tables 6.13 and 6.14:

Case 1: HRLSO_ECOVL = "Blank"

Sequence	Course	Selected schedule date	
1	Principles of Management	01 Jan - 02 Jan 10 Jan - 11 Jan	The system displays the dates for this Course first, as this is first in the sequence. Let's say the schedule starting on 10 Jan is selected.
2	Organizational Behavior	03 Jan - 05 Jan 13 Jan - 15 Jan	The system now displays both the schedules for the 2nd Course, as the value for overlap is "blank". Let's say the schedule starting on 03 Jan is selected.
3	Finance for Non-Finance Managers	06 Jan - 08 Jan	Now the system displays the 3rd Course. There's only one schedule available for this Course and it starts after the end of the 2nd Course. So, this schedule can be selected.

Table 6.13 Curriculum Example One

Case 2: HRLSO_ECOVL = "x"

Sequence	Course	Selected schedule date	
1	Principles of Management	01 Jan - 02 Jan 10 Jan - 11 Jan	Let's say the schedule starting on 10 Jan is selected, again.
2	Organizational Behavior	13 Jan - 15 Jan	The system now displays just the schedule starting on 13 Jan for 2nd Course, as only this schedule begins after the 1st Course, and the value for overlap is "x."

Table 6.14 Curriculum Example Two

Sequence	Course	Selected schedule date	
3	Finance for Non-finance managers	No dates	The system does not display any dates for the 3rd Course, as the only schedule available for this Course begins before the schedule dates selected for the 2nd Course. So, the Curriculum cannot be scheduled with this choice of Course dates.

Table 6.14 Curriculum Example Two (Cont.)

Note
Web-based Courses that are usually time independent can also be sequenced in a Curriculum.

6.13.5 Course Program

The concept of the Course Program object (Object EK) is much closer to that of the university Curriculum discussed in the previous section. The Course Program is an ideal tool for delivering continuous and adaptive learning programs to your learners.

A Course Program is a group of related Courses and Curriculums. In this way, it is similar to a Curriculum. However, a Course Program offers a few other capabilities that are most suited for long-term progressions through Courses: It does not require a learner to complete the elements within a set time frame and it allows the program to be structured into reusable elements called *blocks*.

Course Program Structure

The Courses and Curriculums in a Course Program are grouped into logical learning units called blocks. So, a Course Program can be visualized as made up of one or more blocks. Segregating Courses into blocks gives a well defined structure to the Course Program. For example, the blocks might be used to indicate the different levels of learning in a subject area (see Figure 6.11).

Course Programs are ideal tools for developing learning programs to support career planning and succession planning programs of organizations. This example shows how blocks support progression.

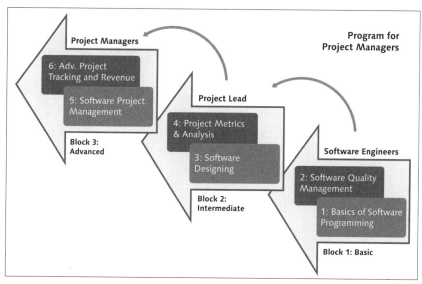

Figure 6.11 Course Program

It is important to know that blocks may have specific sequence order, if needed, and that they may also be made as *mandatory*. Mandatory blocks should contain the most essential Courses that learners should take to acquire those qualifications imparted by the Course Program. Setting some blocks as mandatory helps in preparing a program that will combine both essential, as well as "nice to know" Courses.

> **Tip**
>
> Blocks can be reused across Course Programs. For instance, a block on "Marketing Essentials" can be used in a program for "Sales Effectiveness." The same block can be used, as is, in a program for "Product Management and Leadership."

Course Programs are also ideal when the program structure evolves over a period of time owing to changes in business processes or priorities or depending on how learners progress and interest shown in different areas. For instance, the Course Program might include a few basic topics at the beginning. Learners can start subscribing to the Course Program and attend these Courses. Over a period of time, new topics can be added as the subject evolves and as learners start showing more specific interests. These new Courses will be pushed to the learners automatically, as part of the program they are subscribed to. The Curriculum functionality does not have this flexibility — if a Curriculum type is changed, the changes do not flow down to already scheduled Curriculums (see Figure 6.12).

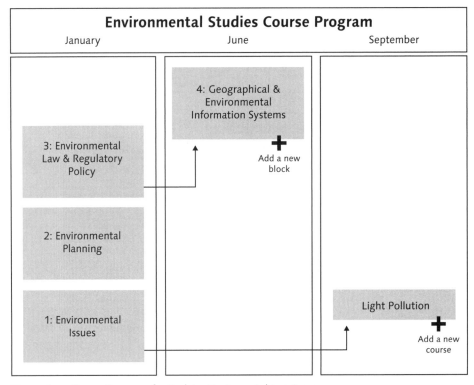

Figure 6.12 Course Programs for Evolving Topics or Subject Areas

Course Programs and Curriculum: A Comparison

We've identified some of the differences between Curriculum Types/Curriculum, and Course Programs. Table 6.15 provides an easy-to-use tool to help you decide when you need to create a Curriculum type with a scheduled Curriculum and when a Course Program might better suit your needs.

	Course Program	Curriculum
Structuring	A Course Program offers not only to group Course/Curriculum types, but also structure them logically into blocks. Each block, is thus a group of related Course/Curriculum types.	A Curriculum is a string of Courses. No separate grouping of Courses is possible.

Table 6.15 Differences Between Course Programs and Curriculums

	Course Program	Curriculum
Essential vs. "Nice-to-know" Courses	Blocks can be selectively set as mandatory. It is sufficient for learners to finish the mandatory blocks to be deemed to have completed the program.	All the Courses in a Curriculum are by nature mandatory.
Scheduling and Enrolling	Administrators have to define only the structure of the Course Program. Courses need not have to be scheduled specifically for the Course Program. Learners can subscribe, even when the comprising Course/Curriculum types have not been scheduled. Learners can enroll to the comprising Course/Curriculum types whenever they are scheduled.	Courses in a Curriculum should be scheduled prior to scheduling the Curriculum. Specific Course schedules are to be picked and grouped when scheduling a Curriculum.
Exclusivity	Even when Courses are grouped in a Course Program, they need not be exclusive to any specific Course Program.	Courses can be marked as exclusive to a Curriculum. Such Courses can be booked only by booking the Curriculum itself.

Table 6.15 Differences Between Course Programs and Curriculums (Cont.)

Value Proposition for Course Program

The main advantage of a Course Program is its flexibility. Training administrators can just define the structure and the comprising Courses of a Course Program. They do not need to schedule these Courses separately (unlike a Curriculum). They can schedule the Courses as per their normal plans. This eliminates the usual administrative tasks associated with scheduling such group of Courses.

Thus, a Course Program has only validity dates and has no exclusive schedule. This allows learners to go through the Courses in a Course Program in a self-paced manner, at times that are the most convenient to them.

System Access and Configurations

Learners can subscribe to Course Programs through the Learning Portal (see Figure 6.13). The Learning Portal helps them know the mandatory blocks and Courses as well as the status of individual Courses — if Courses have been booked or not.

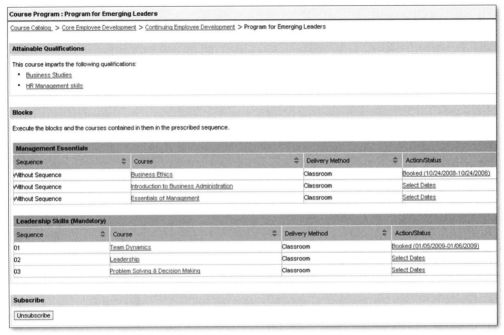

Figure 6.13 Course Program Overview Page

Administrators can also subscribe learners to Course Programs through the SAP LSO backend system. They can also follow up Course Programs just as they would do for other Courses. Administrators need to know if learners have successfully completed all the mandatory Courses to determine if they can be marked as having completed the entire programs. The *Learning Progress of a Learner* report provides this information (see Figure 6.14).

Completion Progress of Learner

Attendee Name	AttdeeID	DelMethod Long	Course Type Name	Group	Start Date	End Date	Required	Partic. Status	Pass	Attendance	Fc
Mrs Carmen Green	00100055	Classroom Training	Team Dynamics	2	11.07.2007	12.07.2007	X	Booked	⊗	⊗	
			Leadership	1	27.06.2007	28.06.2007					
			Problem Solving & Decision Making	3	16.07.2007	17.07.2007					
			Leading High Performance Teams	2	25.06.2007	27.06.2007		To Be Booked			
			Business Ethics	3				No Dates Available			
			Introduction to Business Administration	1	02.07.2007	03.07.2007		Booked			
			Essentials of Management	2	25.06.2007	26.06.2007		To Be Booked			

Figure 6.14 Learning Progress Report (LSO_RHPPROGRS)

6.14   Reporting

A major advantage of an integrated learning system in general, and the SAP Enterprise Learning specifically, is having a single system of record for training activities. The ability to report on these records is a significant benefit of any LMS implementation.

For this reason, SAP offers multiple options to meet reporting needs in the SAP Enterprise Learning. These options include but are not limited to:

▶ Delivered reports: Over forty reports are provided by SAP.

▶ SAP Query: An application to help create reports not delivered as standard. *Ad Hoc Query* is a subset of this option.

▶ Custom ABAP reports: Can range from simply copying and enhancing a delivered report to complex reports that meet unique requirements.

▶ Business Intelligence (BI) reports: Provides On-Line Analytical Processing (OLAP) reporting capabilities. Data must first be extracted from the source system; thus, reporting is typically not for real time data. SAP Enterprise Learning provides a wide variety of predefined BI queries and key figures, which can be well used to create powerful analytical reports, such as to analyze learner participation data, cost Vs revenue comparisons, etc.

In this section, we will discuss the delivered reports, at a high level, specific applications of the query tool, and information on the delivered BW queries and data extractors.

6.14.1   Delivered Reports

Reports delivered with Enterprise Learning are categorized into three major areas:

▶ Participation

▶ Courses

▶ Resources

Participation reports generally provide information about an attendee, the attendee's training history, and his progress through a Course. The selection variables are usually based on the attendee object (e.g., person, external person, contact person) or a group of attendees (e.g., organizational unit, company, or customer). The report data is usually presented in an Active List Viewer (ALV) format, which is extremely customizable and provides the ability to set up display variants for individual or global use. The data may be filtered, summed, and sorted as necessary and is easily downloaded to Microsoft Excel.

Table 6.16 provides a list and brief description of participation reports that are available.

S. No	Title	Transaction	Report description
1	Participant List	LSO_RHXTEILN	Displays list of all participants in a Course.
2	Attendance List	LSO_RHXTEILA	List of confirmed participants with an extra column for class signature. Can be used as a roster.
3	Employee List	S_PH9_46000432	List of employees of an organizational unit. Useful when deciding replacements for Courses.
4	Bookings per Participant	LSO_RHXBUCH0	List of Courses enrolled by a participant.
5	Participation Prerequisites	LSO_RHXKVOR0	Lists the prerequisites required for a Course.
6	Participant's Qualifications	S_PH9_46000429	Lists the qualifications held an attendee (including completed Courses).
7	Prerequisites Matchup	LSO_RHXQANF0	Performs a match-up to compare the required qualifications for Course vs. actual qualifications of a participant.
8	Participant Appraisals	S_PH9_46000452	Appraisals that are completed by participants.
9	Prebookings per Course Type	LSO_RHXVORM0	Lists the prebookings made for a Course Type. This is used to forecast demand.
10	Prebookings per Participant	LSO_RHXVORM1	Lists the prebookings made by participants and the costs associated with the Course Types.
11	Participants for Rebooking	LSO_RHXUMBU0	Lists the participants that are registered but do not have a confirmed place. These participants need to be rebooked.
12	Participation Statistics	LSO_RHXKURS2	Lists the number of participants for a Course.
13	Participation and Sales Statistics	LSO_RHXKURS3	Lists number of participants and fee associated for a Course.
14	Participant Cancellations per Course	LSO_RHXSTOR0	Lists the participant cancellations for a Course.

Table 6.16 Participation Reports

S. No	Title	Transaction	Report description
15	Cancellations per Participant	LSO_RHXSTOR1	Lists the Course cancellations per participant.
16	Budget Comparison	S_PH9_46000423	Compares the budget for an organizational unit with the training costs incurred by the organizational unit.
17	Participant Results Overview	LSO_TAC_PART_RESULT	Lists the Course results for a participant.
18	Participant's Training History	LSO_RHXTHIST	Displays the training history for a participant.

Table 6.16 Participation Reports (Cont.)

Reports in the *Course* category usually provide data specific to the Course. The selection criteria are usually based on a selected Course Group, Course Type, Curriculum type, Curriculum, Course, or e-learning object. Output for these reports is also presented in an ALV format.

Table 6.17 provides a list and brief description of Course reports that are available.

S. No	Title	Transaction	Report description
19	Course Demand	LSO_RHXKBED0	Lists the number of required and planned Course dates per Course Type. Used to identify demand per Course Type.
20	Course Schedule	LSO_RHABLAUF_OLD	Lists the schedules for Courses.
21	Course Appraisals	LSO_RHXEVALV_OLD	Displays the results of the Course appraisals.
22	Course Hierarchy	LSO_RHXCGRP0	Displays the Hierarchy of the Courses starting from the selected Course Group or Course Type.
23	Participation Statistics	LSO_RHXKURS2	Lists the number of participants for a Course.
24	Course Brochure	LSO_RHXKBRO0	Creates a Course brochure with information such as Course Duration, Prerequisites, Objectives, etc.

Table 6.17 Course Reports

S. No	Title	Transaction	Report description
25	Course Information	LSO_RHSEMI60	Displays detailed information about Courses such as instructor, location, etc.
26	Course Dates	LSO_RHXKBRO1	Displays a list of Course dates scheduled per Course Type.
27	Resource List per Course	LSO_RHXERESO	Displays a list of required resources for a Course.
28	Resources Not Yet Assigned per Course	LSO_RHXORES1	Displays a list of resource types that are required for a Course but still not assigned.
29	Material Requirements per Course	LSO_RHXMARPO	Displays a list of materials (resources of type material) required for a Course.
30	Course Prices	LSO_RHXKBRO2	Lists the internal and external Course prices.
31	Course Results Overview	LSO_TAC_TRAIN_RESULT	Lists the Course results such as test results, objectives achieved, etc. for a specific Course Type.
32	Test Item Statistics	LSO_TAC_ITEMSTAT	Displays the item statistics for a specified test. This report can be used to improve the quality of questions by analyzing the responses to the questions.
33	Completion Progress of Learner	LSO_RHPPROGRS	Lists the learner progress statistics for a Course.

Table 6.17 Course Reports (Cont.)

The Enterprise Learning Solution also delivers a few reports that allow you to analyze *resource* usage and availability. Because some of these reports provide graphical analysis, they are not all delivered with ALV formatted output.

Table 6.18 provides a list and brief description of resource reports that are available.

S. No	Title	Transaction	Report description
34	Resource Equipment	S_AHR_61016224	Displays a list of resources (equipment, etc.) available to a specified resource (Room).

Table 6.18 Resource Reports

S. No	Title	Transaction	Report description
35	Resource Reservation	LSO_RHRBEL00	Displays a table of the reservations for a selected resource type.
36	Instructor Information	LSO_RHSSREF0	Displays instructor information associated with the Course.
37	Graphical Resource Reservation	LSO_RHXRBEL1	Graphical display of reservation of a resource type.
38	Available/Reserved Resources	S_AHR_61016225	Displays a list of available/reserved resources.
39	Resource Reservation Statistics	LSO_RHXRESO0	Displays a list of resources and their reservation details.
40	Resources Not Yet Assigned per Resource Type	LSO_RHXORES2	Displays a list of Courses that still require the specified resource type.

Table 6.18 Resource Reports (Cont.)

Tip

As mentioned previously, many delivered Enterprise Learning reports present their results using the SAP List Viewer (ALV). If the field you need in the output does not display, click CHANGE LAYOUT `Ctrl`+`F8` button. The field you need may be available but not be included in the current layout. Fields in the right Column Set can be added to the Displayed Columns. Sort orders and filters can be changed. The new layout can be saved as a general default or a user specific default.

6.14.2 Business Intelligence

Apart from the standard reports, SAP also provides standard Business Intelligence (BI) Queries. The data extracted with these queries can be used to create powerful analytical reports. The reports used here are typically not for real time data, so there is usually a time lag, but this will depend on how often your organization extracts data to SAP NetWeaver BW. In this section, we will provide an overview of the standard queries and standard BW Reports that are offered by SAP. (Note that SAP NetWeaver BI was recently renamed SAP NetWeaver BW.)

Architecture

SAP NetWeaver BW has multiple layers and tools required to convert transactional data into meaningful reports.

▸ *Extraction, Transformation, and Load* (ETL) — This layer is responsible for extracting the data from HR systems, applying transformation rules and loading the data into the BW system.

▸ *Data Warehouse* — This layer is responsible for storing the data in the form of Infocubes

▸ *Reporting* — This layer is responsible for presenting the data in the form of meaningful reports.

Structure of Data

Data in SAP NetWeaver BW is stored in the form of *Infocubes*. Infocubes contain two types of data:

▸ *Key Figures* — These are quantifiable values such as number of employees.

▸ *Characteristics* — These are required to determine Key Figures based on different criteria. Examples of Characteristics are reporting organizational unit or gender of employees.

SAP Enterprise Learning provides two Infocubes by default:

▸ *Training Management* — Stores data regarding training such as Courses.

▸ *Resource Management* — Scores data regarding Resources used.

The data in the Infocubes can be analyzed by displaying various views via a query.

Queries

SAP provides default queries for analyzing the data in the Infocubes. SAP Enterprise Learning provides the following queries out of the box:

▸ Query: Amount of participations and cancellations

▸ Query: Comparison of bookings per year

▸ Query: Quota of participations and cancellations

▸ Query: Training duration

▸ Query: Training fees for participations and cancellations

▸ Query: Assignment of training fees per internal/external bookings

▸ Query: Training fees

▸ Query: Comparison of earnings per year

▸ Query: Comparison of training costs per year

- ▸ Query: Education per organizational assignment
- ▸ Query: Training fees per organizational assignment
- ▸ Query: Training per target group
- ▸ Query: Training costs per target group
- ▸ Query: Test results
- ▸ Query: Comparison of resource costs per year
- ▸ Query: My cost center: actual training costs
- ▸ Query: My cost center: training costs per year
- ▸ Query: My cost center: quarterly training costs

BW Reports

SAP provides default BW Reports that can be used to obtain information in a meaningful format. Table 6.19 lists the reports provided by SAP NetWeaver BW.

S. No	Title	Report description
1	Annual Comparison of Bookings	Provides comparison of booking data with previous years.
2	Annual Comparison of Course Costs	Provides comparison of Course cost data with previous years.
3	Annual Comparison of Resource Costs	Provides comparison of resource cost data with previous years.
4	Annual Comparison of Revenues	Provides comparison of revenues from Courses with previous years.
5	e-Learning: Cancellations by Organizational Assignment	Provides cancellation data by Organizational Unit.
6	e-Learning: Fees by Organizational Assignment	Provides data on fees collected (Attendance Fee, Cancellation Fee) by Organizational Unit.
7	Fee Distribution by Internal and External Bookings	Provides data on fees collected based on internal and external bookings.
8	Fee Rates	Provides data on the all fees (cancellation, participation, etc.).
9	My Cost Centers - Education and Training Costs - Current	Provides data of cost by cost center.

Table 6.19 Reports Available in SAP NetWeaver BW

S. No	Title	Report description
10	My Cost Centers - Education and Training Costs - Quarterly	Provides quarterly comparison of training cost data by cost center.
11	My Cost Centers - Education and Training Costs - Yearly	Provides yearly comparison of training cost data by cost center.
12	Number of Participants and Cancellations	Provides data on participants and cancellations.
13	Participation and Cancellation Fees	Provides data on participation and cancellation fees.
14	Participation and Cancellation Rate	Provides data on participation and cancellation rate.
15	Test Results	Provides the test results.
16	Training and Education by Organizational Assignment	Provides training data by Organizational Unit and compares data with previous years.
17	Training and Education by Target Group	Provides training data by Organizational Unit, cost center, etc., and compares data with previous years.
18	Training and Education Fees by Organizational Assignment	Provides fee data by Organizational Unit and compares data with previous years.
19	Training and Education Fees by Target Group	Provides fee data by Organizational Unit, Cost center, etc., and compares data with previous years.
20	Training Duration	Provides data regarding training duration.

Table 6.19 Reports Available in SAP NetWeaver BW (Cont.)

Enterprise Learning BW Reports

Enhancement package P04 is delivering four *DataSources* for the Course appraisal data. An SAP DataSource is a set of fields that provide the data for a business unit for data transfer into SAP NetWeaver BW. From a technical viewpoint, the DataSource is a set of logically related fields that are provided to transfer data into SAP NetWeaver BW in a flat structure (the extraction structure), or in multiple flat structures (for hierarchies). These are unique in that SAP delivers the DataSources, which reside on the R/3 side. However, no Infocubes or reports are delivered. So, those would have to be built.

The four DataSources are:

▸ **0LSO_APP_DOC_ID_ATTR**
Extracts the master data of the appraisals

▸ **0LSO_APP_ROW_ID_TEXT**
Extracts the text of the appraisal criteria

▸ **0LSO_APP_VA_TEXT**
Extracts the text of the appraisal template

▸ **0HR_LSO_4**
Extracts the *transactional* data of the appraisals

Conclusion

SAP NetWeaver BW, if implemented correctly, can provide data that is vital to the success of the system. Typically, Business Warehouse data is not real time but provides insight into information that can be used to enhance the system. SAP provides multiple tools in order to extract and analyze such data.

6.14.3 Using Ad Hoc Query for Enterprise Learning

While a variety of different reports are delivered with the Learning Solution for participation, Course, and resource analysis, sometimes these reports do not meet an organization's reporting requirements. Usually, organizations turn to BW or custom ABAP reports to meet these additional needs. The following section discusses the advantages and use of SAP Ad Hoc Query to meet unique reporting requirements.

SAP Query/Ad Hoc Query

SAP Query is an inclusive term covering a broad range of options for developing custom SAP reports. These options do not require knowledge of the SAP programming language, ABAP. One subset of the SAP Query tools is InfoSet Query. This tool is suitable for supporting the development of queries (reports) as well as the creation of ad hoc reporting. The specific tool for HR is sometimes referenced as HR InfoSet Query but is more commonly called Ad Hoc Query.

To investigate the use of Ad Hoc Query for SAP Enterprise Learning, we will discuss a specific example. Assume there is a business requirement to show all of the Courses (dates) under a given classroom Course Type. In addition, the names of attendees and their email addresses must be included in the report output. This report might be required to support Kirkpatrick Level 3 Evaluations between 90 to 120 days after a Course date.

To create the required report, we will first use the following tools that support Ad Hoc Query:

▶ Transaction SQ01 (SAP Query) to select the Query Area

▶ Transaction SQ02 (InfoSets)

▶ Transaction SQ03 (UserGroups)

Query Areas

Upon entering Transaction SQ01, first set the Query Area that should be used. Selecting Environment • Query areas provide a pop-up screen to select the Query area, also called the Work area (see Figure 6.15).

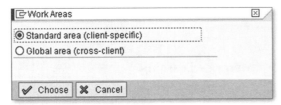

Figure 6.15 Selecting the Query Area

SAP Queries can be stored in either the *Standard Area* or the *Global Area*.

▶ The Standard Area is typically used to support ad hoc (one time) reporting. It is client specific and has no direct connection to the SAP transport system.

▶ The Global Area is cross-client (client independent) and is typically used for queries that will be transported to other systems. Objects generated in the Global Area are registered with the Workbench Organizer and use the normal transport procedure. All SAP delivered objects are contained in the Global Area.

> **Helpful Hint**
>
> Transports can be manually generated for objects in the Standard Area using transaction SQ02 Environment • Transports. It is also possible to use this transaction to download the objects and then upload into another system or client.

InfoSets

InfoSets are created from a logical database. They allow the ultimate query to access only a limited, pre-defined set of data tables and fields.

Typically, reports for SAP LSO will be generated using the PCH logical database. In choosing the starting object type, consider that other object types, which are connected by a relationship, can also be included. Thus, using the Course (E) object type as a starting point allows the inclusion of Course Type and person (attendee) object types. Note that the object types are selected based on their specific relationship to the starting object (see Figure 6.16).

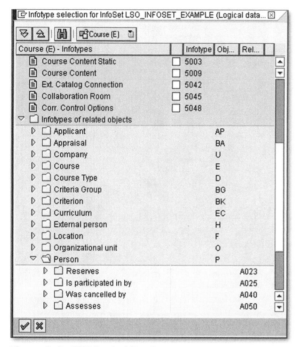

Figure 6.16 PCH Logical Database

The PCH logical database allows the selection of Infotypes that are directly assigned to the starting object type, such as Course (E). It also allows the selection of related objects, such as Person, via the specific relationship, such as *Is participated in by*.

Specific fields can be included in or excluded from the InfoSet. The fields that are available from the selected object types and infotypes display on the left. If these fields are added to a Field Group on the right, then they are available for reporting within the InfoSet. For example, the email address required in our theoretical report is stored in Infotype 0105 (Communications) in the field USRID_LONG. Thus, that field must be included in a field group. The field USRTY (Communication Type) is included to allow the selection to be limited to Subtype 0010 for email (see Figure 6.17).

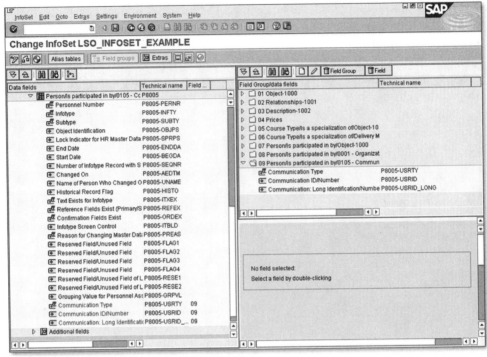

Figure 6.17 Specific Data Fields and Field Groups

> **Note**
>
> Although the InfoSet limits the data that is available for the report, it does not make a separate copy of the data, so Ad Hoc Query is reporting on real time data.

User Groups

Reports created within Ad Hoc Query honor the SAP assigned authorizations. In other words, a user can only report on data to which he has authorization access. However, as seen previously, InfoSets can be used to limit the data available for reporting. User Groups can be used to limit access to InfoSets, so the Ad Hoc Query can be thought of as providing an additional layer of protection that can be applied to the reports.

Specifically, User Groups can control:

► What users have access to a query

► Whether the user has access to create or change a query

► What InfoSets are available to the query

For example, the User Group could limit a user to a single InfoSet and to only the ability to run the report without creating new queries or changing existing queries. The authorization object S_QUERY controls the authorization to create or change queries. However, this authorization can be *revoked* for a given user within a User Group by not checking the available box. In the example, only user C7002 can create or change a query within the User Group. Other users could only execute existing reports (see Figure 6.18). One or more InfoSets are assigned to the User Group and this determines the data that is available for reporting.

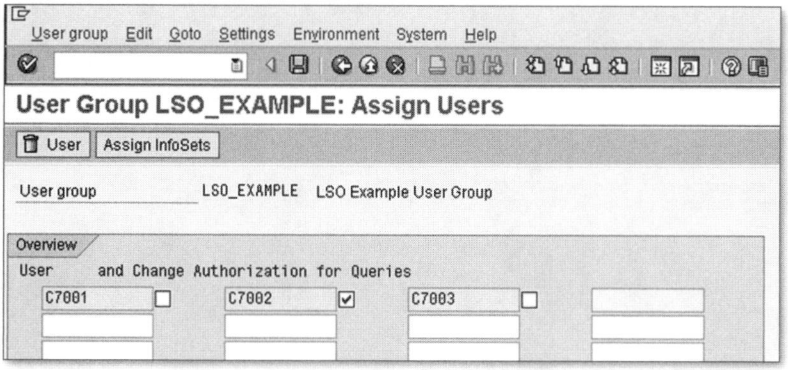

Figure 6.18 Adding User ID

Adding the User ID allows the user to execute reports in the User Group. Checking the box also allows the user to change or create reports.

> **Tip**
>
> Users with S_QUERY field ACTVT set to 02 (Change) and 23 (Maintain) will have access to all user group queries even if they are not specifically assigned. This could be used to provide broad access for reporting super-users.

Ad Hoc Query

To this point, all of the activities have set up Ad Hoc Query reporting. Ad Hoc Query can be accessed in several ways that direct the user to a particular Work Area and User Group. For this discussion, assume the transaction S_PHO_48000513 is being used. (SAP Easy Access menu path: HUMAN RESOURCES • INFORMATION SYSTEM • REPORTING TOOLS • AD HOC QUERY.) The first step is to select the Work Area (Standard Area for this example), the User Group (LSO_EXAMPLE), and the InfoSet (LSO_INFOSET_EXAMPLE).

The user can now utilize the fields available in the InfoSet (upper left) to create the selection criteria and the output results. (Refer to Figure 6.19.) In this example, the field Communication Type is chosen as a selection criteria. This allows the selection to be limited to 0010 (email). These selection fields appear in the upper right section. The field Communication LongID is selected for output and appears in the layout preview at the bottom of the screen. The reporting period can also be selected. In this example, the report is limited to Courses in September in addition to being limited to a particular Course Type. Once a suitable query has been created, it can be saved for later reuse or to use as a template.

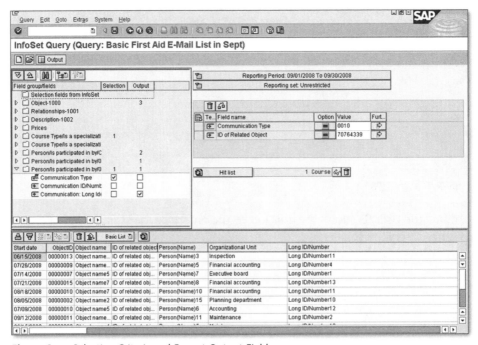

Figure 6.19 Selection Criteria and Report Output Fields

Clicking Output will run the report and open the result in an SAP *List Viewer* (ALV). (See Figure 6.20.) At this point, standard ALV functionality is available. For example, clicking the Excel icon ([Ctrl]+[Shift]+[F7]) will open the report in Excel format. From there, email addresses could be easily cut and pasted into an email with the Kirkpatrick Level Three Evaluation instructions, meeting the original reporting requirements.

To conclude, as demonstrated with the specific case example, Ad Hoc Query represents an important tool in the reporting solutions provided by SAP. Knowledge of ABAP is not required; queries can be created and run from a single screen; and set operations (not discussed) can be used for more complex reporting such as populations without certain data.

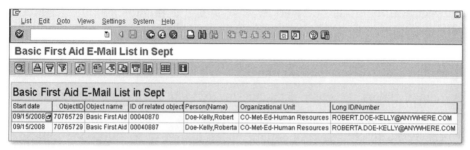

Figure 6.20 Report Results in SAP List Viewer

There are limitations to Ad Hoc Query. As shown, InfoSets and User Group must first be defined. This may require intervention by a reporting super-user. Also, multiline output lists cannot be produced. Despite these restrictions, Ad Hoc Query remains an important solution and should be considered when delivered reports are insufficient and before custom ABAP reports are developed.

6.15   The Training Administrator Portal

With enhancement package 4, Enterprise Learning provides a new administration interface, the Training Administrator Portal. The Training Administrator Portal lets administrators manage the majority of their day-to-day administrative activities through a dedicated portal interface. These include activities such as:

- ▶ Course Management
  - ▶ Scheduling Courses and managing resource allocations
  - ▶ Tracking Course preparation statuses
  - ▶ Following-up Courses
  - ▶ Managing correspondences
- ▶ Participation Management
  - ▶ Monitoring Course capacity statuses
  - ▶ Managing participations
- ▶ Other Administrative Activities
  - ▶ Mandatory Course assignments management

- Content Administration
  - Publishing e-learning content

The Training Administrator Portal provides a convenient, easy-to-use interface that allows the administrator easy access to training information and enables him to take quick, information-driven actions such as:

- Course administrators may perform their day-to-day, frequent, and regular activities through the portal interface.
- Administrators are able to get a quick overview of the training activities occurring in their organization.
- They can quickly assess situations related to Course readiness and capacities and act appropriately, in a timely fashion.
- Training administrative tasks can be easily delegated to several people in the training department.
- Novice users who are not trained on using the SAP GUI (SAP LSO backend system) will easily understand the navigation of the Course Administrator portal and its functions, without the need for extensive training.

The Training Administrator Portal is designed to support users in performing routine work or day-to-day activities. It does not support the creation of master data such as resource types, Course Groups, Course Types, and Curriculums. This more intensive work is better done in the SAP Enterprise Learning Backend System.

6.15.1 Structure of the Training Administrator Portal

The Training Administrator Portal (see Figure 6.21) is organized into four logical *Work Centers*:

- Courses
- Participation
- Correspondences
- Content Administration

These Work Centers, as the name indicates, are specific areas of work that are designed for performing a logical set of related business activities. They provide a central point of access to all such work-related content and tasks and aggregate the most important information in that area for the training administrator.

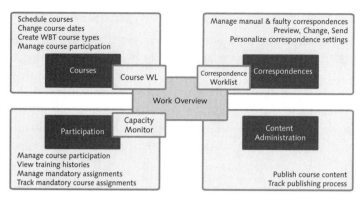

Figure 6.21 Training Administrator Portal

Apart from these Work Centers, the central Work Overview page serves as the home page for the training administrator, providing quick access to the most accessed information and most used activities. The Work Overview consists of two important work lists that simplify the training administrators to information considerably: the *Course Work List* and the *Capacity Monitor*. (Content Administration functionality will be discussed in Chapter 8.)

The Course Work List

The Course Work List (*see* Figure 6.22) helps administrators to:

▶ Gain an overview of training activities in the organization over different time periods — dates, location and language, preparation status of such Courses, capacity situation, resource fulfillment statuses, follow-up statuses, etc.

▶ Perform certain context-oriented activities for a Course — change Course details, manage participation, follow-up, and manage correspondences

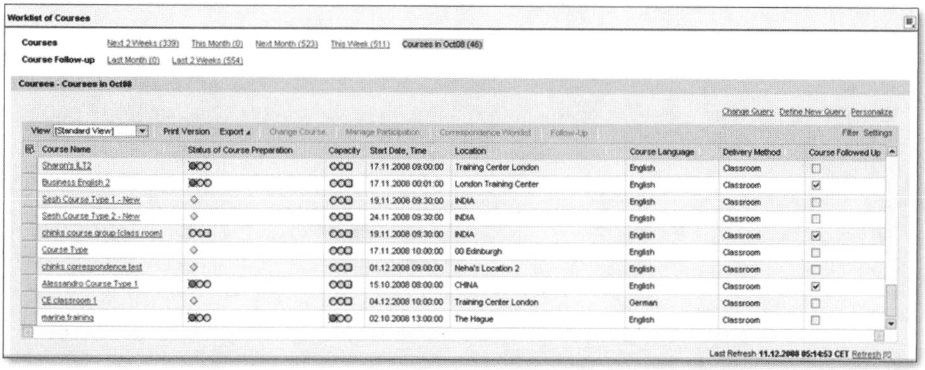

Figure 6.22 Course Work List

Booking, Pre-Booking, Waitlist Monitor (or) the Capacity Monitor

Course capacity status is an important indicator that provides triggers to an administrator, so he knows that specific actions need to be performed. For instance, if an administrator observes that Courses' participation levels are nearing maximum capacity levels, he can ensure that all resource assignments are confirmed and that all material requirements will be met. On the other hand, if an administrator observes that a Course is not going to meet minimum participation requirements, he may decide to cancel the class or may instead decide to publicize the Course dates more vigorously.

The *Capacity Monitor* helps in tracking four different situations, helping administrators to act in a prompt and appropriate manner (see Figure 6.23).

The Capacity Monitor supports this functionality using *Alert Types*. These alert types allow an administrator to easily see areas of concern and make rapid decisions to alleviate any possible issues.

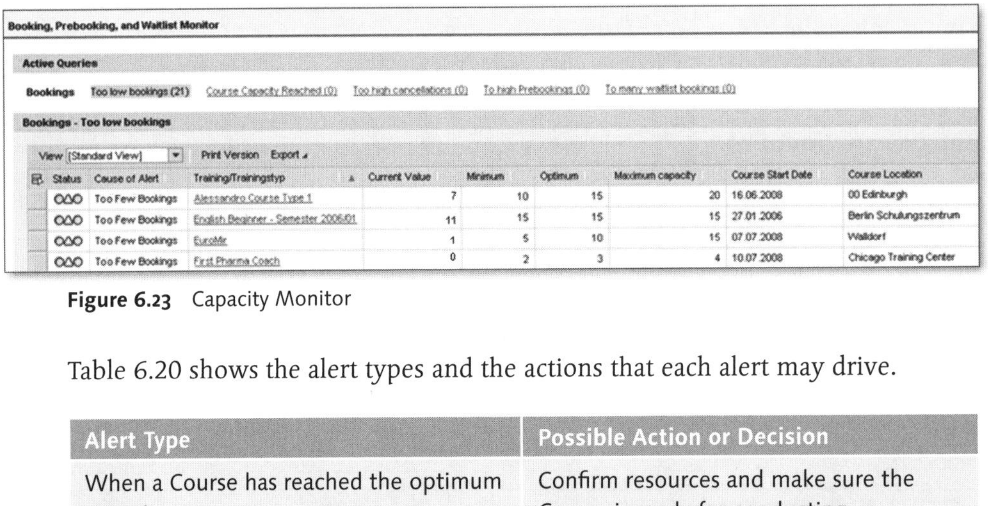

Figure 6.23 Capacity Monitor

Table 6.20 shows the alert types and the actions that each alert may drive.

Alert Type	Possible Action or Decision
When a Course has reached the optimum capacity	Confirm resources and make sure the Course is ready for conducting.
When a Course has too few bookings	Publicize the Course or cancel the Course.
When a Course has too many waitlisted bookings	Arrange for one more schedule of the Course to include waitlisted participants.
When a Course Type has high pre-booking.	Assess demand and schedule Courses accordingly

Table 6.20 Alert Types

Correspondence Work List

The Correspondence work center also has a work list — the *Correspondence Work List* helps administrators manage notifications and communication to different people such as learners, instructors, managers, etc. (See Figure 6.24.)

Because correspondences that are set as automatic are sent without any manual intervention, the Correspondence Work List mainly serves to manage manual correspondences and correspondences that have failed because of errors during generation or during delivery. Administrators can also change or preview correspondence before sending them.

> **Note**
>
> Correspondences can be set as manual or automatic in the SAP LSO backend. Administrators can also personalize an automatic correspondence type to manual through Stopmark customizations.

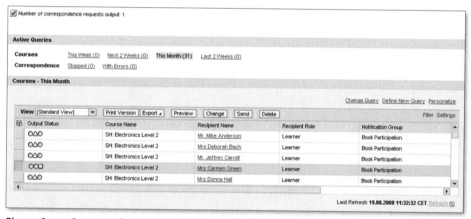

Figure 6.24 Correspondence Work List

The Correspondence Work List helps to effectively manage and dispatch correspondence to different members such as learners, instructors, and managers.

Personalizing the Work Lists

Some generic personalizing options are available for all work lists. End users can create their own queries for the items to be seen in the work list. Every work list provides a list of standard parameters based on which queries can be created. End users can also change the standard queries provided for a work list (see Figure 6.25).

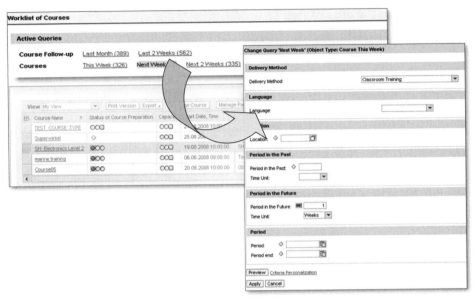

Figure 6.25 Work Lists

End users may also choose to create their own views of information that they want to see in the work list. For instance, it is possible to select hide or display information columns, change the order of columns, freeze columns, etc. (See Figure 6.26.)

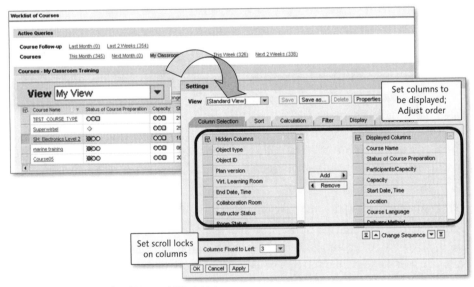

Figure 6.26 Personalized View of Work List

6.15.2 Scheduling Courses, Assigning Resources, and Managing Participation

Users who are familiar with the SAP Enterprise Learning Backend functionalities of scheduling Courses, assigning resources, and managing participation may find it possible to start using the new portal interface almost without any training. Users, who might not be familiar with the Backend functionalities, may also find the new interface easy to use and intuitive.

The Create Course Schedule is the key activity that leads users to the Course Schedule page (see Figure 6.27). This page is organized into logical information tabs that group related sets of information. This enables administrators to quickly access the piece of information that they want to view or change.

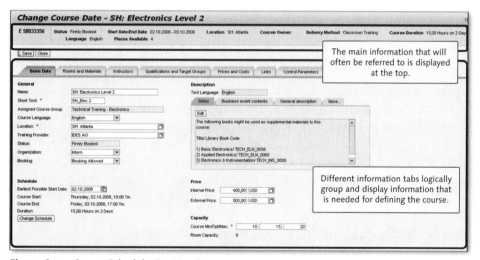

Figure 6.27 Course Schedule Creation Page

The Basic Data information tab is the main tab that holds the most essential information that is necessary for scheduling a Course. This includes information on the Course description and details, the location and schedule, price, and capacity information.

Most of such essential information is derived from the Course Type master. In most cases, it would be sufficient for an administrator to specify the Course location and the starting date (for typical classroom training) to create a new Course schedule.

The Basic Data page takes slightly different looks depending on the delivery method of the Course. For instance, in the case of a Course delivered as Virtual Learning

Room training, the basic data page contains additional information for specifying the Virtual Learning Room through which the Course will be conducted.

Resources requirements of a training Course are managed through two separate info tabs — one for rooms, materials, and other resources and the other one for instructors.

Both of these information tabs have the same layout and similar functions. Through these information tabs, it is possible to assign instructors and resources, either automatically or through a manual search. It is also possible to delimit such resources to specific time periods of the Course schedule.

Changes in these information tabs reflect on the resource status columns in the Course Work list and also affect the overall Course preparation status.

Through the Participants information tab administrators can manage Course booking. This tab clearly displays the number of booked, waitlisted, and cancelled participants at any point in time. An important functionality is that it also displays participants who have pre-booked the Course and enables administrators to quickly book them to the current Course schedule.

Course administrators can book new participants to the Course either with the default fee and payment method as specified for the master Course Type, or they could also change these if required. Payment methods can be specified either in terms of activity allocations (typically used for internal learners) or in terms of billing documents or payment cards (typically used for external learners). The normal checks that are performed during booking are also performed. The system also automatically adjusts the booking priority depending on the Course capacity.

6.15.3 Configuring the Training Administrator Portal

The main advantage in using the Course Administrator Portal is that it does not necessitate any process changes or changes to any system configuration. No specific business process configurations have been introduced for the Course Administrator Portal. This means that customers, who have been using the training administrative functionalities in the SAP EL Backend System, can start using the new Portal application without any additional configurations.

6.16 Development Plans

Development Plans support organizations as they plan and track development activities for their employees. An organization may use Development Plans for a variety of reasons:

- To help employees perform better in their current role
- To provide fast tracking for high potential employees
- To deliver a path to aid all employees in their career growth planning
- To support performance improvements for employees who are not executing to the organization's expectations

These motivations ensure that training Courses are an integral part of any Development Plan. Through such plans, learning opportunities may be identified for individuals to support their development. The status of these learning opportunities is tracked via the Development Plans.

There are several possible ways of realizing development plans in SAP Human Capital Management:

1. Through Individual Development Plan functions in the SAP HCM backend system
2. Via the Development Plan function available as a part of Talent Management and Development features with EhP4
3. Using SAP Performance Management templates

6.16.1 Individual Development Plan function (SAP HCM backend)

Individual Development Plan functionality has long existed in SAP HCM, and is available as a part of the Personnel Development module. This feature allows organizations to create different templates or formats for development plans. These templates (Development Plans) are then assigned to employees and customized as Individual Development Plans, which are unique to each employee.

A development plan may consist of development activities such as Course attendance requirements, time in specific positions or jobs, and time spent in certain locations. Once a development plan is associated with an employee as an Individual Development Plan, the individual elements may be left as is or enhanced with other learning or development activities. These Individual Development Plans may be accessed as part of an employee's master data on the Qualifications Infotype (Infotype 0024) or via the Profile View transaction (Transaction PPPM.)

The integration of SAP Enterprise Learning with this Development Plan facilitates the following activities:

1. Adding Course Types as development plan items
2. Updating the status of these learning related development plan items automatically, from *Planned* to *In progress* to *Complete* as a learner completes activities

in the Portal or an administrator updates learning status in the backed (e.g., a Course Type status in an Individual Development Plan is automatically updated, based on Enterprise Learning activities, such as when booking via the Portal or completing Course attendance.)

3. Supporting direct interaction with Enterprise Learning through the development plan to update the status of the development plan item (e.g., an administrator may choose to book an employee directly to a scheduled Course from the Course Type in the individual development plan). See Figure 6.28 to illustrate this integration.

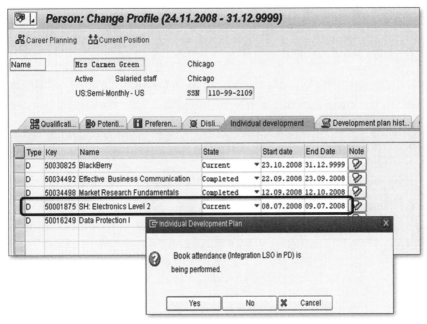

Figure 6.28 Team Manager Integration

6.16.2 Talent Management and Development

The area of Talent Management in SAP ERP HCM has seen major enhancements with the last few releases and enhancement packages. The processes of succession planning, talent review and assessment, talent development, and their interrelationships have received considerable attention in the enhancement pack 4 for SAP ERP. Part of the new functionality is a new object Development Plan in Talent Management. This new development plan has no relationship to the old development plan functionality.

The Development Plan function in Talent Management allows managers and talent development specialists to chart out well-structured Development Plans for their organizational members (see Figure 6.29). Such Development Plans can be integrated with competency catalogs from SAP Personnel Development as well with the Course catalog from SAP Enterprise Learning. Managers can access Development Plans of their team members through SAP Manager Self-Services. This Web-based interface for development plans enables easy visualization of development plans, the progress, and simple assessment of achievements.

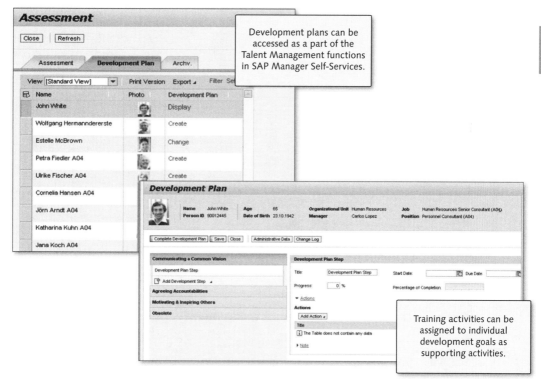

Figure 6.29 Talent Management Functions

For each development goal, it's also possible to define actions that are to be taken by the individual. These actions can represent activities that could facilitate the individual in achieving the goal set. For example, a training activity from the organization's Course catalog can be added as an action item for the individual. See Figure 6.30 for an illustration of this.

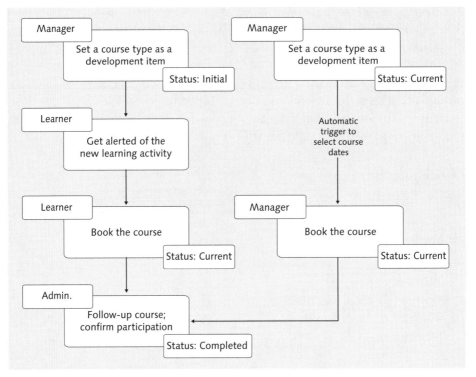

Figure 6.30 Adding Development Items

Through SAP Enterprise Learning, managers can add Courses as development items; the status of the Course progress is automatically updated by the system.

6.16.3 Using SAP Performance Management

Development Plans can also be realized through SAP ERP HCM Performance Management. In many ways, this integration is similar to the previous alternative of using alternate development plans, but it can be realized in earlier releases of Talent Management (EhP4 is not required).

The SAP Performance Management solution provides a flexible framework that helps organizations develop different appraisal formats for different processes, such as regular appraisals, employee potential assessments, performance improvement plans, or development plans (see Figure 6.31). The templates are designed by the organization to support their specific appraisal requirements. These templates govern the nature, content, and process flow of the assessment or development plan document.

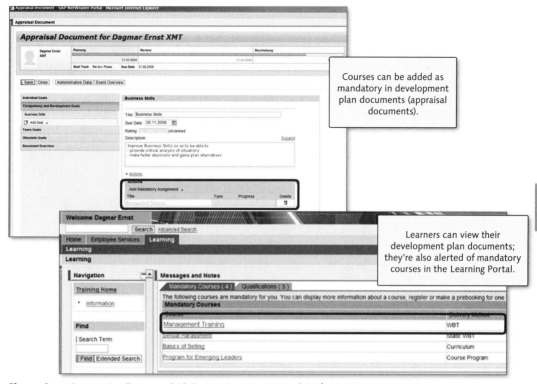

Figure 6.31 Integration Between SAP Enterprise Learning and Performance Management

In this manner, it's quite possible to design a Development Plan document that could consist of the following items:

1. Free-form learning or development objectives and measurement criteria.

2. Competency gaps that the manager would like to track and would want the individual to improve; these gaps can be identified by comparing the individuals' competencies with his current job requirements or with any other job or position that is in his career path.

3. On-the-job performance assessment objectives.

4. Mandatory Courses that the individual should participate in; managers can also specify such mandatory Courses as a supporting activity for a development or performance objective. Individuals are alerted of such mandatory Courses through the Learning Portal.

5. Current training activities in which the individual is participating.

6.17   Summary

This chapter outlined the Training Management process in SAP Enterprise Learning. The life cycle of the training process includes preparation, setting up the Training Catalog, Day-to-Day Activities, and Recurring Activities, including configuration and integration. Specific attention is given to Course Programs and Curricula, which can be used to direct the Course of learning within an enterprise. Finally, this chapter outlined Reporting as well as the new Training Administrator Portal and Development Plans. In the next chapter we will learn about the Virtual Learning Room.

"Conversation has magic to it. Dialog is the most powerful learning technology on earth. Conversations are the stem cells of learning for they both create and transmit knowledge. Frequent and open conversation increases innovation and learning." — From Informal Learning, by Jay Cross

7 Virtual Learning Room

The Virtual Learning Room is an online meeting room used to conduct scheduled, instructor-led learning events. Virtual Learning Rooms are an evolving approach to teaching and learning in an educational setting. While originally created for meetings, they are now often used to supplement traditional face-to-face classroom training, particularly in the business environment.

These classes are usually conducted over the Internet and provide a collection of tools such as those for screen sharing, document sharing, chat, polling, whiteboards, and collaborative notepads.

The Virtual Learning Room enables a subject matter expert to provide informal context to formal content. It also enables conversation between a participant and the subject matter expert and among the participants via voice, video, or text. Such real time open conversation significantly improves learning and innovation within a company without the expenditure associated with a classroom training session.

7.1 Virtual Learning Rooms are Important Business Tools

There will always be a role for a teacher, professor, or a subject matter expert to teach and entertain in a classroom; instructors convey enthusiasm, expert knowledge, experience, and context in live sessions. The interaction between the instructor and the learner also adds value to the live classroom environment. However, such classroom learning is happening less frequently in the business world due to cost constraints and practical problems such as the geographic distribution of learners. When learners are located throughout the country or around the world, instructor-led training cannot be scaled to this audience due to physical classroom constraints. Often, content cannot always be developed and delivered in a timely fashion due to the need for more instructors and various time and location offerings. Instructor-led classroom training also cannot always be produced and replicated quickly or cost effectively to meet critical business needs.

While instructor-led physical classroom sessions are necessary for certain types of training, relationship building, and culture development in an organization, a significant portion of training can be delivered via Virtual Learning Rooms more efficiently and effectively.

7.1.1 Types of Learning for Which the Virtual Learning Room is Best Suited

According to Josh Bersin, a renowned learning and talent management expert, there are four types of corporate training programs: information broadcast, critical skills transfer, skills and competencies development, and certification (see Figure 7.1).

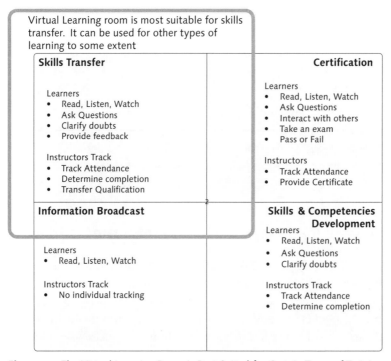

Figure 7.1 The Virtual Learning Room is Best Suited for Certain Types of Training

The Virtual Learning Room approach is best suited for critical skills and critical knowledge transfer to learners. For example, a Virtual Learning Room–based

Course can teach critical information about a product to the sales team. The sales team can read the information presented in the room, listen to the speaker providing informal context to the factual content, watch the demonstrations, if any, and ask questions to clarify doubts. The participants can also answer quick polls to either convey feedback, such as their levels of comfort with the information shared and their readiness level to execute on the information provided.

When Virtual Learning Rooms are used for certifications, the Course conducted in a Virtual Learning Room can be bundled with an assessment in a Curriculum. Learners can attend a Course in the Virtual Learning Room and then take an assessment, which will be a separate item in the Curriculum, to demonstrate their knowledge and get the certification.

7.1.2 A Virtual Learning Room is for Synchronous Events

A Virtual Learning Room is meant for synchronous events where the instructor and learners are present at the same time in an online learning room. It is not meant for asynchronous collaboration. In other words, it is not a place where learners can go any time to learn about a topic.

While the Virtual Learning Room sounds a lot like a classroom session conducted online, it has several advantages over an instructor-led physical classroom session.

7.1.3 The Virtual Learning Room Can Surpass Classroom Training

The Virtual Learning Room approach even surpasses instructor-led physical classroom training in some areas. For example, an instructor teaching in a large physical classroom may not be able to reliably keep track of learner feedback to questions and polls. A Virtual Learning Room can record the feedback to questions and polls at an individual level and at a question level in a database. An instructor may not be able to keep track of time spent by each and every learner in a classroom, especially in a large classroom. Virtual Learning Rooms can accurately track the time spent by learners in a classroom.

Questions and Polls

For example, if an instructor in a physical classroom wants to find out how many students in a class have attended a session on a certain topic before, the instructor usually asks the class to raise their hands to get an idea. However, the instructor in a virtual learning room can create a quick poll to get a response from all the students in a class. The entire class can view the responses and the instructor can access the responses later from the database for reporting purposes.

7.2 SAP Enterprise Learning Virtual Learning Room

The SAP Enterprise Learning Virtual Learning Room is pre-integrated, and powered by Adobe Connect Professional (see Figure 7.2). It is an integral part of SAP Enterprise Learning. Customers do not have to buy the product separately or get a separate license from another vendor for the product.

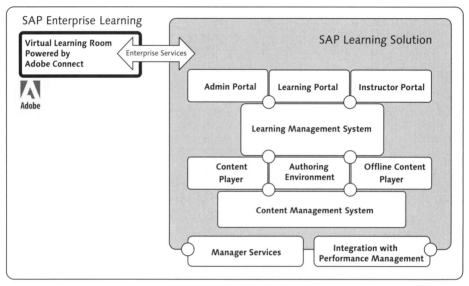

Figure 7.2 The Virtual Learning Room is an Integral Part of SAP Enterprise Learning

7.3 How Adobe Connect is Integrated with SAP Enterprise Learning

In this section we will look at the various roles that use the Virtual Learning Room and elaborate on how the integration helps with their tasks.

7.3.1 Learning Portal

Once a Course is set up, learners can easily register for and launch a Course conducted in the Virtual Learning Room, using the Learning Portal. Only learners who are registered for a Course conducted in a Virtual Learning Room can enter the room. Those who are registered can enter the Virtual Learning Room 10 minutes before the Course starts, and then launch the Course by clicking the Start Now button in the Learning Portal. They will seamlessly enter the Virtual Learning Room. No separate authentication is required (see Figure 7.3).

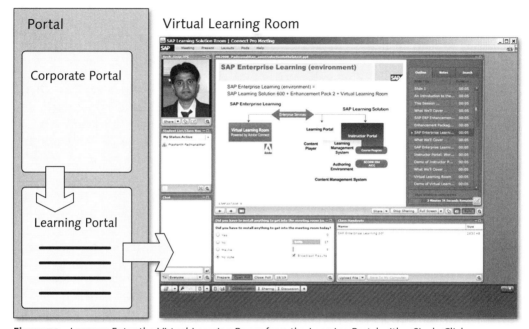

Figure 7.3 Learners Enter the Virtual Learning Room from the Learning Portal with a Single Click

7.3.2 Instructor Portal

An instructor can enter a Virtual Learning Room, change the properties of the room such as description, and change the room assigned to a Course using the Instructor Portal.

In SAP Enterprise Learning, every instructor owns at least one room, which he can enter at any time to prepare for a future training session. He can also create more rooms and assign the newly created rooms to the Courses he teaches. For example, an instructor who trains sales teams in a company may own a room where he teaches sales teams from the Americas, but he can also create another room for training the sales teams from Europe.

Instructor's Virtual Learning Room

For example, if an instructor teaches a class on statistics, the instructor can prepare his room with Course material related to statistics. If the instructor also teaches a Course on marketing, the instructor can create another room, and populate that room with Course materials related to marketing. This saves the instructor preparation time. It also preserves the content created during a previous class. Such content can be saved and used in future sessions. Think of it as a blackboard in a classroom that is never erased and never runs out of space.

A normal class session conducted in a Virtual Learning Room is modeled after a class session in a physical classroom. The instructor can start a lecture session by making a presentation or drawing on the whiteboard. Other instructors can join the presentation. A learner can make a presentation to demonstrate his work. The instructor manages and controls the session like a regular classroom.

A Typical Session in a Virtual Learning Room

In a Virtual Learning Room session, an instructor enters the room and starts his presentation by displaying the Course content. Content could be a document such as a Microsoft PowerPoint presentation or a Microsoft Word document. The instructor will then share his desktop and display an application or website to elaborate on the concept. The instructor can invite other instructors to present to the class. The instructor can also ask a learner to share his screen and make a presentation or demonstrate an application. The session is synchronous. All instructors and learners have to be present in the room at the same time. The Virtual Learning Room is not used for asynchronous collaboration.

The content in a Virtual Learning Room is preserved even after the session. Content placed in the room before the session and content created in the room during a session are preserved and never removed unless the instructor chooses to do so.

Content in a Room is Preserved for Future Sessions

You can think of the Virtual Learning Room as a room that belongs to one instructor and is dedicated to a particular topic. It is a place with unlimited whiteboard space and shelf space with content relevant to the topic, not only from documents but also from conversations and discussions in the past sessions. Instructors can upload as much content as they want into the room to create mini-libraries that are relevant to the class. Instructors can create as many whiteboards as they want, draw on those whiteboards, and preserve them for future sessions. Chat content, notes content, and presentation content are also preserved and retained at the end of the session.

7.3.3 Administrator Interface

A training administrator can create Course Types conducted in a Virtual Learning Room from the training administrator interface. A training administrator can assign resources such as instructors to a class conducted in a Virtual Learning Room from the SAP training administrator interface. The Delivery Type is 0014 (see Figure 7.4).

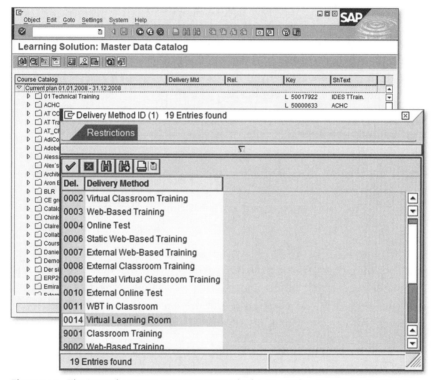

Figure 7.4 The Virtual Learning Room is Treated Like Any Other Course by the Training Administrator.

Assignment of a Virtual Learning Room to a Course

When a training administrator creates a Course that is conducted in a Virtual Learning Room and assigns an instructor to the Course, the room that is associated with that instructor is assigned to the Course automatically. If the instructor does not have a room, a room is created for him automatically.

7.3.4 Tracking of Information with the Virtual Learning Room

The Learning Management System tracks the name of the participant, and the amount of time the participant spent in the class. Additional information such as individual answers to poll questions is stored in the Adobe Connect database and can be accessed by the administrator.

7.4 Features of the Virtual Learning Room

We recommend that you don't use the Virtual Learning Room like a PowerPoint presentation with voiceover. Instead, take advantage of the vast selection of collaboration features, including multiple instructors and participants, chat, polls, whiteboards, content library, and application sharing.

Multiple Instructors and Expert Participants

A Virtual Learning Room enables the seamless participation of multiple instructors and expert participants in a class. Because instructors and experts do not travel, it is easy to invite and accommodate instructors and experts even if their contributions are limited to a few minutes. Such expert participation enriches the conversation.

Polls

Polls in the beginning of a class can give the instructor an understanding about the level of knowledge about the subject matter. This will help the instructor dynamically decide on the portions of the lecture that he needs to spend more time on and the portions that can be skipped or skimmed.

Polls during the class provide instructors and learners an understanding of how much learners have understood the topic.

Chat

Chat functionality enables users to ask questions to the instructor and chat with each other privately about topics.

Application Sharing

Application sharing functionality enables presenters to share applications in their computers with learners. This feature enables the quick delivery of demos and software training without long and expensive content development.

Video or Image of the Speakers

The Virtual Learning Room enables the display of video or still images of presenters and learners.

A video or an image of the instructor adds significant value to the session. The ability to see the instructor enagages the learners. We recommend that you use video with caution based on the bandwidth constraints of learners.

Questions and Answers

Learners can ask questions to the instructor, to the entire class, or to other learners privately. This is a very useful feature that allows learners to pose their questions without interrupting the flow of the class.

Instructors can manage the question and answer sessions by directing all questions to the instructor. Instructors can then choose to answer the questions during the session or after a session. It is also possible for a second instructor to answer questions via chat while the main instructor is delivering his lecture.

7.5 Installation and Configuration

This section covers the high-level steps in installation and configuration of the Virtual Learning Room.

Step 1: Installing Adobe Connect

The Installation document is available from the following link: *http://www.adobe. com/resources/acrobatconnect/server/pdf/connect_enterprise_install.pdf.* This installation location is provided for reference, so you can read the documentation before you receive the physical shipment of the software. It is always advisable to follow the installation document that accompanies your software once you start the installation process.

▶ **System Requirements**
- ▶ Microsoft Windows 2003 SP2 32 bit
- ▶ Server processor - Dual Xeon, 3 GHz processor
- ▶ Memory - 4GB RAM
- ▶ Hard Drive - 100 + GB

▶ To install the Connect Enterprise Server (Adobe Connect Server), a license number is needed.

▶ MSSQL 2005 needs to be installed as mentioned in the documentation.

▶ **Installation and Implementation Steps**
The installation process takes about two hours. The configuration process may take several calendar days based on the customer's infrastructure requirements. Installation is usually not performed by SAP Enterprise Learning consultants.

▶ **Additional software required**
Microsoft Windows 2003 SP2 32 bit is not provided by SAP. A scaled-down version of MS SQL is provided. This version can be used for installation test and piloting purposes. Production version of the system should have a separately licensed version of MS SQL.

▶ **Database requirements**
MS SQL

Step 2: Configuration of Adobe Connect

Configuration of Adobe Connect involves three steps: creating an admin user and adding user to the administrators group, identifying the trusted servers, and modifying the Servlet configuration.

▶ **Creating an Admin User for EL**
A generic admin user is needed for communication with SAP Enterprise Learning.

▶ Log on to the Adobe Connect administrator interface and create an admin user.

▶ Then add the admin user to the administrators group.

▶ **Identify the Trusted Servers**
The next step is to identify and get the names of the trusted servers where SAP Learning Solution is hosted.

▶ **Configure the Servlet**
The next step is to configure the Servlet by modifying the appropriate xml file. (see Figure 7.5).

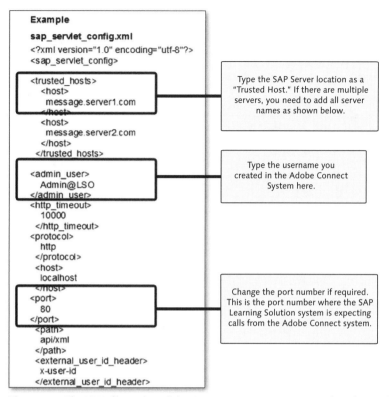

Figure 7.5 The XML file in the Adobe Connect Server Location Needs to be Configured

Step 3: Configuration of the SAP Backend

Configuring the SAP Enterprise Learning Backend system includes activating the business function HCM_LSO_VLR, copying the Logical Ports into the target client, and creating the SM59 RFC destination.

▶ **Activate Business Function**

  ▶ It is necessary to activate the following Business Functions in order to use the Virtual Learning Room functionality. For SAP Learning Solution, activate Business Function HCM_LSO_CI_1 HCM, Learning Solution 01.

  ▶ For SAP Enterprise Learning, activate Business Function HCM_LSO_VLR HCM, Enterprise Learning. The Business Function HCM, Learning Solution 01 is a prerequisite for HCM, Enterprise Learning.

▶ **Copy the Logical Ports into the Target Client**
  For the Virtual Learning Room, some logical ports are required (see Figure 7.6).

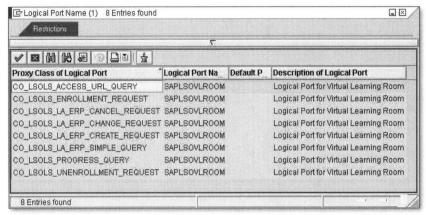

Figure 7.6 The List of Logical Ports Required by the Virtual Learning Room

The Logical Ports are delivered in client 000 and have to be transported into the target client where you want to set up SAP Enterprise Learning.

▶ Launch Transaction LPCONFIG in client 000 and transport all logical ports one by one to the target client.

▶ **Create the RFC Destination**
The next step is to create the RFC destination (see Figure 7.7).

Figure 7.7 Type Transaction SM59 and Create the RFC Destination

Step 4: Portal Configuration

The SAP Portal needs to be configured to add the link "Manage Virtual Learning Room" to the Instructor Portal. Once the Virtual Learning Room integration is configured completely, the Instructor portal will display the link named "Manage Virtual Learning rooms."

Step 5: Testing and Troubleshooting

The configuration can be tested from the SAP Backend by running the connection test. Click on the Connection Test button (see Figure 7.8).

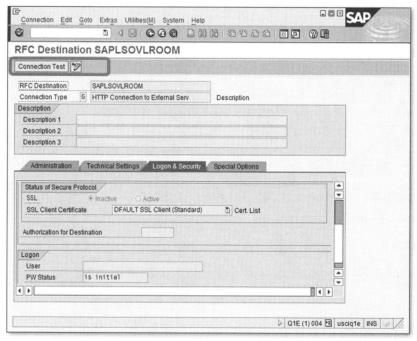

Figure 7.8 Click on the Connection Test Button to Test the Configuration

7.5.1 Troubleshooting Tips

If the configuration is successful, you should see the success message screen. If the configuration is not successful, check the following things:

▶ **Connection Test Not Successful**

  ▶ This indicates a lack of connection with the Adobe system. This could be due to various reasons such as an incorrect server name, lack of network connectivity, or system nonavailability. Check these things to ensure that the connection test is successful.

▶ **Trusted Host Not Successful**

    ▶ Check whether all message-servers of the SAP Learning Solution system are registered as trusted hosts in the file sap_servlet_config. xml.

▶ **User Test Not Successful**

    ▶ Check if the user has been created and has been assigned administrator rights.

    ▶ Check if the user name in the SAP Servlet configuration file in the Adobe system has the right user name added to it.

The response body tab will display the test results (see Figure 7.9).

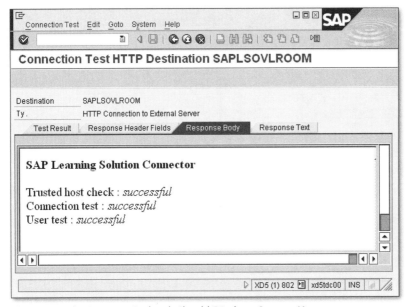

Figure 7.9 The Response Body tab Should Display a Success Message

7.6 Infrastructure Planning for Adobe Connect

This section refers to sizing for Adobe Connect servers. It does not refer to sizing for the other SAP Enterprise Learning components. While there are elaborate documents available from Adobe on the Adobe Connect architecture, the following quick rule of thumb approach helps during initial implementation discussions.

Adobe Connect needs one server per 500 concurrent users. If you do not have prior information based on the actual number of concurrent users, you could take a simple, yet effective, approach to arrive at the possible number of concurrent users. For example, to arrive at the number of concurrent users a company might have, let's start with a target company that has offices in the United States and India. The U.S. offices have 5,000 employees and India offices have 3,000 employees. It is reasonable to assume that U.S. employees work while India employees are asleep. At any given point of time, say 10 percent of the company is in training programs. Twenty percent of training programs are conducted using Adobe Connect. The United States has more employees. 10 percent of 5,000 is 500. Twenty percent of 500 is 100. So, under normal circumstances, there will be about 100 concurrent users in the system. One server for Adobe Connect should be enough for this situation. Even if the number of people who attend training programs conducted using Adobe Connect doubles, they are still well within the server capacity. Because there are 3,000 employees in India, this capacity should serve them fine as well.

This, of Course, is a simple approach. While implementing, the IT team should take into account other factors such as unusual events and connectivity levels of users.

7.7　More Resources on This Topic

Documentation for Consultants

▸ Configuration of SAP Learning Solution and SAP Enterprise Learning, Enhancement Package 2 for SAP ERP 6.0. *http://service.sap.com/learningsolution/* Look for the "Media Library-Enterprise Learning" link.

▸ Master Guide SAP enhancement package 2 for SAP ERP 6.0. Search for material number 50084482 in *http://service.sap.com/instguides.*

▸ The following SAP Notes are relevant for the virtual classroom installation and configuration. Note 1070578: General info on installing and troubleshooting Enterprise Learning Virtual Learning room.

▸ This material is intended to be used together with the Configuration Guide for SAP Enterprise Learning. The configuration guide can be downloaded from the link provided in SAP Note 1070578.

▸ Adobe Servlet configuration is documented in SAP Note 1070578.

References and More Readings on the Topic

- Jay Cross, *Informal Learning*, 2007, Pfeiffer, John Wiley, NY.
- Josh Bersin, *The Blended Learning Book*, 2004, Pfeiffer, JohnWiley, NY.

7.8 Summary

The Virtual Learning Room powered by Adobe Connect is an integral part of SAP Enterprise Learning. It is an effective delivery mechanism for skills transfer training and information broadcast. It can be used for certifications and technical training to some extent. The Virtual Learning Room is tightly integrated with SAP Enterprise Learning and does not require any additional development work. The configuration steps for Adobe Connect and SAP Enterprise Learning were covered in this chapter. In the next chapter we will learn about content design, development, and delivery methods.

7.9 Contributors

Aron Kornhall contributed to this chapter. Aron is part of the SAP Enterprise Learning development team and is one of the lead architects of this integration.

If training administration is the heart of the learning management system, content is the lifeblood of the system. Creating, delivering, and managing content is one of the most critical activities for a training organization. If content is not managed effectively, your training organization will come to a standstill.

8 Content Design, Development, and Delivery in the SAP Learning Solution

8.1 Introduction

The primary function of a Learning Management System (LMS) is to deliver content to learners. Regardless of the solution chosen, the implementation of LMS is not complete without content. Content integration is usually seen as the most difficult part of an LMS implementation, regardless of the solution chosen. If you review LMS literature, you will find that content integration is one of the most commonly noted pain points for all customers during integration and from a support perspective. To relieve this, the implementation team must have a strategy to support content creation and delivery during the implementation that can be rolled out as a support model, once the implementation is complete.

The SAP Learning Solution supports five methods for content delivery:

1. The use of the Authoring Environment (AE) to support the creation of internally hosted, properly structured, SCORM2004 compliant content

2. The use of the AE to validate third-party content that is compliant with either the SCORM standards (1.1; 1.2; or 2004) or the AICC standard and to import standards compliant content into your content management system

3. The use of the Rapid Content Publishing Tool, to quickly publish compliant or single-file content

4. The use of other tools such as XI to allow learners to access third-party hosted content easily, and to ensure that their progress results are passed back to the Learning Solution

5. The use of a static Web-link from any central location to deliver noncompliant content (Note: This method does not support any progress tracking.)

Figure 8.1 shows each of these methods. As we progress through this chapter, each method except the static solution will be discussed in detail.

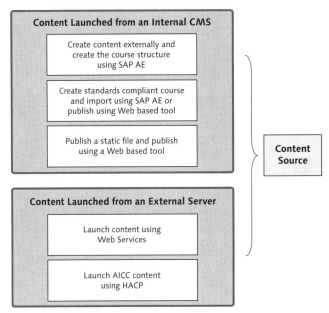

Figure 8.1 Five Methods for Content Delivery

8.2 Content Design

The best way to develop and deliver your content depends on multiple factors, including the concept that is being taught, the learning method of the student, required evaluation methods, and budget. The SAP Learning Solution supports multiple delivery methods, which were discussed in detail in Chapter 6. For the purposes of this section, we will discuss content design and delivery for the delivery methods Web-Based Training and Online Test. In later sections of this chapter, we will discuss the External Delivery Methods.

Content Development Strategy

Content Development involves significant investment in terms of time and resources. Content development often requires a dedicated team within the organization, particularly if the organization maintains a large catalog of internal content or plans to grow into this, to support its LMS implementation. Because content development requires expertise in development tools, design processes, and standards, some organizations prefer to use a third-party vendor to create and maintain content. As noted earlier, we will discuss this option later in the chapter.

As you know, a well-balanced team is critical for the success of any project. If you chose to develop your content in-house, an internal Content Development team with a variety of skills is probably necessary. The number of resources required for each skill will vary, depending on the volume and the type of content being created by your organization. The AE within the SAP Learning Solution supports these different roles, as noted below and discussed in more detail later in this chapter. Following is a list of the typical members involved in the content development and delivery process.

▶ **Instructional Designer**: defines the Course outline to ensure it delivers the required learning objectives to the target audience. The AE provides a role for the Instructional Designer that allows him access to those functions that support his job.

▶ **Subject-Matter-Expert (SME)**: Although usually not a permanent member of the content team, the SME provides the knowledge that will be imparted upon delivery of the content. He helps identify the knowledge objectives and provides the detail behind each objective. The AE also provides an SME role that provides access to the functions required by this role.

▶ **Media Development Specialist/Visual Designer**: creates the user interface and supporting media for the content, including the graphics and audio, with a focus on usability.

▶ **Instructional or Copy-Writer**: scripts the e-learning content, activities, and assessments for the Course.

▶ **Content Architect/Engineer**: determines the best authoring tools to leverage for the Course and the final Course format.

During the implementation of your LMS, you may not have your entire content team identified. However, you will need key implementation team members who have the skills required to develop content standards for your organization. Your standards must be defined before you go-live, to ensure that content is developed and delivered consistently. Common elements that are included in an organization's standards include layout and format, instructional design and strategy, and project management methodology. See Table 8.1 for a discussion of these elements.

Strategy Element	Essentials
Layout/Format	Ensures that your content has a consistent look and feel in terms of branding and format; the navigation appears in the same way on all your content; tests are designed optimally; and other media guidelines such as screen resolution and bandwidth requirements.
	From an SAP AE perspective, this also supports your authors as they leverage meta-data and content tagging.
Instructional Design	Addresses both the methodology you use to create content (The ADDIE model, for example, or Rapid Prototyping) as well as the key players needed to implement this model (see roles information, above). It also includes your organization's guidelines on usability.
Project Management	Identifies the deliverables and timeframes for each deliverable, based on your selected methodology, for each phase of the content creation project: for example, work plan, needs analysis, design plans, story boards, Courseware, and evaluation methodology.

Table 8.1 Strategy Elements

Once your standards are defined for internal content development, you can leverage these as you develop Course content for your go-live and on a post-go-live basis.

8.3 The SAP Authoring Environment (AE)

We've mentioned the AE, but we haven't talked about its functions in detail until now. The SAP Learning Solution provides the AE to support content integration during the implementation of the Learning Solution and to provide a structure to ensure content is created consistently and cleanly post-go-live. The AE is commonly represented as a content creation tool, but this is not the case. It is, instead, a content structuring tool that allows you to leverage any best-of-breed content creation tool you wish to develop content. It then supports your content development team in applying your corporate standards to ensure the content is structured appropriately and delivered to your learners successfully.

The AE is also used as a conversion tool when you wish to bring third-party content in-house. It runs through a series of checks to validate that the content is standards compliant and then converts the content into a format the Learning Solution Content Player supports. This ensures that third-party created content is in a format that adheres to required standards.

Let's take a tour of the AE, so we can understand how it works to support the content creation process.

Important! Without the AE, there is no e-learning on the SAP Learning Solution prior to enhancement pack 4. AE is an integral component of SAP Enterprise Learning that is required to pass content to the Content Management System (CMS). It may be used as a:

▶ Structuring tool to create a Course structure and attach existing content

▶ Test Author

▶ Tool to import existing SCORM/AICC–compliant content

With the advent of enhancement pack 4, the Administrator Portal provides basic publishing functionality. It does not support test creation. This is discussed further in the section on Rapid Content Publishing.

The AE Layout

As mentioned, the AE is a standalone (Figure 8.2), Java-based application that is installed on each instructional designer/content creator/publisher's desktop or laptop. The tool has multiple panes in the main application that support Course structure development, meta-data tagging, learning strategy design, and error processing. These panes are defined in Table 8.2.

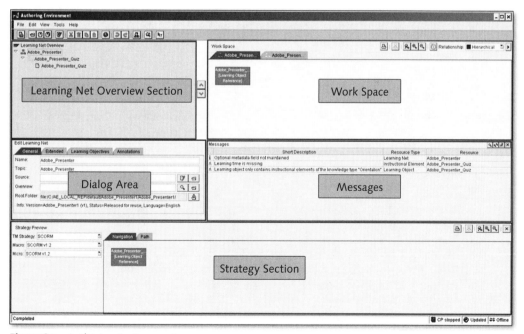

Figure 8.2 Authoring Environment

As noted earlier, the Authoring Environment supports two separate roles: the Instructional Designer and the Subject Matter Expert (SME). During the initial setup of the AE, the end-user must select the appropriate role required to use the AE. These roles are delivered for usability purposes only; there are no authorizations associated with them. Each role is configurable by the end user to allow more or less functionality than delivered and the end user may switch between the two roles.

▶ **Instructional Designer** — This role provides full functionality within AE and supports development of the Course structure, design of learning objectives, and publishing functions.

▶ **Subject Matter Expert** — This role provides limited functionality within the AE. This role is typically provided to the content developer who creates content for the Course.

Section	Description
Learning Net Overview	Used to create the Course outline. If the Workspace is not used to create Macro-strategies among the objects, the structure created in the Learning Net Overview drives the format of the content as it appears to the learner.
Dialog Area	Used to manage content meta-data, such as key words and micro-strategy. Content media is associated with Instructional Elements in the Dialog Area.
Workspace	Supports the creation of Macro-strategy, which drives the path the learner may take through content. This may be used to "force" a learner through content in a linear manner.
Messages	Informational, Warning, and Error messages appear here to help guide you through the content development process. This may be turned off in your personal settings.
Strategy Section	If the Workspace is used for Learning Path development, this section shows how the content will appear based on the selection of different Learning Strategies. This may also be turned off in your personal settings.

Table 8.2 Authoring Environment Functions

> **Note**
>
> From an Authorizations perspective, you may limit a user's ability to publish. Users who have selected the Instructional Designer role may not publish if they are not given Read/Write access to the content folders designated for e-learning Content in your CMS as well as an ERP backend user role that includes the authorizations in the delivered role: SAP_HR_LSO_AUTHOR.

Creating Content in the Authoring Environment (AE)

As an author, once you have assigned yourself a role in the AE, you must decide whether you want to create your content independently of the AE, using one of the supported standards and then importing it or whether you want to create your content within the AE, using it as a content structuring tool. There are pros and cons to both methods. As we discuss content in this chapter, we will refer to the first option, creating content outside the AE as *Independent Authoring* and refer to the second method, creating content within the AE, as *Integrated Authoring*. These are not SAP terms, but they illustrate the difference between the two methods and make reference to one or the other as a simpler process.

Many experienced content developers prefer Independent Authoring because it allows them to use the tools they are familiar with in the same way they have always used them. However, there are some advantages to Integrated Authoring that may not be immediately obvious to the novice user of the AE. See Table 8.3 for details.

Feature	Independent Authoring	Integrated Authoring
Uses Content Player navigation	Does not support	Supports
Sequencing	Supports through SCORM 2004 calls	Workspace supports via Drag and Drop functions
Consistent Navigation	Must be designed with Content Creation tool	Inherent
Support of all Mandatory SCORM elements	Must be developed with Content Creation tool.	Inherent
"Bookmarking"	Inherent to the Learning Object level. Additional detail will depend on the tools provided by the content.	Inherent to the Instructional Element level
Progress Tracking	Depends on the tool and standard. Additional information may be provide leveraging a BadI.	Inherent

Table 8.3 Independent vs. Integrated Authoring

If you choose to leverage Independent Authoring, once you've created the content, you will import it, convert it, and publish it using Wizards in the AE or use the Rapid Publishing functions available with enhancement pack 4, which is discussed in more detail later in this chapter.

If you chose to use Integrated Authoring, you will instead create the content outline within the AE and fill it in with detail and media content, using the AE the entire time. To do this, you must understand the content structure SAP supports. It closely aligns with the SCORM structure, so, if you are familiar with this structure, you may recognize some of the following elements.

The highest level structure element supported in the AE is the *Learning Net*. A simple way to think of a Learning Net is as the "book" you are writing for the Course (Figure 8.3). Within a book, you normally have "chapters" and these are represented within the AE structure by *Learning Objects*. If you are familiar with the SCORM standard, a Learning Object maps directly to a Shareable Content Object (SCO). A Learning Net that is derived from imported, third-party content generally has only one Learning Object because most content creation tools package all their content into one SCO. A Learning Net that you create within the AE will probably consist of multiple Learning Objects, because these enhance navigability for your learners and provide more tracking information from an analytics perspective.

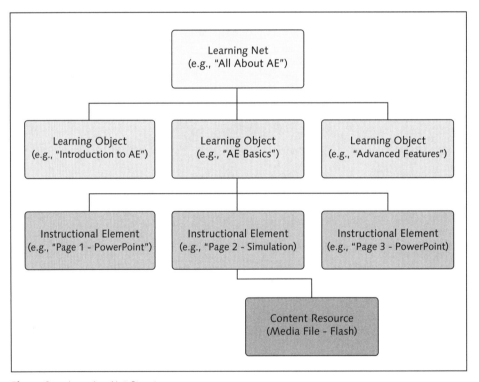

Figure 8.3 Learning Net Structure

Every Learning Object consists of at least one *Instructional Element*. Following the "book" example, think of the Instructional Element as a page. Because neither SCORM nor AICC support the breakdown of content to this level, an imported Course created by a third-party tool will have one Learning Object with one Instructional Element. The content will be associated to the Instructional Element. However, content that is created via Integrated Authoring may have multiple Instructional Elements, each of which becomes a page that the learner progresses through. Because of this flexibility, your instructional development group can create a reusable Instructional Element with the Introduction page your company uses in every Course. Each author can leverage this same page again and again, as they create content. If this page is revised, a simple workflow may be used to update the introduction across all content throughout your organization.

Learning Strategies and Adaptive Learning

Different people learn differently. So far, we have discussed linear content and not talked about how content can be structured to support this requirement. Since the release of Learning Solution 1.0, the AE provides this capability using *Learning Strategies*. Learning strategies support adaptive learning by allowing a learner to leverage a preferred learning path (the sequence in which the learning objects are presented to the learner), based on how the learner prefers to have content presented in the browser, as he progresses through a Course. If you are familiar with SCORM 2004, you know that one of the main differences of this standard is that it supports sequencing, navigation, and the ability to create branching content. Learning Strategies provide a similar functionality to authors who do not use the SCORM 2004 standard when they create their content (Figure 8.4).

As authors create content within the Authoring Environment, they may choose to link the objects and elements of the content with "Relationships" and flag the elements of the content with "Knowledge Categories." Relationships are created between learning objects and then are leveraged by Macro-strategies to determine the sequence in which learning objects are displayed. Examples of Relationships include "before" and "consists of." Relationships work in conjunction with Knowledge Categories to derive a Learning Strategy for content. Knowledge Categories can be used to identify the type of content an Instructional Element contains during the content creation process, such as "Summary" or "Procedure."

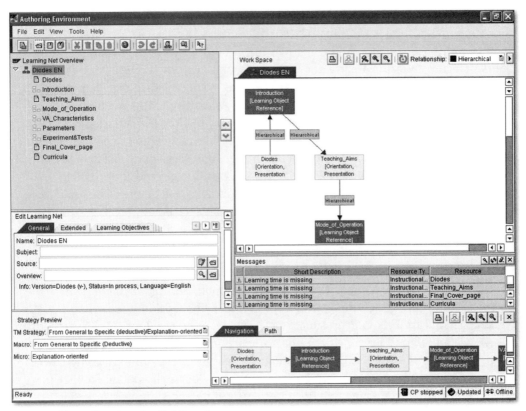

Figure 8.4 Learning Net Overview

At runtime, content is analyzed by the Content Player, which uses an algorithm that selects the most suitable learning objects and instructional elements for an individual learner's learning strategy according to the relationships and knowledge types. It reads the Macro-strategy to determine how the objects should be presented to the learner and then reads the Micro-strategy to determine which instructional elements should be presented to the learner. Not all Micro-strategies are valid for all Macro-strategies, so only those that are valid are able to be selected. You may choose to let the learner select the appropriate Learning Strategy or you may assign a Learning Strategy to content. See Table 8.4 for the Macro-strategies and Micro-strategies.

> **Note**
>
> You may not add new Micro- or Macro-strategies to the system. Each element is pre-defined by SAP.

Macro-Strategies	Definition
Table of Contents	This strategy only uses the table of contents of the Learning Net, ignoring relationships. This means that the learning objects are displayed in the sequence in which they are arranged in the Learning Net.
General to Specific — Deductive	In this strategy, the learner works through the hierarchy between Learning Objects from the top down. You work through the hierarchy from the top down. For example, "Consists of" and "Generalizes."
Specific to General — Inductive	In this strategy, the learner works through the hierarchy between Learning Objects from the top down. There is only a brief orientation given for each learning object. Then the learner works his way up through the hierarchy again with the desired level of detail.
SCORM Learning Strategies	Use with third-party SCORM Courses to ensure materials are presented correctly.
AICC	Use with third-party AICC Courses to ensure materials are presented correctly.
Linear	These strategies generate a linear display sequence so no alternatives are offered in the path. The learner must follow the path specified.
Orientation only	Only the orientation knowledge of the Learning Objects is displayed. No other Knowledge Types are displayed.
Initial orientation	Orientation knowledge is displayed to start with and then the other Knowledge Types.
Explanation-oriented	Explanatory knowledge is displayed to start with and then the other Knowledge Types.
Task-oriented	Practical instruction is displayed to start with and then the other knowledge types.
Example-oriented	Example knowledge is displayed to start with and then the other Knowledge Types.
Table of contents	The table of contents format is used and knowledge types and relationships are ignored.
SCORM	Used with the corresponding SCORM macro strategies. Use with third-party SCORM Courses to ensure materials are presented correctly.
AICC	Used with the corresponding AICC macro strategy. Use with third-party AICC Courses to ensure materials are presented correctly.

Table 8.4 Creating Tests in the Authoring Environment

Supported Macro-Strategies

In addition to the creation of content for use in online Courses, the AE also has a TEST EDITOR function that supports the creation of tests. These tests may be standalone or delivered as part of an online Course, as a pre-test, a post-test, or a self-test. Each of these test types is defined in more detail in Table 8.5.

Test Type	Test Characteristics
Pre-Test	Test appears at the beginning of the Course content. Pass/Fail results as well as test item results are recorded in the backend TAC tables. Can impact progress through a Course.
Post-Test	Test appears at the end of the Course content. Pass/Fail results as well as test item results are recorded in the backend TAC tables.
Self-check	Test appears within the Course content, usually at the end of sections. Pass/Fail is recorded but test item results are not stored in the TAC tables.
Standalone Test	Delivered as an "Online Test" delivery method. Pass/Fail results as well as test item results are recorded in the backend TAC tables.

Table 8.5 Test Types and Characteristics

Tests are structured, just as content is structured. Each test must consist of the highest level element, a *Test* that acts as a folder to contain the test structure, questions, and characteristics of the test. A test must also have items or questions. Two other elements, "Sections" and "Item Groups" are not mandatory but provide structure options. If they are used, Sections are superior to Item Groups in the test structure and Item Groups are superior to Items in the structure (see Figure 8.5).

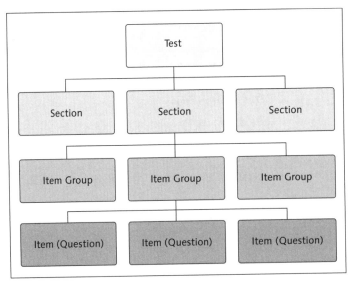

Figure 8.5 Test Structure

> **Note**
>
> You may create reusable Test Items. This function supports the creation of a test bank of reusable questions.

Table 8.6 describes some of the more popular functions the Test Editor supports.

Test Features	
Reusability	A pool of reusable questions may be created and used across multiple tests.
Randomization	Questions and Answers may be randomized. Randomization of questions may occur within the Item Group, the Section, or the Test, depending on your test structure.
Question Pool	The test will select questions from a question pool at the Item Group level. You may create 20 questions to test knowledge and configure the test, so it randomly selects 10 of these questions for the test taker.
Test Results	You may choose whether the learner should see his results at the Test Level, the Section level, and/or the Item Group level.
Pass	You determine the percentage required for pass/fail results. You may require that the learner pass a certain Section or Item Group to pass the test.
Timing	You may set a timer at the test level. After the timer runs out, the learner will be locked out of the test.
Layout	You choose how the test will appear — each question may be presented on its own page, item groups may be on their own page, sections may be own their own page, or the entire test may appear on a page.
Question Features	
Weighting	You may weigh questions, so they are evaluated differently when results are calculated.
Question Types	The following question types are supported: Multiple Choice, Multiple Response, Multiple Response-Explicit, Fill-in-the-Blank, Rating.
Beta Questions	You may flag a question as a Beta question and chose to not have answers calculated in the test results.
Feedback	You may provide general feedback (e.g., Pass/Fail) at the question level or choose to provide the answers to the learner. You may also direct the learner to further information, via a URL, for example.

Table 8.6 Test and Question Features

Learning Objectives

Although not often used, Learning Objectives serve an important purpose for an organization. They provide the ability to test out of areas of content based on pre-test results and they allow learners to skip content that they have already absorbed from previous classes. Although Learning Objectives are generally thought of as statements that describe what a learner is expected to achieve as a result of completing the learning content, from a Learning Solution perspective, Learning Objectives act as "knowledge tags." You may tag Learning Nets, Learning Objects, and/or Item Groups with Learning Objectives. Learning Objectives may be marked as *attainable* (they are associated with the learner's profile once they have progressed through the content tagged with them) or as *not attainable*, in which case a learner can skip content sections tagged with these objectives if he already have them in his learner account.

A common example of the use of Learning Objectives is through a Pretest. The pretest is structured into collections of similar questions collected into Item Groups to reflect the content covered in a Learning Object. The Item Group is tagged with the same Learning Objective as the Learning Object. At the Item Group level, a Learning Objective is always attainable if the Item Group is passed. At the Learning Object level, the Learning Objective is not marked as attainable. Thus, when the learner takes the pretest, he achieves Learning Objectives for the Item Groups passed. When he reaches the Learning Object with the same Learning Objective, the Content Player considers the Learning Object complete and the learner skips it. When the learner reaches a Learning Object that has a Learning Objective not achieved during the pretest, the learner will progress through the content as usual, but the Learning Objective will not be attained. It may be attained in a post-test, if the post-test has Item Groups tagged with the same Learning Objective.

Publishing Content

Once you've created your content, you must publish it to your CMS and create content type pointers in the backend ERP system, so a training administrator can access the pointer when a Course Type is created that leverages the content in question. You may publish in one of two ways: through the Repository Explorer or via Rapid Content Publishing (RCP), depending on the type and location of the content. We will discuss the Repository Explorer first and then cover RCP functions later in this section.

The content publishing process is fairly straightforward. Content is created by the author locally and stored in a designated folder known as the Local Repository. This is set up during the initial installation of the AE. Once content is complete, the author or another person who is a designated publisher, publishes the content. Publishing the content causes the content files to be placed in the Central Repository of the CMS, where they may be viewed and used by any other author with access rights to the folder in which they are stored. Publishing also creates a pointer in the backend system, called a Content Type. This Content Type is stored in a variety of LSO tables and also creates an entry in the Publisher Database, so Training Administrators may link the content to a Course Type and push it out to learners via the Learning Portal. Publishing is a three-step process: Content is first "Checked-in" to the Central Repository. It is then "Released," which allows other authors to reuse it if necessary. If the content is a simple media-object or a reusable chapter, it may only be released. However, if the content is a complete Course, it is "Published" and available to be linked to a Course Type. Figure 8.6 illustrates how the Repository Explorer works with the rest of the SAP AE architecture.

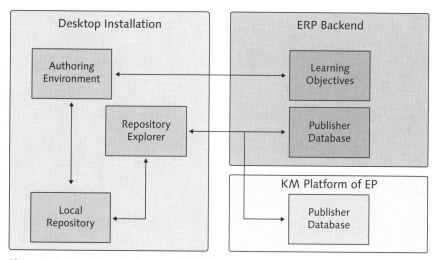

Figure 8.6 Repository Explorer and SAP Enterprise Learning Architecture

In addition to supporting the publishing process, the Repository Explorer also supports "content versioning" (Figure 8.7). When content is published to the Central Repository for the first time, it is automatically versioned as Version 1 by the system. If corrections, revisions, or other updates need to be made, the content is copied out of the Central Repository to the Local Repository, where changes are made. Once editing begins on the copy, it is versioned as a new version (Version 2, in this example). Once editing is completed, the new version is checked in to the Central Repository and possibly released and published as the new version. It is important to note that any other content that was referencing the original content is still referencing Version 1. You must manually implement a process that updates all referencing content. SAP designed the process this way on purpose. With the first release of the Learning Solution (LSO100), content was "checked out," changes were made, and the new, checked-in content automatically updated all referenced materials. However, this lead to issues with authors not knowing that sections of their content was updated. Because of this, SAP moved to the "copy" process with the release of Learning Solution 2.0.

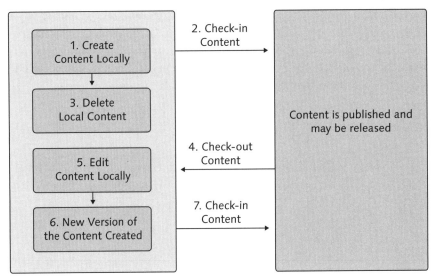

Figure 8.7 Check-in and Versioning Process

Online Publishing Tool

As of enhancement package 4, the SAP Learning Solution provides an online publishing tool that supports Rapid Content Publishing (RCP).RCP is a Web-based tool accessed via the Training Administrator Portal. Using RCP, the content publishing process is reduced to a few clicks. To leverage RCP, the content publisher accesses the interface and selects the content type and language (see Figure 8.8). The publisher then selects the current location of the content file and the target location and selects "Publish" (see Figure 8.9).

This simplifies the publishing process for those who create their content independently of the AE or who purchase their content from a third-party provider. These users have no need for the full suite AE and require a rapid process to publish.

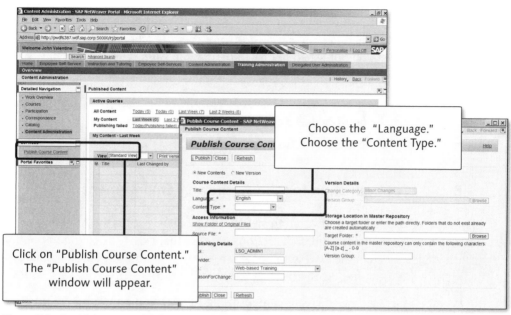

Figure 8.8 Rapid Content Publishing Process Step 1

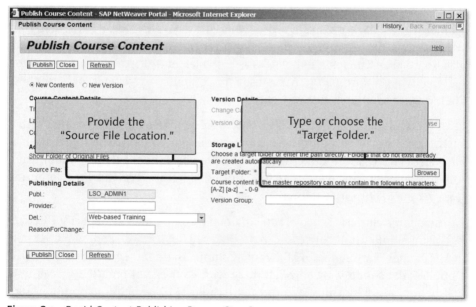

Figure 8.9 Rapid Content Publishing Process Step 2

Advantages of RCP include:

▶ Files are published in rapid succession, one after the other. There is no need for the first file to be published before initiating publishing for the next file.

▶ SCORM and AICC content packages are supported.

▶ Any single document (e.g., Microsoft Word, Adobe Flash, Microsoft Power-Point) may be published as a Learning Net.

▶ No need for the AE to publish Course content.

8.4   Configuration for the Authoring Environment

There are only a few configuration switches to be managed for the AE; however, it is important to understand the functions of those that exist. The configuration for the AE is located in the IMG with the other LSO configuration: TRAINING MANAGE-MENT • SAP LEARNING SOLUTION • AUTHORING ENVIRONMENT.

As mentioned earlier, to create content using the AE, you only need AE installed on your workstation. However, to publish the content, you need credentials to allow the Repository Explorer to connect to the backend and access to the CMS to publish the content. The first entry, "Perform Separate Logon to Training Management and CMS," contains a switch that allows you to indicate whether your architecture setup requires a separate login for the CMS and the backend system or whether the same login will work for both elements. Separate logins are often required when a third-party CMS is used for content management, because these often require additional authentication.

In the second IMG entry, "Specify CMS Address," enter the URL location of the basis folder that is set up in the CMS to store your content. The folder itself is manually created in the CMS, usually by a member of your Portal Admin team. Any additional breakdowns of the folder (subfolders) are created by the authoring team via the Repository Explorer.

The next three entries: "Specify Name of Course Content Index," "Specify URL Prefix for Communication between CM and Master Repository," and "8-bit Support in File Names" are used for TREX configuration, as are the entries under "Search Options." You would work through these with your expert on TREX, because he will be responsible for this setup. Note that the TREX search function only supports searches through the CMS for content. It has nothing to do with searching for Courses via the Learning Portal.

The entry "Enter Address of Central Storage Location for Templates" allows you to indicate where you are storing your common templates, so authors can access them when creating content in the AE. This supports requirements for a global look and feel across all content, as does the final entry in this section "Activate Confirmation when Publishing Course Content." Here, you indicate which fields are required fields when publishing content. This ensures that all required data is maintained as content is added to the CMS. For more detail on the setup and configuration of the AE, please review the Installation Guide for the release of the Learning Solution you are implementing. This includes detailed information on each of the settings as well as a guide to the TREX setup. Installation Guides are found on the SAP Service Marketplace: *http://service.sap.com/instguides.*

8.5 Third-Party Content and the Authoring Environment

We have discussed content as it pertains to in-house content. If content is created within the AE directly, it automatically adheres to SCORM 2004 requirements. If you use a third-party tool to create your content in a SCORM-compliant or AICC-compliant format and then import it into CMS using either the AE or the RCP process, it will be converted to the SCORM 2004 standard. This section of the content chapter will discuss third-party content as delivered to your organization by a content provider. We will discuss SCORM-compliant content first and then AICC-compliant content.

8.6 SCORM Course Delivery

The specifications for the SCORM standard are defined by the Advanced Distributed Learning (ADL) group; although in 2008, the International Federation for Learning-Education-Training-Systems-Interoperability (LETSI) took over the standard. This international organization is currently working on the SCORM 2.0 standard and expects to see conformant products by the end of 2009. ADL still supports the earlier standards.

SCORM content may be imported directly into the AE or it may be hosted remotely, using the Exchange Infrastructure (XI) technology. In this section, we will discuss importing the content directly. Hosting options were discussed in the section "Delivering Third-Party Hosted Content."

8.6.1 SCORM Versions

The SCORM specification has evolved over a period of time and for this reason, there are multiple versions.

SCORM 1.1

This was the first production version of the specification. This version was largely based on the AICC specifications for defining Course specifications in a XML format; although it also drew from other standards groups, including the Institute of Electrical and Electronic Engineers (IEEE) and the Instructional Management Systems Project (IMS).

SCORM 1.2

This is the most commonly and widely adopted SCORM specification.

SCORM 2004

SCORM 2004 is the current version that has many enhancements over the previous versions. This version also supports adaptive sequencing, which was missing from the previous versions.

The SAP Learning Solution supports SCORM 1.2 as well as SCORM 2004 (EhP2 onward). Content creators can create SCORM content and readily import these into the AE to publish the Courses or directly publish the Courses using the online publishing tool.

SCORM support

Table 8.7 lists the SCORM data elements supported by SAP Enterprise Learning:

Element	Mandatory	Supported	Comments
cmi.version	Yes	Yes	
cmi.core.student_name	Yes	Yes	
cmi.core.student.id	Yes	Yes	
cmi.core.lesson_location	Yes	Yes	
cmi.core.credit	Yes	Yes	
cmi.core.lesson_status	Yes	Yes	

Table 8.7 SCORM Data Elements

Element	Mandatory	Supported	Comments
cmi.core.entry	Yes	Yes	
cmi.core.score.raw	No	Yes	
cmi.core.score.min	No	Yes	
cmi.core.score.max	No	Yes	
cmi.core.total_time	Yes	Yes	
cmi.core.lesson_mode	No	Yes	Only field value "normal" supported
cmi.core.exit	Yes	Yes	
cmi.core.session_time	Yes	Yes	
cmi.suspend_data	Yes	Yes	
cmi.launch_data	Yes	Yes	
cmi.comments	No	Yes	
cmi.comments_from_lms	No	No	
cmi.objectives	No	No	All sub-elements are also not supported.
cmi.student_data	No	No	All sub-elements are also not supported.
cmi.student_preference	No	No	All sub-elements are also not supported.
cmi.interactions	No	No	All sub-elements are also not supported.

Table 8.7 SCORM Data Elements (Cont.)

8.6.2 SCORM Course Creation

Creation of a SCORM Course consists of three activities: creating the content, creating the meta-data files, and creating the IMS packaging specification. Content files consist of the usual media and html files. The meta-data files are elements specified by the SCORM standard that describe the content. They are contained in a single file, the IMS packaging specification or *imsmanifest.xml*, or in an external file, referenced by the imsmanifest.xml file. In addition to meta-data, this file also contains information about the content files used for the Course, their structures, and possibly their sequences. The file must be present in the root folder of the Course for all SCORM 2004–compliant Courses.

More information about the SCORM standard and specifications for the manifest file are available in the ADL website (*www.adlnet.gov*).

8.6.3 Deploying and Launching a SCORM Course

A SCORM Course, once created, may be imported to the SAP Authoring Environment and converted to Learning Net and published using the Repository Explorer. The zip file is pulled into the AE via a Wizard that manages the import and conversion process quickly and easily. The AE automatically identifies the type of Course (SCORM for the purposes of this discussion) based on the meta-data files. As mentioned earlier, a SCORM Course usually appears as a single Learning Net with a single learning object in the AE.

The steps to import and convert a Course, using the Wizard, are as follows:

1. Call the Wizard via: Tools • Wizards • Import as Reusable Media Object (see Figure 8.10).

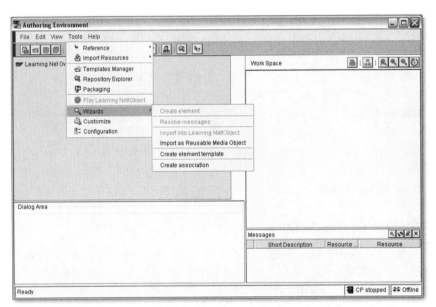

Figure 8.10 The Import Wizard Guides You Through the Import and Conversion Process

2. In the Wizard dialog box, select the types of files you are importing (e.g., zip, folder, individual files – see Figure 8.11).

3. Search for the files you wish to import and select. The Wizard lists all the files you have selected, which you may modify if necessary (see Figure 8.12).

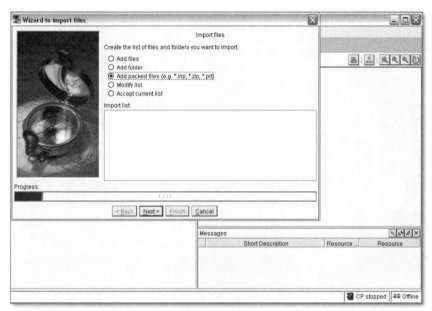

Figure 8.11 Allowable Files are Individual Files, Folders, or Compressed Files, Such As .zip Files

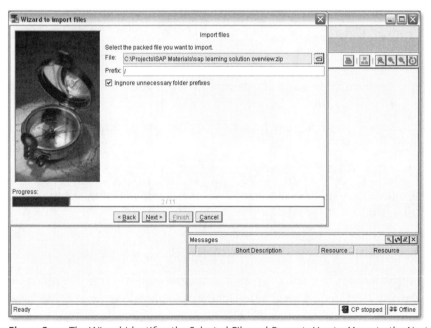

Figure 8.12 The Wizard Identifies the Selected File and Prompts You to Move to the Next Step

4. Validate the import method. If the files are SCORM-compliant or AICC compliant, the system will automatically default to the appropriate standard (e.g., SCORM or AICC.) See figure 8.13 for an example of a SCORM Course.

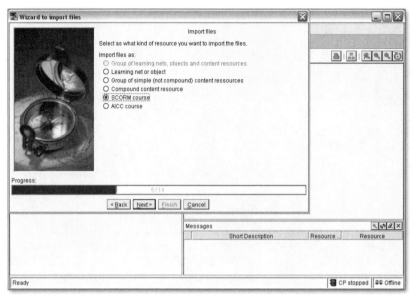

Figure 8.13 Because of the imsmanifest.xml, the System Recognizes the Course as a SCORM Course

5. Select the appropriate location and storage folder in your local repository. You may create a new folder or select an existing folder.

6. The Wizard will copy all the files as reusable media objects to the local repository.

> **Note**
>
> In the SCORM zip file, the imsmanifest.xml file, which is required of the SCORM standard, must be stored in the root folder.

8.6.4 SCORM Tests

With the support of the SCORM 2004 specifications, Enterprise Learning now supports the ability to store test results from third-party tests that are SCORM 2004 conformant. This provides additional analytical data from tests that are not created with the Test Editor. However, SAP provides more robust analysis for Test Editor tests simply because they can fully use the fields in the backend testing tables (TAC tables). SCORM tests must only pass the results as required by the SCORM standard. More information is available in the section on Question Mark Perception Assessments later in the chapter.

8.7   AICC Course Delivery

AICC is a standard maintained by the Aviation Industry CBT Committee. AICC develops guidelines and standards for training content. This standard is an older standard than the SCORM standards and historically has had wider adoption by content providers. This is changing, but you will still find providers who have been in the industry for a long time with extensive AICC content libraries.

SAP Learning Solution, as of EhP2, adheres to AICC Standards (up to Level 4). When an AICC Course is delivered via the Learning Portal, it may be deployed or hosted (in a different server). This section discusses both the options and the benefits of each option.

8.7.1   AICC Course Creation

Just as with SCORM content creation, the creation of an AICC content file consists of creating the content and creating the meta-data files. AICC content structure is similar to SCORM content structure, because the SCORM standard was based on the AICC standard. However, AICC does not use the IMS packaging specification — instead, structure information is in a specific meta-data file. For AICC Courses, the following files need to be created:

▶ .AU file — has information about the Assignable Units

▶ .CST file — has information about the structure of the Course

▶ .CRS file — has information about the Course such as Course title, Course description, etc

▶ .DES file — has information about the content modules

More information and specifications for these files are available on the AICC website (*www.aicc.org*).

8.7.2   Deploying and Launching an AICC Course

An AICC Course, once created, may be imported to SAP AE and converted to Learning Net and published using the Repository Explorer. AE automatically identifies the Course as AICC based on the meta-data files and converts it to a format that can use the LSO tables. The process is exactly the same as the process used for importing SCORM Courses.

8.7.3 Hosted AICC Content

The AICC standard uses HTTP AICC Communication Protocol (HACP). This allows content to be hosted on a different server than the server on which the LMS resides. This is one of the key advantages of AICC over SCORM (which uses a JavaScript-based API); AICC Courses may be deployed directly in your LMS or they may be hosted in some other server and launched remotely. In the hosted scenario, only the meta-data files (.AU, .CST, .CRS, and .CST) files are deployed in the LMS and the .AU file has the URLs to the content. Before deciding on hosting AICC content remotely, you must consider the following:

The vendor system must comply with AICC CMI 1 Version 4.0, AGR 10.

The SAP system and the vendor system must be able to communicate to transfer data. In some cases, firewall restrictions may need to be removed to allow communication between the systems. The most common solution is to allow communication from specific IP addresses to minimize the exposure.

Some advantages and decision points for the two approaches are listed in Table 8.8.

Deployed Content	Hosted Content
This approach is chosen when the content is created in-house within the organization.	This approach is chosen when the content is created by a third-party vendor and is hosted by the vendor.
The LMS provides the end-user content delivery interface.	The content uses interface provided by the vendor.
The LMS provides all tracking data.	Some data may be passed to the LMS, but the third-party vendor system may maintain additional data that are not passed to the LMS.

Table 8.8 Deployed vs. Hosted Content

Figure 8.14 shows how SAP Enterprise Learning launches a Course hosted in a third-party server and illustrates how data is passed back to the system.

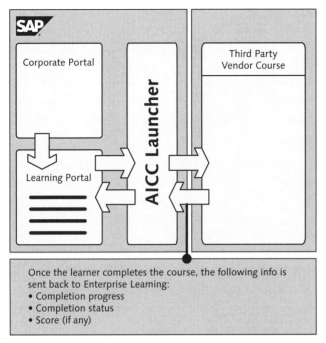

Figure 8.14 SAP Enterprise Learning and the AICC Launcher Integration

8.7.4 AICC/HACP Error Codes

Table 8.9 explains the common error conditions. Every communication will have an error code.

Error Code	Error Text	Error description	Potential Resolution
0	Successful	No error	
1	Invalid Command	The system did not recognize the command/function.	Check the method name and/or parameters passed.
2	Invalid AU Password	The AU password is incorrect.	Check the password that is passed.
3	Invalid Session ID	The AICC_SID is either incorrect or is not recognized by the LMS.	Check if the parsing of the string is correct. If the parsing is correct, check if the correct Session ID is being passed.

Table 8.9 Error Codes

8.8 Content delivery

Once content is created and published to the CMS, a Training Administrator or other professional user with access to the catalog in the backend must associate the published content with a Course Type. Once this is done, as long as the administrator has indicated that the Course is ready to be accessed, the Course is available for learners to book to and launch via the Content Player.

The Content Player provides a frame for content. It may be used to support navigation between instructional elements and Learning Objects in content created using the AE and may be used to provide navigation between SCOs in content created with a third-party tool. The Content Player also reads Learning Strategies (see next section) and ensures content is presented to the learner appropriately. Figure 8.15 is an example of content shown in the Content Player.

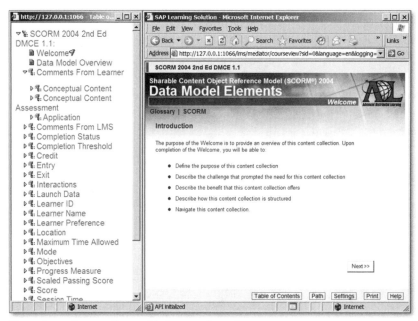

Figure 8.15 Content Player with Content Example

Courses created with a third-party tool or created by a third-party provider often have their own navigation designed within the content. If this is the case, you may modify or disable the navigation functions of the Content Player using the Application Programming Interface (API) of the content player. SAP provides detailed documentation on this in the help documentation for the Authoring Environment.

8.9   Configuring the Content Player

The Content Player requires configuration done on both the Enterprise Portal and the backend system. We'll talk through Enterprise Portal configuration first and then highlight the configuration requirements on the backend.

Configuration on the Portal

The configuration steps performed through the Enterprise Portal are part of the installation process of the Online Content Player. All the setup described in this section is usually performed by a BASIS consultant. However, it is good for everyone on the implementation team to understand the process because installation information is used in the backend configuration.

First, an RFC destination called "SAP_LSO_BACKEND" must be created using the transaction code "sm59." This RFC ensures that the Online Content Player is able to communicate with the backend system. This is important, so Learning Progress can be recorded in the backend system.

You must also create a Communication User with a copy of the delivered role SAP_HR_LSO_COURSEPLAYER. This user should not be a dialog user. It will be used to access the backend system and pass data to the LSO tables.

Finally, you must call the configuration interface via the URL *http://<J2EEservern ame>:<portnumber>/lms/mediator/config*, where *<J2EEservername>:<port number>* equals the path for your WebAs Java installation. On the configuration interface, you will choose the option New Configuration and enter the following information from Table 8.10.

Field	Description	Example
System	Name of the SAP ECC system used (backend or training management system)	EL1
Client	Client used in the backend system	100
Application Server	Address of the message server	105.265.73.71 or myserver.domain.com or myserver
System Number	System number of the backen system used	00

Table 8.10   New Configuration

Field	Description	Example
User	User who writes learning progress to the backend system	EL_USER
Password	User's password	*****
Language	Logon Language (Optional)	EN
CMS User	User who downloads learning content from the CMS. If the CMS does not require the user to log on, then this field can remain empty.	CMS_User
CMS User Password	CMS user's password If the CMS does not require the user to log on, then this field can remain empty.	****

Table 8.10 New Configuration (Cont.)

Once the configuration is complete, select Update and then Check to ensure your configuration is correct.

Configuration on the Backend

Configuration on the backend system may be completed by the BASIS team or by a functional consultant working with the BASIS team to ensure the values are correct. The configuration takes place in the same IMG location as the rest of the Learning Solution configuration: TRAINING MANAGEMENT • SAP LEARNING SOLUTION • LEARNING PORTAL • CONTENT PLAYER.

The first entry that is important in the setup of the content player is the entry. Specify the URL Address for Playing Courses. This entry should contain the value for the URL location of the Content Player. The URL must comply with the following syntax: <Transfer log>://<Server address>: <Server port>.

> **Example**
>
> If the WAS is installed on the system cp001.acme.com and configured for HTTP accesses on port 50080, the address of the Content Player is *http://cp001.testserver.com:50080*

The next entry that is required to enable the content player is the entry Specify CMS Address, used by the Content Player to access CMS to load all the files related to a Course. It is the WebDAV URL of the CMS on the Enterprise Portal. This entry should contain the same CMS address specified in the IMG to indicate where the AE should access CMS.

8.10   Offline Player

Content-rich multimedia e-learning Courses are engaging. However, such content may be hundreds of megabytes in size. Multiple users accessing the content from a central server may consume limited and expensive network bandwidth. Many organizations, such as those in the retail or finance industries, have office locations with low-network bandwidth allocated for training activities. Slow downloads will impact the user experience and may keep learners from accessing or completing a Course.

One approach to resolving this issue is to have a hardware-based content caching solution where content is automatically downloaded to multiple locations. This is good solution, but it is expensive and time consuming to implement. Discussion of this solution is beyond the parameters of this book, but SAP and Castify provide a good white paper that discusses this solution, available on Castify's website (*www.castify.com*).

If this solution is not viable, SAP also provides the Offline Player. Although the Offline Player is a not a replacement for content caching solutions, this feature provides a cost-effective solution that meets the needs of most organizations. This approach speeds up delivery of content to those connected using a low-bandwidth network and preserves valuable network bandwidth for other critical activities. It significantly reduces the need for expensive and effort-intensive implementation of hardware solutions. It can meet the need of workers in home offices who don't benefit from hardware-based solutions.

With the release of EhP4, SAP Learning Solution will also provide the functionality for Offline Course Distribution, which will allow customers to provide Courses to learners via CDs and synchronize results online once they are connected to the network. The functionality is similar to that provided by the Offline Player.

Using the Offline Player

As previously mentioned, Offline Course Distribution via the Offline Player enables the distribution of e-learning Courses to the local hard drives of learners who are connected to the network via low-bandwidth networks. This enables them to view Course content quickly and easily and resynchronize their Course progress with the backend when they complete the content or when they are back on a high-speed connection.

When a learner accesses the Learning Portal, he can easily see those Courses that are flagged as available for Offline usage. A simple click will start the download process for the learner. Once the download is complete, the learner can start the Course immediately or choose to start it later, during business travel on an airplane, for example. Once the learner completes the Course (or decides to stop taking the Course offline), he may reconnect to the network and synchronize Course progress and performance results. If the learner did not complete the Course offline, this is indicated to the backend and the learner may complete the Course online, starting exactly where he left off.

From a navigation perspective, the Offline Player has a similar look and feel to the Content Player. This is by design and allows a learner to switch between the two methods of displaying content with little to no learning curve.

Using Offline Course Distribution

Offline Course Distribution is enabled for content in the same way it is enabled for the Offline Player: When content is published, the author flags the content available for offline distribution and the Training Administrator indicates that the Course is available offline. However, the author must also create a content package of these e-learning Courses (an .OCD file) and package it. This file is then sent to remote office or home office locations, often via CD. Learners in these locations may then download the content from their local drives or from the CD, rather than from the central server. These learners may use the Offline Content Player to view the Course content. They synchronize their Learning Progress and performance results back to LMS once they are online.

> **Note**
>
> The limitation to this process is that there is an extra step for the Training Administrator. The Training Administrator must manually create and send the files to the remote office location and home office users.

8.11   Tracking and Reporting Progress in e-Learning Courses

As we've discussed, the Content Player is the component used by the end user to launch and view Courses. The learner-specific Course sequence is generated at run-time based on the specified Learning Strategies and the Content Player keeps track of the Learning Objectives achieved. The Content Player communicates and sends progress information in real time once the user launches the Course. The Learning Progress is displayed in the portal for the user.

8.11.1 Progress Tracking in the Learning Portal

After enrolling and starting a Course, the learner can view his progress information in the Learning Portal, either on the main page, in the "My Training Activities" section or in the Course detail, in the "Learning Progress" section. Figure 8.16 provides an example of the learner view for Course progress.

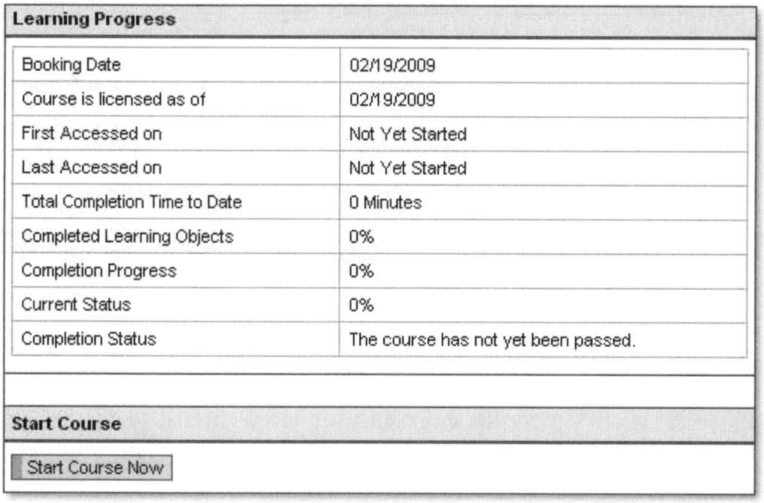

Learning Progress	
Booking Date	02/19/2009
Course is licensed as of	02/19/2009
First Accessed on	Not Yet Started
Last Accessed on	Not Yet Started
Total Completion Time to Date	0 Minutes
Completed Learning Objects	0%
Completion Progress	0%
Current Status	0%
Completion Status	The course has not yet been passed.

Start Course

Start Course Now

Figure 8.16   Learner Course Progress in the Portal

Table 8.11 lists each progress parameter and provides a definition of the parameter in question:

Parameter	Definition
Completed Learning Objects	Indicates the number of Learning Objects completed with respect to the total number of Learning Objects in the Course content. Information is displayed as a percentage. For example, if a Course has 10 Learning Objects and 1 Learning Object is completed, then the displayed value is 10%.
Completion Progress	Shows the number of Instructional Elements completed with respect to the total number of Instructional Elements in the Course, again displayed as a percent value. If the Learning Object has multiple Instructional elements, it is marked as complete only after the final instructional element is complete. For example, if a Course has 10 Learning Objects and 1 Instructional element per Learning Object, if 1 Instructional Element is completed, the displayed value is 10%.

Table 8.11   Progress Parameters

Parameter	Definition
Current Status	Displays the relative number of Learning Objects completed with respect to the number of Learning Objects to be completed in the Course. Again, this value is displayed as a percentage. For example, if a Course has 10 Learning Objects and the Completion Threshold is set at 80% and 1 Learning Object is completed, then the displayed value is 13%.
Completion Status	Displays whether the Course is passed.
Achieved Score	Online Tests: Presents the score achieved on a test in terms of total number of points.
Achieved Percentage	Provides the score achieved on a test in terms of a percentage value (points achieved divided by total number of points).
Minimum Pass Score	Shows the minimum score required to pass the test, in terms of a percentage value.

Table 8.11 Progress Parameters (Cont.)

The results shown in the above table are also passed to the backend. They populate a series of LSO tables that may be accessed by your technical team and are displayed for your functional users in delivered SAP reports, which are discussed later in this section.

8.11.2 Learning Progress BAdI

With Learning Solution 6.0, a BAdI, LSO_LEARNING_PROGRESS, is available to calculate a learner's progress through content for SCORM and AICC Courses, as well as other data that may be needed for analysis purposes. This calculation is then able to be displayed in the Learning Portal, in the view for Learner's Progress as shown in the previous section.

Because AICC- and SCORM-compliant Courses are generally delivered as one single SCO and thus imported as a single learning object, SAP Learning Solution is unable to determine progress within the SCO. Because of this, progress in the standard solution is returned either as 0% or 100%, which can be confusing for a learner checking his status on the Learning Portal. Additionally, only the SCORM data *lesson_status* is evaluated; other elements are not passed. The BAdI allows the system insight into progress within the SCO. It also supports the calculation of completion time and completion status, as well as other elements that may be relevant. SAP delivers an example implementation of the BAdI, LSO_SINGLE_SCO_EXAMPLE, which can be used to create custom implementations. The delivered implementation calculates progress within a single-SCO Course based on delivery method. If you need to calculate progress differently for different Course Types, create a delivery method for each calculation method.

SAP Note 1032103 provides detailed information on this BAdI.

8.11.3 Content Reports

SAP provides reports that are relevant to the content as well as progress of students. The delivered reports were discussed in the Administration section. Three of these reports deserve to be highlighted again in this section, because their results are focused on content results.

These reports are listed in Table 8.12.

Report Title	Transaction	Description
Participant Results Overview	LSO_TAC_ PART_RESULT	Lists test results for a participant, including analysis question level. Results include all test results (Pass/Fail) within the selection period, percentage learning objectives attained, the participation document, test scores, and item level or question level analysis.
Course Results Overview	LSO_TAC_ TRAIN_RESULT	Lists Course results, including test results (Pass/Fail), percentage learning objectives attained, the participation document, test scores, and item level or question level analysis.
Test Item Statistics	LSO_TAC_ ITEMSTAT	Displays the item statistics for a specified test. This report can be used to improve the quality of questions by analyzing the responses to the questions. Results are provided in the format of the test structure and include: number of participant results evaluated, mean value of results at all levels of the test, and total score achieved by all participants at the level of the item.

Table 8.12 Content Reports

A fourth report is new with Enhancement Package 2: the SCORM Data Report (transaction LSO_SCORM_REPORT). This report provides data based on selected SCORM elements, such as completion status or suspend data information. As long as the content passes the information to the backend and it is a supported SCORM field, you are able to report on it. If your content was originally AICC-compliant content, the conversion process will have translated the AICC data elements to SCORM data elements.

8.11.4 Publisher Database

While not a true report, the Publisher Database provides content-related data to the backend administrator. As mentioned earlier, when content is published, it updates both the CMS and the backend. Specific LSO tables are populated and the Publisher Database reads these tables and assembles the content data into a usable format. The Transaction for the publisher database is LSO_PUBLISHER.

The Publisher Database contains information on Learning Nets and reusable objects, such as test items or instructional elements that are flagged as "reusable." When accessing data from the Publisher Database, it is provided in views. Information includes:

▶ **Learning Nets (Content)** — This displays information such as title, author, publisher, estimated completion time, etc. This also displays information such as the Course that has this Learning Net and the associated Learning Objective.

▶ **Learning Objects** — This displays information such as Learning Net and Learning Objective that correspond to the Learning Object.

▶ **Tests** — This displays information such as the hierarchy for the tests as well as information about the test itself.

▶ **Learning Objectives** — This displays information at a Learning Objective level and provides the associated Learning Nets, Learning Objects, the Course, and the corresponding Qualifications.

▶ **Qualifications** — This displays information at a Qualification level and provides the associated Courses that impart the Qualification, associated Learning Net, and the Learning Objectives.

A training administrator can use the information from the Publisher Database in a variety of ways. Some common usage examples include:

▶ Which Courses impart a specific Qualification?

▶ Which tests impart a specific Learning Objective?

▶ What is the latest published version of a Learning Net?

▶ Which Learning Strategy is associated with a Course?

▶ Which Learning Objectives are used by selected Learning Nets and Objects?

8.12 Delivering Third-Party Hosted Content

In the last section, we discussed how content created in-house content created by a third-party vendor are successfully delivered to your learners via the Learner Portal from your CMS. However, not all organizations have the infrastructure or the desire to create and/or host their content in-house. Other organizations create the vast majority of their content in-house but purchase libraries of specific content, such as Management Development or IT Skills training, from providers who specialize in these areas.

If either of these scenarios describes your organization, you have a decision to make as to how you will handle the library from the third-party content provider. Obviously, if the content is SCORM or AICC compliant, you may import the content as outlined in the previous chapter and store it in your CMS. However, you may decide that you'd prefer to have your provider host the content, for a variety of reasons: your provider may not allow customers to bring their content in-house, your provider's content may make calls back to their LMS that can't be supported if it's not stored on their CMS, you may not have allocated the space for their library on your CMS, or you may not wish to invest time and effort in converting their content if you have a short-term contract. If this is the case, the SAP Learning Solution provides a solution using the Exchange Infrastructure (XI) that allows your learners to view and access the third-party content library on the Learning Portal. However, when they launch the content, they will launch it from the provider's site. As they progress through the content, completion data may be passed back to the Learning Portal, so you can report on progress, test scores, and any other elements you are interested in tracking.

> **Note**
>
> As discussed in the previous chapter, the AICC standard uses HTTP AICC Communication Protocol (HACP), which allows content to be hosted on a different server than the server on which LMS resides. This precludes the need for leveraging XI with AICC-compliant content.

Table 8.13 summarizes the options available for content and provides some considerations when determining how your organization will manage the third-party content. The first option for providing third-party content to learners is via a static URL. The static option does not require the use of the AE or a formal CMS. Instead, it requires a centrally accessible storage location for the content. This option does not use the Content Player and does not require that the content adhere to any standards. For these reasons, if you use this option, no progress or completion data is tracked; scores, time spent, Pass/Fail, and other tracking elements will not be passed to the backend LSO tables.

	Third-party content				Internal Content Created Using the AE
	Legacy Content (static URL) (e.g., CBT)	SCORM Content (Converted and Imported via the AE)		Third-party Hosted (Web Services)	
		Single SCO	Multiple SCO		
Repository	WebServer or CMS	CMS	CMS	External CMS or Webserver	CMS
Reusable Learning Objects	No	Complete Courses are reusable – not Learning Object	Yes	No	Yes
Versioning	No	Complete Courses may be versioned.	Yes	No	Yes
Tracking	No	At 0% or 100% unless BadI used.	Yes	Yes, via XI	Yes
Learning Objectives	No	At the Complete Course level	Yes	No	Yes

Table 8.13 Content Options

8.13 Using the SAP Exchange Infrastructure (XI)

SAP provides the SAP Exchange Infrastructure (SAP XI) as its strategic process integration platform, used to implement cross-system processes. SAP XI is based on open architecture, uses general standards, and provides basic Web services that enable you to integrate different systems with SAP.

From a Learning Solution perspective, you may leverage SAP XI to allow learners to seamlessly access content hosted on a third-party system via the Learning Solution Portal. The third-party system may then pass the progress results back to the SAP backend. SAP delivers Web services to support this process:

▶ Course Enrollment Request

▶ Course Access URL Query

▶ Course Enrollment Cancellation Request

▶ Learning Progress Query

Although these services are provided by SAP, it is important that you understand that there are no standard Web service definitions LMS functions. Your third-party provider may not provide any interfaces and they will have to be built on the provider side to support this interface, or they may provide some of these services but not all, or they may provide all the services, but they don't map to SAP's services. Regardless of the scenario, it is quite likely that your provider will have to create new services and the delivered SAP services will have to be modified to meet the needs of the interfaces offered by the third-party provider.

8.13.1 XI Examples

The following are some examples of implementations using XI for SkillSoft, a well-known content provider, and Questionmark™ Perception™ , one of the more popular test creation tools. These implementations are examples only and are to be used as guidelines when creating your own implementations.

Delivering e-Learning Courses Hosted by SkillSoft

SkillSoft is a leading provider of on demand e-learning Courses. SAP and Skill-Soft announced the successful integration between the learning platforms of the respective companies in 2008. This integration enables customers who use both SAP Enterprise Learning and SkillSoft hosted Courses to provide a seamless user experience to their learners. Once implemented, learners are able to do the following from the Learning Portal:

▶ View SkillSoft hosted Courses from the Course catalog of SAP Enterprise Learning

▶ Book SkillSoft hosted Courses from the Learning Portal of SAP Enterprise Learning

▶ Cancel booked Courses from the Learning Portal of SAP Enterprise Learning

▶ Launch SkillSoft hosted Courses from the Learning Portal of SAP Enterprise Learning

▶ See the following tracking information in the Learning Portal of SAP Enterprise Learning

▶ Course progress

▶ Course completion status information

▶ Date accessed

▶ Time spent in the Course

Integration Overview

Before beginning the integration, the customer must have the SAP Learning Solution 6.00 or higher with the appropriate SAP notes and support packages implemented as well as SAP Exchange Infrastructure, which is licensed separately and not provided as part of SAP Enterprise Learning. They must also have purchased access to the SkillSoft Courses directly from SkillSoft.

The integration itself leverages standard XI-based Web services, which are delivered with the solution for SAP Learning Solution and SAP Enterprise Learning customers. Web services are available for: booking a Course, canceling a Course, launching/starting a Course, and the transfer of learning progress back to LMS (includes progress as well as completion information).

Figure 8.17 illustrates the passage of data between SAP and SkillSoft using the XI interface.

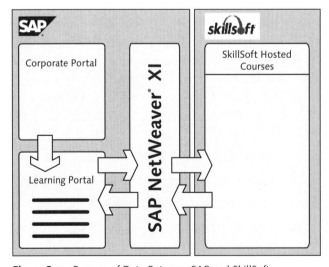

Figure 8.17 Passage of Data Between SAP and SkillSoft

IMG Configuration Guide

The configuration for this integration is done in the IMG by your configuration team. Usually, this configuration is completed by a functional resource, although this person will need to work with your XI expert to ensure some of the values entered are correct. The following process outlines the configuration requirements in the order they must be completed:

1. TRAINING MANAGEMENT • SAP LEARNING SOLUTION • COURSE PREPARATION • TRAINING PROVIDER • EXTERNAL TRAINING PROVIDER • SPECIFY EXTERNAL PROVIDER

In the table that appears upon executing this step (Table LSOLSP), enter the name of the provider (SkillSoft, in this example) and assign a table identifier (a number in the 9000-series) as shown in Figure 8.18.

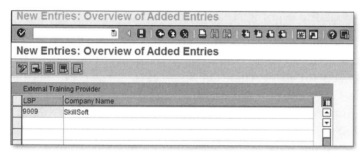

Figure 8.18 Table LSOLSP Configuration

2. TRAINING MANAGEMENT • SAP LEARNING SOLUTION • COURSE PREPARATION • TRAINING PROVIDER • EXTERNAL TRAINING PROVIDER • SPECIFY EXTERNAL SERVICE

After executing this step, you will associate the *External Provider* (SkillSoft) created in the previous step with the services you wish to support as part of the integration in table view V_LSOLSP_XI. This is illustrated in Figure 8.19.

New Entries: Overview of Added Entries

LSP	Company Name	ID	Service
9009	SkillSoft	1	Start External Course
9009	SkillSoft	4	Read Learning Data

External Training Provider: Services

Figure 8.19 External ProviderServices Configuration in table view V_LSOLSP_XI

8.13.2 Master Data Requirements

Two types of *master data* elements are required to support this integration: the Company object, representing SkillSoft, and Course Type data, representing the SkillSoft catalog. As with all Training Management master data, these elements may be configured and transported or created directly in your production system. Most organizations treat this data as true master data and create it directly in the production environment prior to going live with the integrated solution.

You must create a *Company* (object type "U") to represent *SkillSoft*. The Company will be associated with all Course Types from the SkillSoft catalog. The company information maintained includes address information as well as a link to the service provider you configured in the IMG (see Step 1 in the previous section). The Company object provides the linkage that allows the system to know which services are supported by Course Types associated with it.

Once you have identified the Courses you wish to provide to your learners from the SkillSoft catalog, you will need to create Course Types to represent these Courses in the Learning Solution Course Catalog. These Course Types comprise the catalog the learner will see as he searches for Courses. It is up to your organization to determine exactly what information should be displayed to the learner (e.g., Course descriptions, estimated time to completion, navigation tips) and to include this in the Course Type information. Most likely, you will pull the information directly from SkillSoft's catalog. There is no supported interface to pass Courses or descriptive information from SkillSoft to the SAP Learning Solution, so this is usually a one-time, manual process.

Other information that must be entered for each Course Type representing a Course from the SkillSoft catalog:

- Delivery Method: External Web Based Training
- External Catalog Connection: Enter the SkillSoft Course ID as provided by SkillSoft
- Relationships: Associate Company SkillSoft as the Provider
- Auto Progress Update: Enter the value Automatic Update, to enable auto update of progress data in the Learning Portal

Additional Implementation Information

SAP consulting has implemented this integration internally at SAP and can bring significant experience and knowledge to the table. Implementation of the integration usually requires the following skills:

▶ SAP Learning Solution functional resource: approximately 40 hours

▶ SAP XI resource: approximately 80 hours

▶ SkillSoft technical contact

The previous estimate is for the implementation of this solution only. It does not include testing of all the Courses a customer plans to implement or the effort required for the master data setup. For example, if a customer wishes to support a catalog of 500 SkillSoft Courses, a training administration team needs to be involved.

There is an appendix available on the book's web page at (*www.sappress.com*) that contains a step-by-step guide for the XI integration configuration.

Additional information may be found in the following link:

▶ SAP Exchange Infrastructure

http://help.sap.com/saphelp_nw04/helpdata/en/14/80243b4a66ae0ce10000000a11402f/frameset.htm

8.13.3 Questionmark™ Perception™ Assessments Integration

The Questionmark Perception assessment management system enables educators and trainers to author, schedule, deliver, and report on surveys, quizzes, tests, and exams for various delivery types (PDA, secure browser), various mediums (CD, web, paper) and provides very detailed analysis (for psychometricians) of test results and behavior. Many of the advanced assessments features it provides are not available in tests created via the AE using the Test Author. Because of this, customers who have advanced assessment needs may consider an integration of the SAP Learning Solution with Questionmark Perception.

Table 8.14 compares some of the test features delivered by the two tools.

	SAP Enterprise Learning	Questionmark Perception
Authoring	Supports five types of questions.	Supports 22 types of questions.
Delivery	Supports browser-based delivery	Supports delivery via multiple mediums.
Security	Supports regular browsers.	Supports secure locked down browsers required for stringent certification purposes.
Standards	No QTI support.	Supports QTI standards.

Table 8.14 Test Features

	SAP Enterprise Learning	Questionmark Perception
Reporting	Standard Course reporting.	Provides detailed reporting meant for psychometricians. Normally corporations do not do such analysis unless they are a for-profit education and testing organization such as Prometric.

Table 8.14 Test Features (Cont.)

Because Questionmark Perception is such a powerful tool, SAP worked to develop integration between SAP Learning Solution and Questionmark Perception. This integration uses XI functionality and a standard developed by the IMS Global Learning Consortium, an industry and academic consortium. This standard, the IMS Question and Test Interoperability specification (QTI) supports the exchange of test questions among authoring systems, learning management or other delivery systems, and repositories. This specification was developed based on a proprietary language initially developed by Questionmark™ Perception™.

Integration Overview

Before beginning the Integration, the customer must have the following SAP and Questionmark software:

▶ SAP Learning Solution 3.00 or higher with the following SAP Notes implemented: 1093463, 1087959, 1065834 or the respective Support Package levels

▶ SAP Exchange Infrastructure, which is licensed separately and not provided as part of SAP Enterprise Learning

▶ Questionmark Perception version 4.3 or higher and a Questionmark SAP Connector license (See *www.questionmark.co.uk* or *www.questionmark.co.uk/perception/help/v4/knowledge_base/sap/sapls401.aspx*)

Using this integration allows learners to launch assessments hosted in a Questionmark server from the Learning Portal using standard Web services, which are delivered with the solution for SAP Learning Solution and SAP Enterprise Learning customers. Web services are available for: booking an assessment, canceling an assessment, launching an assessment, and transferring learning progress back to the Learning Solution. This supports the passage of Course access dates, completion progress, completion status, and time spent in assessment to the SAP Learning Solution.

Figure 8.20 illustrates the passage of data between SAP and Questionmark leveraging the XI interface.

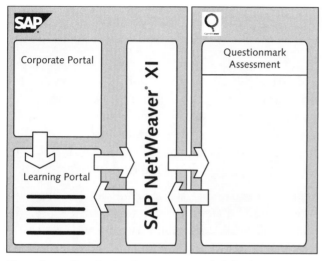

Figure 8.20 Data Passing Between SAP and SkillSoft

IMG Configuration Guide

The configuration for this integration is done in the IMG by your configuration team. Usually, this configuration is completed by a functional resource, although this person will need to work with your XI expert to ensure some of the values entered are correct. The following process outlines the configuration requirements in the order they must be completed:

3. TRAINING MANAGEMENT • SAP LEARNING SOLUTION • COURSE PREPARATION • TRAINING PROVIDER • EXTERNAL TRAINING PROVIDER • SPECIFY EXTERNAL PROVIDER

In the table (LSOLSP) that appears upon executing this step, enter the name of the provider (Questionmark Perception, in this example) and assign a table identifier (a number in the 9000-series).

4. TRAINING MANAGEMENT • SAP LEARNING SOLUTION • COURSE PREPARATION • TRAINING PROVIDER • EXTERNAL TRAINING PROVIDER • SPECIFY EXTERNAL SERVICE

After executing this step, you will associate the External Provider (Questionmark Perception) created in the previous step with the services you wish to support as part of the integration in table view V_ LSOLSP_XI.

There is a detailed Questionmark Perception integration guide with animated tutorials to demonstrate the configuration. Contact the support team or product team at SAP to get the guide and animated tutorials.

Master Data Requirements

Two types of master data elements are required to support this integration: the Company object, representing Questionmark, and Course Type data, representing the Questionmark tests. As with all Training Management master data, these elements may be configured and transported or created directly in your production system. Most organizations treat this data as true master data and create it directly in the production environment prior to going live with the integrated solution.

First, you must create a Company (object type "U") to represent Questionmark. The Company will be associated with all Questionmark test Course Types. The company information maintained includes address information as well as a link to the service provider you configured in the IMG (see Step 1 in the previous section). The Company object provides the linkage that allows the system to know which services are supported by Course Types associated with it.

After you create an assessment using the Questionmark Perception tool, your Training Administrator must also create a Course Type in the Course Catalog to associate with the Questionmark assessment. There are a few data elements, specific to the Questionmark assessment, which the training administrator needs to take care of:

▶ Delivery Method: Either External Web-Based Training or External Online Test

▶ External Catalog Connection: Enter the assessment ID from the Questionmark system

▶ Relationships: Associate Company SkillSoft as the Provider

▶ Auto Progress Update: Enter the value Automatic Update to enable auto update of progress data in the Learning Portal.

Configuring SAP Exchange Infrastructure

This configuration is done by an SAP Exchange Infrastructure (XI) support resource in collaboration with a functional configuration expert for the Learning Solution.

Make sure you have a WSDL file from Questionmark and know the XI mapping files before you begin the tasks outlined below:

- System Landscape directory
  - Set up the general system landscape to Questionmark
- Integration Builder
  - Upload the WSDL file you received from Questionmark and configure the integration
  - Perform interface mappings and message mappings
- Integration Builder Configuration
  - Link the ID of the external provider in the backend
  - Configure the sender agreement
  - Configure the receiver agreement

The Appendix contains a step-by-step guide for the XI integration configuration.

Additional Information may be found in the following links:

- SAP Exchange Infrastructure

http://help.sap.com/saphelp_nw04/helpdata/en/14/80243b4a66ae0ce10000000a11402f/frameset.htm

- Questionmark SAP Connector

www.questionmark.com/uk/connectors/sap.aspx

8.14 Summary

As we mentioned in the beginning of this chapter, content integration is usually the most difficult part of an LMS implementation, regardless of the LMS selected. SAP Enterprise Learning provides tools to ensure that your internally hosted content, whether created in-house or purchased from a third-party content provider, works seamlessly with SAP Enterprise Learning. This is one of the major benefits gained by using the Authoring Environment to structure content and to convert and import content – it validates that content is standards compliant. If you choose to have an external provider host your content, SAP Enterprise Learning is delivered with standard web services that will support passing critical data between SAP

Enterprise Learning and the host organization. In the next chapter we will look at common enhancement methods for SAP Enterprise Learning.

8.15 Contributors

Vad Vayntrub and Shirish Yadwadkar contributed to the XI integration section of this chapter. Jason Siesko contributed to the SkillSoft integration section, and Frank Hanfland contributed to the AI CC integration section.

Every organization is different, with a unique set of requirements for the tools that drive personnel development. The SAP Enterprise Learning Solution provides customers with mechanisms to enhance the standard functionality to meet those customer requirements.

9 Enhancing the SAP Enterprise Learning Solution

In this chapter, we will discuss some of the common methods available to enhance the SAP standard functionality. Then we will cover a difficult concept that impacts many users of the Learning Solution: *Structural Authorizations*. And we will wrap up the chapter with a case study of a commonly implemented enhancement that ties many of these concepts together.

9.1 Enhancements and BAdIs

In Chapter 6, we discussed standard configuration options for the SAP Enterprise Learning Solution. This chapter will expand on these functions by identifying areas that can be enhanced by using function modules and BAdIs or by using standard configuration in unusual ways. As in Chapter 6, this section is ordered in the same manner as the IMG. At the end of the sections, we will discuss additional functions that are not in the Learning Solution section of the IMG.

9.1.1 Training Management

Let's begin the coverage by looking at the enhancements available in the Training Management section of the IMG. These include settings to extend menu views, reporting and collaboration functions, as well as user exits you can use to increase fee handling and correspondence functions.

Dynamic Reporting Menu Enhancements

Within the Basic Settings section of the IMG, the function module RH_MORINFO allows you to enhance the Dynamic Reporting Menu view. This function module is located under Basic Settings • Dialog Control • Technical Settings • Dynamic Menus. It allows you to add additional information to the Dynamic Reporting Menu view, such as the name of the Instructor or telephone number for the room where the class is held. To make this sort of enhancement, copy the delivered Function Module and add the code you need to call in the additional information. In order for the custom function module to work in place of RH_MORINFO, the function must have the exact same interface (importing, exporting, etc. parameters) as RH_MORINFO. If you include complicated logic, this could impact the system response time.

Reporting

A second useful enhancement within Basic Settings is the configuration entry "Integrate Customer Specific Reports." This allows you to remove nonused reports from the Dynamic Reporting Menu and add custom reports to the menu. By using this customization option, your administrators will be able to easily navigate to reports they use most often via the Dynamic Reporting Menu, instead of executing custom reports from the Easy Access Menu of the backend. You may also edit some of the pop-ups that appear in the Current Settings section of the IMG using this function. For example, when you select entry Training Provider • Create (LSO_PSVQ), the option "Create Organizational Unit" appears along with the option "Create Company." A Training Administrator is rarely allowed to create an Organizational Unit (and most will not have the authorizations to do so). Removing the entry creates a more usable interface for the administrator. To add or remove entries from these menus:

▶ Navigate to and execute the menu you wish to modify.

▶ Right click on the menu in question.

▶ Select the option Keys ↔ Texts.

▶ Note the technical name of the menu.

▶ If you plan to remove any entries, note the technical name of the entry you wish to remove.

▶ Navigate to and execute the IMG Entry SAP Learning Solution • Basic Settings • Information Systems • Integrate Customer Specific Reports.

▶ Select the menu Settings • Keys ↔ Texts.

▶ Find the menu you identified earlier by its technical name.

▶ To delete an entry, simply highlight the entry and delete it. Note: This is an SAP delivered entry that you are removing.

▶ To add an entry, highlight the menu and select the menu Entry • Create • Level Down.

► In the Select New Entry option, choose New Function.

► Enter the following:

  ► New function you have created for this entry (Personnel Management • Global Settings in Personnel Management • Dialog Control • Set Up Control Parameters for User Interface)

  ► Type of Function being called (usually, this is a report)

  ► Server Name (usually, the technical name of the report is called)

  ► Service

  ► Service SUB_INFO1_LSO will allow you to select on Participants.

  ► Service SUB_INFO2_LSO will allow you to select on Course Group or Course Type.

  ► Service SUB_INFO3_LSO will allow you to select on Course Group or Course Type or Course.

► Save your entry.

► Save the menu.

Collaboration Functions

Within the Integration section of the IMG, three BAdIs exist to enhance Collaboration functionality. These are Assignment User ID to Learner (LSO_LEARNER), Assignment of Learner to User ID (LSO_LEARNER_SET), and Participation in Rooms (LSO_COLLABORATION). In the standard system, the User ID stored on Infotype 0105, Subtype 0001, is used to determine the person (PERNR) participating in the collaboration room. If the system can't find a person, it will use the User ID as the participant instead. BAdI LSO_LEARNER, method GET_LEARNER, may be used to enhance that process or to get other types of learners, such as External Persons. BAdI LSO_LEARNER_SET, method SET_LEARNER, must be used if you leverage LSO_LEARNER for collaboration functions.

This BAdI derives the appropriate User ID for use in Collaboration based on the learner. The BAdI Participation in Rooms allows you to build additional filters to determine who can access collaboration rooms. In the standard system, you can indicate that only learners who are enrolled in a Course, enrolled in a Course that is associated with a particular Course Type, or enrolled in a Course associated with a particular Course Group may enter a collaboration room. The standard functions also allow you to create open collaboration rooms or rooms that may be attended by invitation only. Using this BAdI allows you to filter based on other elements, such as Organizational Assignment or Language.

9.1.2 Resource Management

As you move down the IMG to the Course Preparation section, you will find an entry that allows you to enhance the Resource Management functionality. Under TRAINING MANAGEMENT • COURSE PREPARATION • RESOURCE MANAGEMENT • CONTROL ELEMENTS, you find the value *RH_ALLOCAT* entered in table T77S0, entry SEMIN RESOC. RH_ALLOCAT is another function module that provides you with the opportunity to change the way the resource reservations functionality works. As with replacing RH_MORINFO, any custom function module used here must have the exact same interface definition as RH_ALLOCAT.

An example of how this has been used by an organization is as follows:

A company that provides software training to multiple customers across the world uses one server for many classes. However, the server can only support a finite set number of classes. Therefore, this company has created a setting that allows a resource "Server ABC" to be reserved by a certain number of classes during a time frame. After that number is reached, the system allows no other classes to reserve the server during that time frame.

9.1.3 Fee Handling

In the Day-to-Day Activities section, under BOOKING • FEE HANDLING, table T77S0 contains the entry *SEMIN CCDCT*. This entry points to a function module, *LSO_PRICES*, which drives the method by which the SAP Learning Solution manages training participation charges. In the standard system, if the switch SEMIN CCOST (contained in the same table view of T77S0 as entry SEMIN CCDCT) is set to the value "1," the Learning Solution uses the function module LSO_PRICES to check the attendee type, the prices stored for the Course in question, and, if relevant, the cancellation configuration to determine the attendance or cancellation fee that should be charged for external and internal attendees. If you need to modify the calculation of the fees, you can copy function module LSO_PRICES and enhance it to meet your functional requirements. As with replacing RH_MORINFO, any custom function module created to replace LSO_PRICES must have the same interface as LSO_PRICES.

> **Example of Enhance LSO_Prices**
>
> An organization's corporate university charges cancellation fees for internal attendees who take training offered internally. In the standard system, based on function LSO_PRICES, the fees are derived from the field "Internal Price" in the Infotype "Prices"

(P1021-IKOST) and charged against the attendee's cost center at the percentage defined in table T77S0, entry SEMIN CCDEL, or at the percentage associated with the appropriate cancellation reason in table T77CART (which overrides the entry in T77S0). The business rules in place by the corporate university require that all cancellations within 10 days of the start day of the class should be charged at 100% and those that occur more than 10 days out should be charged at 50% of the internal price. To enable this calculation to take place automatically when cancellations take place in the Portal or in the backend system, the organization chooses to copy function module LSO_PRICES to ZLSO_PRICE, add their calculation logic to the copy, and then replace LSO_PRICES in table T77S0 with ZLSO_PRICE.

9.1.4 Cancellation Reasons

In the same section, under "Participation Cancellation," the "Define Customer-Specific Cancellation Reasons" BAdI is delivered. This BAdI, BAdI LSO_CANCELREASONS_C, is only called for cancellations in the Learning Portal. The most common example of the use of this BAdI is allowing participants to select from a list of cancellation reasons when they self-cancel from the Portal. In the standard system, a default reason defined in Table LSO_T77S0, entry SEMIN WEBST, the learner is provided with no option to choose a reason.

Example of Enhancing Cancellation Reasons

An organization wanted to define cancellation charges based on proximity to the start of a Course. If a learner cancelled within 10 business days of the start of the Course, he was charged; otherwise, cancellation was free of charge. The BAdI for cancellation reasons was implemented and passed back a cancellation, which allocated 100% of the charge if the cancellation was performed within 10 days of the start of the Course. If the cancellation is outside of the charge window, the BAdI returned a cancellation reason that allocated 0% of the charge.

9.1.5 Correspondence BAdIs

Correspondence functions, also found in the Day-to-Day Activities section of the IMG, contain many opportunities for enhancement via a series of BAdIs. In this book, we will only address the enhancements for Request-Based Correspondence (RBC), because SAP script-based correspondence is not SAP's recommended method of correspondence as of LSO600. The delivered implementation (if any) and functionality of each of the RBC BAdIs is defined in Table 9.1:

BAdI	BAdI Name	Implementation	Description
Specify Correspondence Control Options	LSO_CORRESPONDENCE41	GET_OUTPUT_OPTIONS GET_RECIPIENT_OPTIONS	This BAdI allows you to enhance the settings you made in the IMG entry *Specify Correspondence Control Options per Delivery Method (V_LSOCRPCONTROL)*. For example, you might have indicated that all correspondence for learner bookings should occur automatically for email, but you wish to deliver additional information for a certain group (e.g., operators who don't have regular access to the Portal) or deliver the correspondence differently to a group of employees (e.g., you provide a simpler layout to your sales employees and their correspondence is delivered by SMS).
Specify Access to Communication Data	LSO_CORRESPONDENCE46	GET_ADDRESS_READER	This BAdI determines how the system finds the address of the person receiving the correspondence. In the standard system, for example, email address for a person is derived from Infotype 0105, subtype 0010 but you may have created a custom subtype to store this information. This BAdI allows you to read the custom subtype rather than the standard.
Specify Communications Parameters for Recipients	LSO_CORRESPONDENCE45	GET_COMMUNICATION_DATA	Based on output type (automatic or manual) and participant type, you can indicate where the system should look for certain addresses. For example, if an email address is not stored on Infotype 0105, subtype 0010, you might leverage this BAdI to direct the system to look at the user associated with the recipient and check for an email there. Note that the output medium specified has no impact on the address determination.

Table 9.1 RBC BadIs Implementation and Functionality

BAdI	BAdI Name	Implementation	Description
Change Output Control Options	LSO_CORRESPON-DENCE43	GET_SENDCON-TROL CHANGE_PRINT-PARAMS IS_ASYNCHRO-NOUS GET_COUNTRY_FOR_LANGU	This BAdI allows you to enhance output control options based on, for example, participant or country specifications for date formats. It could also support changing the timing of automatic correspondence (e.g., notifications to a certain group may not go out immediately.) All methods are delivered empty but an example of coding using the implementation to change the document title of a correspondence, using method CHANGE_PRINTPARAMS is provided in SAP Help: *http://help.sap.com/*
Determine Sender	LSO_CORRESPON-DENCE44	GET_SENDER GET_SENDER_NAME GET_SENDER_TELN GET_SENDER_FAX GET_SENDER_PAGER GET_SENDER_RMAIL GET_SENDER_EMAIL	This BAdI allows you to specify the sender and contact data for correspondence. You may specify the name that appears as the sender of a notification that is being output as well as the contact data for the sender. This information can change, depending on who the recipient is. For example, you might have notifications going to one department appear with a different return email address than those going to a participant in another department.

Table 9.1 RBC BadIs Implementation and Functionality (Cont.)

9.1.6 Learning Portal

Most of the enhancements in the previous section affect functionality on the backend of the system. We will now discuss some of the delivered BAdIs that impact the frontend – the Learning Portal view.

Learning Portal View

The Learning Portal section of the IMG contains a few BAdIs to enhance functionality as well. One key tool is that because LSO300, table LSPAGE_ALIAS_C has been available to enter customer enhanced copies of the Business Server Pages (BSP). This table is not available in the IMG.

The entries in LSPAGE_ALIAS_C override the entries SAP delivers in table LSPAGE_ALIAS (see following). LSPAGE_ALIAS contains SAP's delivered BSPs. As you can see from the table (Figure 9.1), SAP defines a set number of Aliases, which refer to a particular BSP page within the hcm_learning application. You may view the delivered BSP code via the Object Navigator (transaction SE80) under the BSP Application "hcm_learning" and copy the delivered BSPs to create your own custom BSPs.

Definition of Page Aliases of SAP Learning Solution

Alias	OT	BSP Application	BSP Page
1 Navigation		hcm_learning	navigation.htm
2 Training Home		hcm_learning	traininghome.htm
3 Catalog		hcm_learning	catalog.htm
4 Settings		hcm_learning	settings.htm
5 Profile Matchup		hcm_learning	checkprof.htm
6 Qualifications Profile		hcm_learning	myqualifications.htm
7 Favorites		hcm_learning	favorites.htm
8 Prebookings		hcm_learning	prebookings.htm
9 Activities		hcm_learning	activities.htm
10 Find		hcm_learning	search.htm
11 Info Page		hcm_learning	information.htm
12 Prebook	D	hcm_learning	prebook.htm
100 Details	D	hcm_learning	trainingtype.htm
100 Details	DC	hcm_learning	trainingtype.htm
100 Details	E	hcm_learning	training.htm
100 Details	EC	hcm_learning	training.htm
100 Details	EK	hcm_learning	coursepgm.htm
100 Details	L	hcm_learning	traininggroup.htm
100 Details	Q	hcm_learning	qualification.htm
101 Curriculum		hcm_learning	curriculum.htm

Figure 9.1 LSPAGE_ALIAS View

Note

Only add entries to LSPAGE_ALIAS_C. Do not add entries to LSPAGE_ALIAS because it is an SAP-owned table of class S (System table, SAP maintains this table).

To use LSPAGE_ALIAS_C, copy any of the standard BSPs to "Z" BSPs and make your changes: rework the text, remove functionality, or add custom code. As your custom BSPs are managed in a customer table, there should be no concern that your changes will be lost as you upgrade or apply enhancement packs. However, you should be aware that new functionality will not be reflected on your custom pages.

For example, if you customized a copy of traininghome.htm while you were on LSO300 and then upgraded to LSO600 EhP4, you will not see the Course Program options on your custom page. It is a good idea to review each delivered BSP page as you upgrade. To do this, select the BSP page you are interested in reviewing, right-click, and select "Properties." You'll see the page address with the name of the BSP page at the end of the address. Copy this URL and replace the custom BSP page name with the delivered BSP page name to review the content. Other pages have more complicated flow logic and you may find it easier to remove the custom BSPs from table LSPAGE_ALIAS_C to view the delivered pages.

Additional enhancements that are available via the IMG include a series of BAdIs. The BAdI "Create Customer Specific Personalized Training Proposals" (LSO_LEARNER), found in the IMG directly under the entry LEARNING PORTAL • SETTINGS, is delivered with two methods, *GET_LEARNER* and *GET_ALERTS*. The method GET_LEARNER allows a customer to define a different method to attach a User ID (the attribute known initially to the Learning Portal) to a learner master record. The standard implementation looks for the User ID in Infotype 105 of a personnel master record. If one is not found, the User ID (object type US) is used as the learner master.

The method GET_ALERTS allows you to enhance the "Messages and Notes" section of the Portal. In normal circumstances, training activities are pushed to a learner in this section via the relationship "mandatory for" (A/B 615). In the standard, Courses may be set as mandatory for a learner based on his organizational unit assignment, job assignment, position assignment, or directly to his personnel number (PERNR). But, if you wish to push Courses to a learner based on his Personnel Area assignment? Or, if you wish to push a Course to all learners in a company, you may use LSO_LEARNER.

> **Tip**
>
> The more complicated the logic required to find mandatory Courses, the more processing time the system will take to pull up Messages and Notes with its mandatory assignments. Keep your logic simple and make sure you have a solid business reason for any enhancements to this page. If the logic necessary to push Courses becomes too complex, it may be better to completely replace the home page of the learning portal as just discussed.

Another BAdI located directly below LSO_LEARNER in the IMG is "Define Customer Specific Course Offering" (TRAININGTYPE_ADV_C). This BAdI is delivered active. It uses method CL_DEF_IM_TRAININGTYPE_C, which provides the Top Ten list in the Navigation section of the Learning Portal. This BAdI can be used to provide custom report information to learners as they log on to the Portal. However, it is important to remember that processing time for the report pulled can impact the Portal's response time. As delivered, the method CL_DEF_IM_TRAININGTYPE_C calls function module LSO_TOPTEN_GET_LIST_C, which runs through your entire training catalog and determines which Course Types have the most bookings over the last six months. As you can imagine, as your catalog grows and your learners increasingly use the Learning Solution functionality, this will impact system resources. If you do not have a business requirement to view the Top Ten list, it is strongly recommended that you delete the example implementation, rather than simply hiding it on the Navigation BSP.

User ID

In the Collaboration discussion in this chapter, BAdI Assignment User ID to Learner (LSO_LEARNER) was discussed as it pertains to Collaboration functions. As noted, in the standard system, the User ID stored on Infotype 0105, Subtype 0001, is used to determine the learner and if it can't determine the learner from this, the system will use the User ID as the learner (and track learning data on the object US associated with the logon ID used to access the system). This logic is used when the learner is accessing the Learning Portal as well as when the learner is accessing Collaboration functionality. Just as with Collaboration, the BAdI LSO_LEARNER, using method GET_LEARNER, may be used to enhance this process. A common requirement for an organization implementing the Learning Solution is the need to track external people attending training. These people may be customers of the organization, contractors at the organization, dealers who work with the organization, external instructors who must go through internal certification prior to delivering company materials, or any other type of person who needs to access some or all of the organization's training materials but is not on-boarded into the system as an employee or contractor (i.e., any person who does not have a PERNR and master data file in SAP HCM).

A typical scenario where this BAdI might be used is as follows: An energy delivery organization has a partnership with a university program. The organization has agreed to pay the tuition of students attaining skills relevant to energy delivery roles, with the understanding that upon completion of their university program, they will work for the organization. As part of their education, these students spend two sets of five-week periods working on-site at the organization. They receive required training that they must have to work at the site. The organization is legally (per OSHA requirements) required to track the students' training but is unable to on-board the students as employees, based on company restrictions. So, the organization creates records for the students as "External Persons" (object type H.) It provides them with User IDs to access the company network and the Learning Portal.

To ensure that the records are transferred to the External Person record rather than to the User ID (as the standard system functionality does when no IT0105 for a person is available), the BAdI LSO_LEARNER is used. After checking the User ID against IT0105, the system then checks the User ID against Infotype 1032 to see if the ID is associated with an external person instead. If it is, the training record is then associated with the external person ID as opposed to the User ID that accessed the system.

9.1.7 Content Player and Learning Objectives

When a learner starts a Course in the Content Player, the Content Player calls function module LSO_LA_GET_EBO_C via an RFC-enabled function module. LSO_LA_GET_EBO_C determines the learning objectives that the learner has achieved through tests or progressing through other content and transfers them to the Content Player. The Content Player then skips units whose content the learner already knows, as flagged by Learning Objectives. You may use BAdI LSO_EBO to change the list of achieved learning objectives. The most common usage is to filter out Learning Objectives that were achieved outside of a set time frame, for example, Learning Objectives that are over one year old are not passed. This BAdI has no default implementation provided, but Note 891401 documents an example implementation.

9.1.8 Additional Enhancements

There are a few other BAdIs and function modules available for the Learning Solution that are not found in the IMG. These are summarized in Table 9.2.

Enhancement Type	Name	Function
BAdI	LSO_LEARNING_ PROGRESS	This BAdI allows you to enhance how progress is tracked for Learners in the Portal. It is discussed in detail in Chapter 7.
BAdI	LSO_CHECK_BOOKING	This BAdI replaces RHPV0001 in TEM. It allows you to add prerequisites for booking, cancellation, and prebooking activities, such as "Course may only be booked by an administrator." This BAdI is discussed in detail later in this chapter.

Table 9.2 Enhancements Found Outside the IMG

Enhancement Type	Name	Function
BAdI	LSO_FOLLOWUP	This BAdI is not supported. However, organizations often find it and attempt to use it with no success. SAP has no plans to support this function in the future.
BAdI	LSO_PRICES	This BAdI is not supported. Instead, you should use the function module "LSO_PRICES" as described in the section on "Fee Handling."

Table 9.2 Enhancements Found Outside the IMG (Cont.)

9.2 Structural Authorization Techniques

A variety of standard authorization profiles are provided as templates when implementing SAP Enterprise Learning. It is a good idea to copy these templates and then tweak them to meet your needs. Structural Authorization profiles are not delivered for use with SAP Enterprise Learning, but they offer additional restrictions that many organizations use on both the backend and frontend of the solution.

9.2.1 Configuring Structural Authorizations

Structural Authorization profiles (Structural Authorizations or SAs) are attached to User IDs. There are two very important items to keep in mind with SAs:

- SAP functionality, where any objects are concerned, always checks Structural Authorizations. Objects, strictly speaking, are instances of object types. The list of object types can be found in table T778O. Because most data in Enterprise Learning is related to objects (Course Types, Courses, learners, etc.), virtually all of the data retrieval performed in Enterprise Learning utilizes SA checks.

- Once a user is restricted by any structural authorization, access to all objects is governed by the structural authorization profiles assigned to that user.

This means that you cannot simply apply restrictions to a specific set of object types and objects; you must explicitly grant access to each object type/object that the user will require.

Structural Authorizations can be configured in multiple locations in the IMG. Because we are discussing Enterprise Learning, Figure 9.2 shows the path to SA configuration in the Training and Events sub-tree.

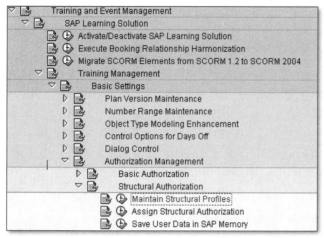

Figure 9.2 One of Many Places in the IMG Where Structural Authorization Configuration Resides

9.2.2 Maintain Structural Profiles

In this configuration step, SA profiles are built. A user can have multiple profiles assigned, each granting inclusive access. Therefore, profile definition depends heavily on the overall authorization strategy a company employs. This is a two-step configuration. First, profiles are defined with an Authorization Profile ID and a text description of the profile (displayed in Figure 9.3).

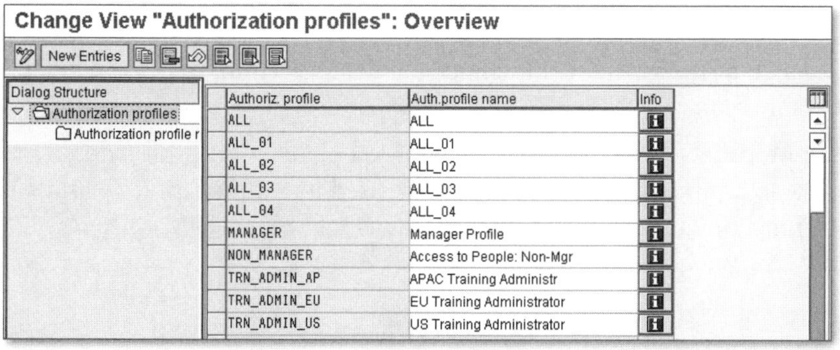

Figure 9.3 Defining Authorization Profiles

The first step in configuring Structural Authorization profiles is "Maintain Structural Authorization profiles." This is where you name the profiles you will use.

Drilling down to an individual profile displays the profile definition (displayed in Figure 9.3). This is the core of the configuration step. Each entry here defines access to an object type for the profile. The fields in the table are:

- **Profile** — This is the SA profile being displayed/maintained.

- **Sequence Number** — This field allows multiple records per profile. The order in which records exist in the table is not relevant, so numbering sequentially from 1 to x will work; there is no need to leave open numbers between records.

- **Plan Version** — Most companies use the standard plan version of "01" as the active (and only) plan version, so we will use that for our purposes.

- **Object Type** — This field is the object type for the start of the structure.

- **Object ID** — This field is the root object ID.

- **Maintenance Flag** — SA access can be for display or maintain. Checking this box in a record will give the user maintenance authority for objects corresponding to this record.

- **Evaluation Path** — The evaluation path can be used to define how the structure should be read.

- **Status Vector** — This field defines the planning statuses of objects to be included. If left blank, all statuses will be included. Each status to be included is entered here. For example, to give access to Active and Planned status, enter "12."

- **Depth** — The depth of the structure included can be limited with this field. In most cases, the field is left blank, but the field can be used to limit the structure read along the evaluation path to any number of levels.

- **Period** — Use of the period field defines the date selection used in authorization determination.

- **Function Module** — If the Object ID field is left blank, a function module can be used to determine the root object(s) to be used in authorization determination. The function module must have a specific interface. RH_GET_MANAGER_ASSIGNMENT is a good example.

Example

A company wishes to control access to the Course catalog for training administrators. All training administrators should be able to see the entire Course catalog, but each should be able to maintain only Courses offered within their respective regions. To do this, the company uses the SAP HCM solutions, so access to people must be limited (keeping in mind that the user might also be a manager of staff).

To create a profile to meet these requirements, you need to determine which objects should be wide open in the profile. In this example, the objects with sequence numbers are 20 - 132 as seen in Figure 9.4.

That leaves the objects that require more specific authorization. In our example, those objects are Course catalog and organizational (staffing) data. For the Course catalog, two entries are necessary. The first entry defines display access to the entire catalog. The second entry defines maintenance authorization to a subset of the catalog. The evaluation path used for both entries in this example defines a path from the Course Group through the Course/Curriculum type and Course Program to Course, Curriculum, and e-learning. The function module will be used to define the root Course Groups. A custom application table, maintained in each environment, can be used to define the root objects for the structural authorization determination. The access to people only requires one entry in the configuration, but the entry is more complicated. To perform certain learning functions (i.e., booking a learner into a Course, assigning an instructor to a Course, etc.), the training administrator will require access to people. To grant this authority, while limiting access to people in other HCM applications, use a function module to define the root. In this case, the function module needs to return the highest level organizational unit if the user is performing a training activity, or the user's own organizational unit(s) for all other activities.

Change View "Authorization profile maintenance": Overview

New Entries

	No.	Plan ...	Obj. ty...	Object I	Maint.	Eval.path	Status...	Period	Function module
Dialog Structure	1	01	0		☑	SBESX	12		Z_HR_STRUCAUTH_P
▽ 🗀 Authorization profiles	7	01	L	50000001	☐	ZLSOSTRU	12		
🗀 Authorization profile r	11	01	L		☑	ZLSOSTRU	12	F	Z_LSO_GET_TA_ROOTS
	20	01	R		☑				
	30	01	G		☑				
	40	01	U		☑				
	45	01	F		☑				
	50	01	OJ		☑				
	60	01	H		☑				
	70	01	01		☑				
	80	01	02		☑				
	90	01	03		☑				
	100	01	04		☑				
	110	01	VA		☑				
	120	01	VB		☑				
	130	01	VC		☑				

Figure 9.4 Example Configuration of Structural Authorization Profile for Training Administrator (Fields Profile, Depth, and Sign are Hidden from the Screen)

In some of the most complex scenarios, custom evaluation paths and function modules may not provide enough flexibility to control authorization across various

HCM applications. If tighter control is necessary then that can be managed through configuration, implement BADI HRBAS00_STRUAUTH. The BADI can be used to grant access to individual objects.

After defining the profiles for Structural Authorizations, the profiles must be assigned to users. There are a number of processes available to accomplish this task. In the IMG, the step below Maintain Structural Profiles is Assign Structural Authorization. This method assigns Structural Authorization Profiles directly to SAP User IDs. This method requires maintenance every time a new user is added to the system. Assigning profiles to jobs and positions — through infotype 1017 (PD Profiles) — requires much less ongoing maintenance; however, the company's organizational structure must be defined to the level that supports the authorization plan. As always, workflow and custom programs can be used to blend the available solutions into an automated process. One SAP customer used a program to generate User IDs for each person in the organization. This process looked for employees and external persons with no User ID attached and then generated the ID. Roles were assigned to grant ESS/MSS permissions and structural authorization profiles were attached based on certain attributes. Only personnel whose job profiles required additional SAP access required manual effort by the security personnel.

9.3 Enhancement Case Study: Controlling Access to the Course Catalog

Many companies implementing SAP Enterprise Learning face a challenge with learners being able to self-register for training Courses. For any number of reasons, companies require the ability to control access to areas of the Course catalog. Structural Authorizations and supervisor approval of bookings through workflow are two methods to address this issue, but there are shortcomings with both approaches.

Structural Authorizations are a standard method available to control access to the Course catalog. The benefit to using this approach is that Structural Authorizations are used pervasively throughout the Enterprise Learning module. If a learner does not have access to a Course Group or type, he will not be able to register for any Course schedules offered. Even if a training administrator performed the registration in the backend as an override, the learner cannot access the training record in the Learning Portal. Unfortunately, that is also a downside of this solution. The inherent rigidness of the authorizations do not allow for any sort of override. In addition, the implementation of Structural Authorizations can have some unintended consequences because some employees may carry multiple roles. For example, a training administrator in one training organization may be granted access to build Courses only in that organization's section of the Course catalog. But in most cases, that administrator would then not have access to register for training offered by another training organization.

Supervisor approval of training bookings can provide another level of control. If a learner attempts to book a Course that is not relevant for his role in the organization, the supervisor can reject a workflow request, blocking the registration. The downside of relying on the supervisor is that it places the burden of interpreting the plan of the training organization on the individual supervisors.

If an organization wishes to control learner registration to reduce costs and optimize performance of training programs, then the proper point of control is the registration process. The system must support job role- and location-based controls of the booking function to ensure that only the target audience of training programs is using those resources.

9.3.1 Enhancement

SAP Enterprise Learning provides prerequisite check functionality, which can restrict learners' access to Courses under certain conditions. The standard functionality can define the severity of the prerequisite check (if a failed prerequisite check results in an error or warning) and assign the Courses, curricula, Course Programs, and qualifications required in order for the learner to participate. In addition, the BADI LSO_CHECK_BOOKING facilitates customization of the checks performed by the system when determining if a learner can book or be booked into a Course.

By extending the standard prerequisite check functionality with a custom infotype, a custom subtype for the Descriptions Infotype (1002), an implementation of the LSO_CHECK_BOOKING BADI, and a customization in the learning portal, it is possible to use additional attributes in the determination of a learner's ability to register. The additional attributes can be defined per organization, but some of the most common elements are: Organizational Unit, Organizational Structure, Job, Location, Employee Group/Subgroup, and whether the learner is a supervisor.

Some customers have used this functionality to differentiate access to Courses for contractors vs. employees. Other customers have used this enhancement to remove access to sections of the Course catalog based on business unit of the company (for example, only manufacturing personnel can access the Courses in a section of the catalog for the manufacturing organization). Other companies have used the basic functionality of the enhancement to allow greater control of Course attendance by the training administrator. In one case, a company had a few Courses that were important to one organization but also of interest to employees across the company. Using the ability to block booking for learners but not for administrators, the training administrators were better able to manage the limited slots available to make sure that the employees most needing the Course could find the available slots.

Example

To best illustrate this functionality, let's consider an example. Company A needs to roll out a training program dealing with regulatory compliance. This training is specific to people in the manufacturing and quality control organizations that supervise others. Additionally, there are variances in regional regulations to a degree that separate Courses will be offered in the different regions of the company.

When the training administrator builds the new Course Type, an additional (custom) infotype is maintained to define the prerequisite check. The organizational attributes of the target audience are defined (see Figure 9.5). The bottom line would allow managers in the U.S. compliance organization to participate in the Course. The middle line would allow managers in the U.S. manufacturing organization to participate in the Course. The top line specifically excludes learners in the Minneapolis plant even though those learners are in the U.S. manufacturing organization.

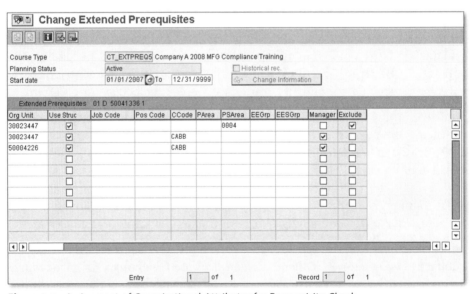

Figure 9.5 Assignment of Organizational Attributes for Prerequisite Check

Next, to help learners better understand the prerequisites of the Course, the training administrator maintains a custom subtype of the Description Infotype. The description entered is a plain-text definition of the entire set of prerequisites. This description will display in the Learning Portal. Figure 9.6 shows the prerequisite displays on the Course Type page for schedule dependent Courses. Registration for Courses of this Course Type occurs on a subsequent page, so the prerequisites are only displayed here; they are not checked. Figure 9.7 shows the results of the prerequisite check.

Prerequisites

Prerequisite	Prereq Type
Company A Introduction to MFG Compliance	Course
Generic Compliance Reporting	Qualification
Extended Prerequisites (see below)	N/A

The **intended** audiance for this course is:
A) Managers in the US Compliance Organization
B) Managers in the US Manufacturing Organization (with the exception of the Minnesota Plant)
In order to register for this course, learners must have taken the global Introduction to Manufacturing Compliance course, and must be qualified on Generic Compiance Reporting.

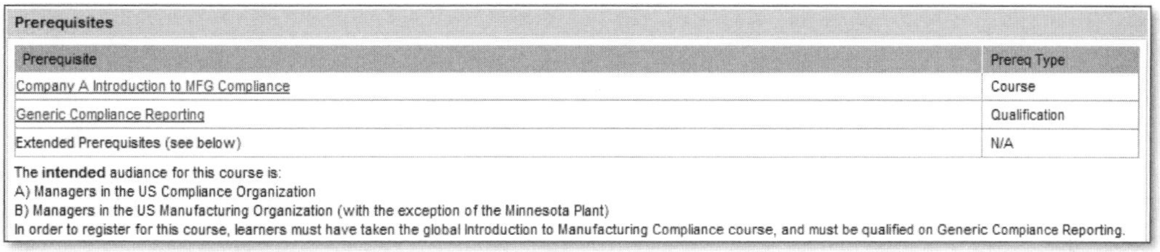

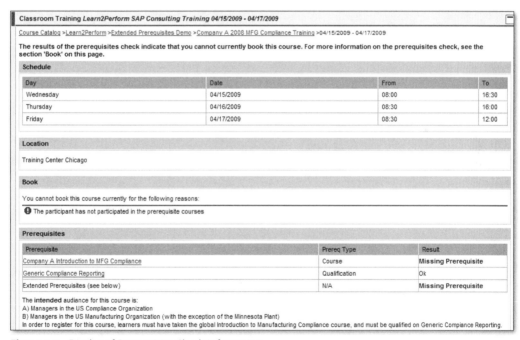

Figure 9.6 Display of Prerequisites of a Course Type

Classroom Training *Learn2Perform SAP Consulting Training 04/15/2009 - 04/17/2009*

Course Catalog >Learn2Perform >Extended Prerequisites Demo >Company A 2008 MFG Compliance Training >04/15/2009 - 04/17/2009

The results of the prerequisites check indicate that you cannot currently book this course. For more information on the prerequisites check, see the section 'Book' on this page.

Schedule

Day	Date	From	To
Wednesday	04/15/2009	08:00	16:30
Thursday	04/16/2009	08:30	16:00
Friday	04/17/2009	08:30	12:00

Location

Training Center Chicago

Book

You cannot book this course currently for the following reasons:

The participant has not participated in the prerequisite courses

Prerequisites

Prerequisite	Prereq Type	Result
Company A Introduction to MFG Compliance	Course	**Missing Prerequisite**
Generic Compliance Reporting	Qualification	Ok
Extended Prerequisites (see below)	N/A	**Missing Prerequisite**

The **intended** audiance for this course is:
A) Managers in the US Compliance Organization
B) Managers in the US Manufacturing Organization (with the exception of the Minnesota Plant)
In order to register for this course, learners must have taken the global Introduction to Manufacturing Compliance course, and must be qualified on Generic Compiance Reporting.

Figure 9.7 Display of Prerequisite Check Information

An additional enhancement to SAP standard functionality details specific checks to the learner, so he can understand which prerequisite has not been met.

The extension of the prerequisite functionality can add efficiency to the training processes. Learners are better informed of the requirements of a Course. Training administrators only need to handle exceptions with manual booking in the R/3 backend. In many cases, rigid structural authorization implementation is not necessary.

9.4 Summary

This chapter outlined several possible enhancements to the Learning Solution. We can adapt to the needs of the client with changes to the Dynamic Reporting Menus, reporting, and many other enhancements. Of particular note is Structural Authorizations, which can be changed to meet the regulatory needs.

In the next chapter we will discuss how to manage your SAP Enterprise Learning implementation.

Once you start to dig into the world of Enterprise Learning, you start to realize how vast it is. Managing an Enterprise Learning project requires an understanding of the business drivers, the content requirements, and the technology requirements. Each of these elements is key to a successful implementation.

10 Managing an Enterprise Learning Implementation

Managing an SAP Enterprise Learning implementation can be a challenge. As discussed in previous chapters, the solution uses functionality from the backend ERP system (Organizational Management, Personnel Administration, Personnel Development, and Training Management), NetWeaver Portal functionality (Collaboration, Content Management, the Learning Portal, the Instructor Portal, and the Training Administrator Portal), and the Authoring Environment and Content Player functions. Additionally, you may choose to use XI, Workflow, Adobe Connect, TREX, or BI to create a comprehensive training and e-learning solution using SAP Enterprise Learning. You may also need to take into account how your SAP Enterprise Learning will complement current or future Talent Management implementations in your organization.

In this chapter, we will discuss some of the differentiators of an Enterprise Learning implementation from a Project Management (PM) perspective, generally following SAP Accelerated Methodology (ASAP). We assume that you are familiar with project management methodologies and will not define each phase of the methodology or address all processes that occur in each phase. We will also not discuss budget or timing in detail, because these elements will vary by project, based on both scope and available resources. We will, however, highlight differentiators from an Enterprise Learning PM perspective as we progress through each phase.

10.1 Project Planning

Comprehensive up-front planning can help alleviate many of the challenges encountered during an Enterprise Learning implementation. In this section, we discuss best practices to be used during this key phase. The discussion points will help ensure that you (1) have the knowledge you need to support project scope discussions; (2) understand the functional and technical resources you will need on-site during the implementation based on the defined project scope; (3) are able to create a project plan that addresses and provides adequate time to implement your desired functionality; and (4) understand the change management requirements that should be planned for during your implementation and the post-go-live period.

10.1.1 Project Goals, Objectives, and Scope

When planning your project, you must ensure the goals and objectives of the project are defined and that you have an agreed-on scope. Your goals and objectives should be the drivers for your project. Generally, the goals and objectives are identified before your project is initiated. Typical goals for an Enterprise Learning implementation may include the following:

▶ Centralize learning processes and standards across the organization

▶ Provide a single source for employee learning

▶ Design a global learning solution to enhance global talent management

▶ Provide a robust solution for required training management

▶ Facilitate the use of e-learning content

These goals should help further define your project scope. Typically, a project's scope is outlined when the project is initiated, to help the organization determine the best solution to meet its requirements. During the planning phase, you provide more specifics around the scope, to help you identify resources and define your timelines. You also validate your scope with the business stakeholders and project sponsor(s).

Defining scope for an Enterprise Learning implementation project can be a relatively complex process. Let's start by taking an example based on these goals.

▶ Centralize learning processes and standards across the organization

　▸ Is there a group that acts as a *learning leader* within your organization currently or are there scattered groups that have no aligned processes?

　▸ If there is a learning leader, does that group have content standards or process standards that should be reviewed?

　▸ If there is no learning leader, do any of the content owners in your group have strong content developers? Are standards supported to any degree within your organization?

▶ If any groups have strong standards, should these continue to be supported or is there a need to revisit all standards?

▶ Is there a group that will be able to support centralizing your learning/content processes? If not, are you able to bring consultants in to manage this aspect of your implementation?

▶ Is there a lot of existing content within your organization?

▶ If so, does this content meet either the AICC or SCORM standards that SAP supports?

▶ If the content does not meet these standards, should you attempt to convert the content to one of these standards or simply provide the content as static when you go live?

▶ If you plan to convert your content, which standard will you support on a go-forward basis?

▶ Provide a single source for employee global learning.

▶ Where is learning content hosted now?

▶ On multiple external sites?

▶ If so, do you wish to maintain external site content externally or do you wish to bring it in house?

▶ If the content will be hosted externally, should the learner access the content through the Portal or will they go directly to the host site?

▶ If you would like them to access content directly via the Portal, does the third-party provider support AICC?

▶ If not, does the third-party provider have Web services to support the use of XI?

▶ On multiple internal sites?

▶ If so, have you involved the internal content owners in the project preparation process?

▶ Is the internal content standards compliant?

▶ Should this content be presented as Learning Content? Or is it more Knowledge Leader? If it's knowledge management, is this part of the implementation or is this a separate project?

▶ Design a global learning solution to enhance global talent management.

▶ Do you have other aspects of SAP Talent Management Solution in place now?

▸ If so, do they have learning requirements?

▸ If not, are there plans to implement any of these solutions in the future? And will they have learning requirements that should be taken into consideration during this implementation?

▸ If there are no SAP Talent Management solutions in place, but there are third-party providers in place, do they have integration needs?

▸ Provide a robust solution for required training management.

▸ Does your organization have formalized regulatory requirements that must be met to make the implementation a success?

▸ If so, what are the governing bodies? Do they have documented standards?

▸ If not, are there any internal trainings that are considered "Required" for any employee bodies?

▸ If there are regulatory requirements, is there a reason your implementation should not leverage qualifications (e.g., another solution is heavily leveraging them; qualifications were determined to be out of scope for the implementation at some point)?

▸ Facilitate the use of e-learning content.

▸ Are there e-learning Courses in existence now?

▸ Which tools are used to develop these Courses?

▸ Is a requirement to identify a content development package in scope for the implementation?

▸ Does your organization have a *Technology Culture* or will e-learning be a new concept to many of your employees?

As you can see, as you start to drill down into your goals to define your scope, things can get complicated. While you may not be able to answer all the questions listed above, you will be able to use the information you derive to manage and define your blueprint sessions. For example, you probably are not aware of all the hosted content that exists in your organization. However, you may know that implementing XI is not feasible during your Enterprise Learning project and determine that any Web-services solutions are out of scope for the implementation. This information will let your consulting team know they must identify all third-party hosted solutions during your blueprint sessions and also have the business users determine if (1) the content could be hosted internally; (2) if you could leverage an AICC-based solution; or (3) if you must simply provide access to the site from the Learning Portal. If you are also moving toward globalization, you may use your project to help your organization phase out third-party hosted content that does not meet specific criteria that was identified during scoping. Or, you may decide to use your Blueprint to decide which criteria should be used to determine if content should be used by your organization or phased out.

Generally, most implementation partners are experienced in scoping out Enterprise Learning implementations. If you are talking with multiple implementers to determine who you will work with to support your project, you will find that they will often offer high-level scoping as a free or reduced-rate service to help you determine your project staffing needs. However, if you have never implemented an LMS before, it might make sense to engage a third-party to finalize scope because there are so many variables that can be determined up front. Your scoping document needs to be as comprehensive as possible to adequately drive project planning and blueprinting and to help you avoid common "gotchas."

10.1.2 Project Staffing

Based on your project scope decisions, you should easily finalize your project staffing decisions. There are some obvious skill sets you will need, that are typical for any LMS or SAP implementation. Table 10.1 attempts to provide a comprehensive list of the roles you might need to staff your project. Some projects may decide that it makes sense to combine two or more roles while other projects may split roles into multiple *mini-roles*, perhaps based on availability. Of Course, if certain functions, such as Workflow, are not in your scope, you will have no need for a role to support this functionality.

Role	Description
Project Sponsor	Acts as project champion. May be part of a Project Steering Committee.
Project Manager - Business	Responsible for managing resources, maintaining the project plan, ensuring project stays aligned with business goals, and maintaining communication with Project Sponsor/Steering Committee/Other Stakeholders.
Project Manager - Technical	Often a resource from your implementation partner. Ensures that technical issues are highlighted quickly, that the development and configuration aspects of the project remain on-track, and that no technical considerations of the implemenation are neglected.
Change Management Lead	Responsible for planning and managing the change to processes, systems, organization structure, and/or job roles as a result of the implementation.

Table 10.1 Roles and Responsibilities in an Enterprise Learning Implementation

Role	Description
LSO Functional Consultant(s)	Responsible for configuration, testing functional requirements in the system, writing functional specifications, supporting business process design in terms of administrative and content processes, providing system documentation and knowledge transfer. Typically an external role with expertise in the LSO. Depending on the scope of the implementation, there may be more than one resource or expertise may be split for training administration and content.
Business/Systems Analyst(s)	Supports the same initiatives as the LSO Functional Consultant and works with this role to gain knowledge needed to support the implemenation on a go-forward basis. Typically an internal role.
Usability Analyst	Responsible for performing usability analysis of the Learning Portal. Generally a web-design specialist.
Subject Matter Experts	Partially dedicated resources who represent the following areas: Business Unit Stakeholders (Required for Blueprint; Proof of Concept; User Acceptance Testing; Master Data Clean-up for conversion purposes). Functional Resources (Expertise in current OM, PA, PD, and other Talent Management solutions that currently exist).
Education Consultant/ Specialist	Responsible for development and delivery of end-user training materials.
Content/ Instructional Design Resource(s)	Responsible for content conversion decisions, establishing content development standards, and non–end-user training based content creation linked to roll-out.
WebDynpro Resource	Responsible for development on Instructor/Tutor and Administrative Portals.
ABAP Resource(s)	Responsible for any reporting, interface, conversion, enhancements, forms required for the implementation.
BSP Resource	Responsible for enhancements to the Learning Portal pages.
XI Resource	Responsible for XI services, if in scope.
Portal Resource	Responsible for integrating the Learning Portal component into the SAP Enterprise Portal. May be responsible for Content Management as well, or this may be a separate resource.
Security Resource	Responsible for adjustments to delivered security roles, creation of new roles, and possibly structural authorizations.
BI Resource	Responsible for enabling the standard data cubes availabile and creating additional extractors/cubes/queries if needed.

Table 10.1 Roles and Responsibilities in an Enterprise Learning Implementation (Cont.)

Role	Description
Basis Resource	Responsible for installing and configuring the add-on components required for the SAP Learning Solution.
Workflow Resource	Responsible for implementing and/or enhancing delivered workflow solutions.
Additional Functional Resources	Depending on integration points, you may need internal expertise in the following areas: CO (Activity and Cost Allocations) SD (External customer billing) MM (Materials management support for resources) Time (Integration to Time Management)

Table 10.1 Roles and Responsibilities in an Enterprise Learning Implementation (Cont.)

It is unlikely that all of these resources will be required. However, you will find that most implementation providers insist on some project management oversight, as Enterprise Learning implementations tend to be complicated.

10.1.3 Project Timeline

You probably had a project timeline going into your scoping process and, if anything drove your scope, it was probably your project timeline. By now, you should have validated that your timeline is reasonable based on your scope and you should feel comfortable filling your timeline in with key milestones.

There is no "perfect" timeline for an implementation. Any good implementation partner will tell you that the timeline "depends." Companies have implemented Enterprise Learning in three months and deemed their projects successes while others have felt they did a perfect 18-month implementation. A rule of thumb for a mostly "out-of-the-box" implementation with a full-complement of resources, a few custom reports, perhaps some minor BSP enhancements, and solid e-learning content that has gone through unit testing is that integration testing and user-acceptance testing is six months from Blueprint to rollout. But again, every project is different and every company has its own project drivers that impact the scope and delivery of its Enterprise Learning implementation. There is no vanilla project plan and no vanilla roll-out because there is no vanilla Enterprise Learning company. Figure 10.1 below illustrates an example of a six-month project plan that you may wish to use as a guideline.

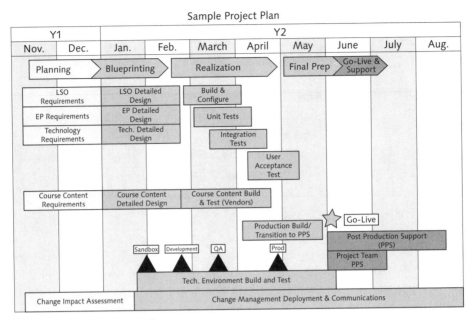

Figure 10.1 Sample Project Plan

10.2 Blueprint

Blueprint, or Requirements Gathering, is just as important as the project planning phase, because it defines your scope and ensures that the project meets your business needs at a detailed level. This is where you validate that you chose the correct implementation partner. Realization is the phase where you begin to understand how accurate your scope document was and how viable your milestones/initial project plan is. The key players during Blueprint are your consultants and your SMEs. Your consultants should be driving your workshops and they should be geared to provide your SMEs with a high-level view of the solution, while, at the same time, providing your consultants with a solid understanding of your functional requirements. Your technical support should be available to answer questions regarding infrastructure, security restrictions, and report and develop processes. Your internal configuration resources/business/systems analysts should be at every Blueprint workshop because they will be your support resources once your consultants have rolled off the project. These are fairly typical expectations for any SAP project, regardless of size or scope. From a topics perspective, you should plan the following workshops. Table 10.2 contains a recommended time frame for each topic, based on a phased implementation for a company with about 10,000 employees and five stakeholder organizations. You should allocate two to three weeks for your consulting team to compile the results of these workshops. The most effective process is to schedule time in between workshops to write up the results.

Workshop Title	Description
Portal 1 to 1.5 Days	Review the Portal functionality and understand usability requirements of stakeholders. Discuss branding and define business use of each section of the portal. If possible, hold this workshop in the beginning of your Blueprint sessions, to introduce stakeholders to the solution, and then review the results of the workshop at the end of your Blueprint sessions and dive in to the requirements. All Business SMEs should participate.
Training Management Requirements 3 Days	Review Administration role and functionality. Understand business requirements from a global perspective. This session should cover roles and this discussion can be used to begin authorization definition. Leave room in your schedule for follow-up sessions for key organizations (e.g., for a Utilities organization, there should be follow-ups for Nuclear and Energy Delivery; for a Pharmaceutical/Life Sciences company, plan a QAC follow-up; for most organizations, follow up with Sales and the Ethics/Compliance organization).
Qualifications 2 Days	Review the Qualifications Catalog functionality and discuss how Qualifications will be used to support regulatory/required training. Note: You may require follow-up workshops as above or you may not require this workshop at all, depending on the project scope.
Reporting requirements/MSS 1 to 2 Days	Demonstrate SAP reporting functionality and review Ad Hoc and BI reports, based on scope. Also provide MSS overview and discuss managerial reporting needs, if in scope. Discuss reporting requirements from a business perspective and define the business needs for each report.
Content 1 to 5 days	The length of this workshop will vary based on existing content. If content is minimal, this workshop should only take one day and most of it should be educational. In this case, the consulting team should be qualified to drive the direction of content development, delivery, and standards, if necessary. If stakeholder groups have extensive content, allocate up to one day per business unit.
Follow-up Session	Allow up to two days for follow-up.

Table 10.2   Roles and Responsibilities in an Enterprise Learning Implementation

As the project manager, as each workshop finishes, you should be working with your consulting team and your technical project lead/manager to flesh out your project plan based on the Blueprint results. You should also review each Blueprint section to ensure that it meets your scope needs and is not allowing "scope creep." For example, as reporting requirements are complete, your consulting team should document those requirements and indicate whether each requirement is delivered, available via Ad Hoc or BI reporting, or an enhancement. Based on the scope set down during the Project Planning phase, your consulting team should estimate whether the requirement is *in scope* or *out of scope*. Regardless of whether the requirement is in scope, out of scope, or outlandish, your consulting team should capture it. This reassures your extended team that they were listened to and understood. A good method for capturing requirements is a Functional Requirements Matrix (FRM). This matrix might be embedded in your Blueprint document or it might be part of the deliverables, as a second document. Table 10.3 is an example of an FRM.

Req #	Cat	Business Requirement	Bus Unit	Gap	Scope	Res Type	Comments
AE00		Authoring and Content Management Requirements					
AE01	ID	Create file structure according to the prescribed standards and guidelines.	ALL	N	Y	4	The content in the CMS must be organized based on a structure documented and maintained by the Learning and Development group that accommodates all participating and future business units.
AE02	ID	Specify how the content needs to be divided within the organization per regulatory practices.	ALL	N	Y	4	Content needs to be separated on the server by use of permissions and folder structure.
AE03	ID	Establish guidelines and coordinate the content creation process.	ALL	N	Y	4	Learning and Development Group

Table 10.3 Training/Learning Administration Functional Requirements Matrix

Req #	Cat	Business Requirement	Bus Unit	Gap	Scope	Res Type	Comments
AE04	ID	Ensure metadata support for content reusability.	ALL	N	Y	4	Establish guidelines for assigning metadata to content for future re-use.
AE05	ID	Publish the whole learning net in the repository, making it available to the training administrator.	ALL	N	Y	4	The publishing process will be handled by a small number of Instructional Designers called "Publishers." They will be responsible for checking the files into the CMS, releasing them, and then publishing them for the training administrators.
AE06	ID	Make finished content (learning net, learning object, or media object) available to other authors, by storing the content in the Content Management System.	ALL	N	Y	4	Support content creation collaboration (Checking-In content) The file is copied to the Content Management System via the Repository Explorer Wizard.
AE07	ID	Check content into the master repository.	ALL	N	Y	4	
AE08	ID	Release content by date preference.	ALL	N	Y	4	This is a manual process.

Table 10.3 Training/Learning Administration Functional Requirements Matrix (Cont.)

Each requirement is numbered and categorized for easy sorting. Relevance by Business Unit is noted, as is whether the item is a Gap, is in Scope, and what type of Resolution is required. There are also comments, when relevant, that discuss how the issue will be resolved. Comments may be used to indicate why something is out of scope, a suggested workaround, or a high-level solution from an enhancement perspective. Again, your Blueprint should not be so high level that it simply lists requirements. It must define the requirements and communicate how those requirements will be met.

10.3 Realization

Realization is the phase where everything starts to come together. From an implementation perspective, you need to ensure that your consultants are managing the configuration, achieving knowledge transfer, and completing their documentation requirements. In addition, your consultants will be writing functional specifications, so your development team can get started on their tasks. If you've managed an SAP project, this is nothing new. Some potentially new elements of a project revolve around content management and change management.

10.3.1 Content Management

We've mentioned content development, content standards, and content conversions already. But we really haven't gone into detail on these aspects. If you review the statement of work from your implementation partner, it is likely that no guarantees are made on content deliverables (unless it's standards development, end-user documentation, and/or end-user training). There's a reason for this, and it is probably not because your implementation partner was trying to ignore your content requirements. Your implementation partner is probably aware that "SCORM compliant" doesn't mean the same thing to all content vendors. And your content provider probably is aware that SCORM-compliant content might not meet your minimum requirements for content — because the standard is more of a guideline than a standard. This means it's easy to do the bare minimum from a content perspective and be SCORM compliant. Because your implementation partner may not have worked with your custom content, your vendor, or your third-party content creation tool in the past, there was no way for them to estimate how long it would take to convert your content, import your content, or manage your content in any other way to meet your specific requirements. And even if they had, it's amazing how quickly things change in the content world.

As a project manager, be conservative as you estimate how long content deliverables will take. And, as you work through Realization, touch base with your content team regularly and be prepared to pare your project deliverables down to the bare minimum prior to go-live. Because SCORM has minimal requirements from a content perspective, your team will have to convert each piece of content from a provider, review it, analyze it, and determine if it's viable for go-live. If the content was created in-house and created using the same development tool, it will probably work the same way each time it's converted for use with Enterprise Learning, but after conversion, your team may decide that the look and feel is not appropriate for delivery to the end users. Large chunks of content may have to be reworked — something you had no way to plan for.

At the same time your content team is working with your existing content, they'll also be working on defining your organization's content standards (unless you came to the implementation with a robust set of standards using current best practices from a content perspective). As the team learns more about content and standards, they will probably become more conservative in terms of what they're comfortable rolling out for go-live. Again, this is a good thing because your content team is thinking about the end-user experience, which we will address in the next section.

10.3.2 Change Management

As a project manager, you should expect to address the same things you've addressed in the past from a change management perspective: How will the new solution impact my organizational role? Will the new solution be intuitive? Does it affect my organizational structure? What about the administrative processes we've used for the last five years?

In addition, because Enterprise Learning provides your employees with a new interface to learning, you will address similar change management issues to those you might address when implementing ESS or MSS, particularly usability. But learning content throws a new variable into the mix. Not only do you need to address content issues for your learners, but you need to teach your help desk to address those same content issues. In fact, you may need to plan for a new organization (perhaps the seeds of a new centralized learning organization, even if this was not one of the original project drivers) to support this.

Content becomes such a big issue with an LMS implementation because your employees, even those who have experience with self-service solutions, are used to everything coming from the organization's corporate intranet to be the same. They expect consistency and process-driven scenarios. If you don't have control over your content, all of that goes out the window. Content integration is one of the biggest causes for the failure of an LMS implementation and one of the leading causes of employee dissatisfaction with LMS solutions, once implemented. This is often not the fault of the solution; it's the fault of the content.

Consider, for example, an organization that goes live with just four pieces of content. Two of the Courses are created by third-party content providers, specifically for the organization in question. Traditionally, employees have accessed this content through an email link. They logged onto a third-party site, were directed to the content, completed it, and were probably provided with a certificate they could print out. Two of the Courses were created in-house, specifically for their Enterprise Learning implementation. One Course was created by the organization's Office of Ethics and Compliance, using PowerPoint through the Authoring Environment. The other one was created as a tutorial on the new solution, using the content creation tool Articulate.

In this example, assume that each piece of content was stored in the local CMS (instead of being hosted by a third party). Because the third-party content was created prior to the initiation of the content standards project, one piece of content has basic, linear navigation and instructs learners to click "Next" as they review each page. The second piece of third-party content is extremely interactive and supports learner navigation via a virtual elevator, which allows the learner "progress" from one scenario to the next.

When your employees log onto the portal for the first time, they will be faced with four pieces of content that provide them with completely different navigation instructions. If one of your employees gets stuck in the elevator (which has happened to employees at one organization), they will call the help desk and ask how they should get out of the elevator. Unless your help desk has content experts who understand how differently configured laptops can impact content navigation, there will probably be minimal support for that employee. If another employee starts each piece of content and spends approximately 20 minutes on each Course, and then logs off without completing the content, the system will tell him that he is 0% complete with the Articulate content and probably 0% complete with both pieces of third-party content as well. Only the PowerPoint content that was structured in the Authoring Environment will give an accurate percentage completion. Your help desk isn't going to be able to support this employee either, at least not with their current understanding of SAP. You are now asking them to venture into the wide world of content. From a change management perspective, you have to decide who you are going to manage: The help desk? The learner? Or each of the four content providers?

When considering this, you need to understand that the reason the SAP AE created content worked the most smoothly was not because SAP is playing favorites — it is because bare minimum SCORM compliance does not require that progress be passed back, beyond "start" and "complete." Unless you had a lot of foresight when planning your project, you probably didn't plan for this, or for the fact that your sales team has a different version of Java installed on their laptops to support a sales application –not the company standard version of Java that supports elevator doors opening as learners navigate through a class. If your content team is good, they will probably catch these issues while they are testing content and developing their standards. And, if they're good, they'll probably request a scope change to support additional development support in the form of Java wrappers for existing content or leveraging BAdIs to enhance progress tracking. As a project manager, you'll have to decide whether your project has the ability to support this scope change as opposed to increased change management. And you'll also want to consider that a decrease in usability, from a learner perspective, generally leads to less satisfaction with a software solution.

10.3.3 Proof of Concept

A "Proof of concept" (also called "Playback" or "Walkthrough") is often cited as a best practice for an SAP implementation. The Proof of Concept is an opportunity for the implementation team to review configuration with the stakeholder organizations in scripted demos, about two-thirds of the way through the Realization phase. This allows the implementation team to validate their work with the stakeholder organizations prior to the User Acceptance Testing (UAT) phase. It also ensures that the end-users in these organizations stay engaged in the long dry spell between Blueprinting and UATs.

One problem often cited with a Proof of Concept during a project is the time it takes to set up the data and script the demos. Often, setup for a Proof of Concept can take a week or more away from an implementation, right in the middle of system testing, last minute configuration, and process documentation and end-user training development. If something has to be cut from a project plan, the Proof of Concept is often the "something" that's cut.

In the previous section, we discussed change management, particularly from a help desk and employee perspective. The Proof of Concept helps address this from an administrative perspective. It ensures that the blueprint, translated into via configuration into system processes, was translated effectively. It also provides the end-users with the opportunity to view the system prior to UAT. This means that UAT does not require as much support from the implementation team because the testers reviewed the system and saw the "big picture" a month or so before the initiation of UAT. And of Course, the Proof of Concept, when done correctly, validates to the stakeholder team that they were listened to during the Blueprint sessions.

10.4 Go-Live Preparation and Go-Live

The last two phases of an Enterprise Learning implementation are generally the most painless for the Project Manager. Most organizations, during Go-Live Preparation, are doing their final content conversions and master data conversions. Generally, master data conversions are simple Excel loads or eCATTs, with the most complicated data being training history.

End-user training also takes place during these last two phases. Formal training for the administration team often takes place in the classroom while employee and MSS training use the new LMS for end-user training. Often, organizations send out a welcome email with a link to the new Learning Portal. As soon as a new user selects the link in the email, he is able to view mandatory employee and (if relevant) manager training that guides them through the new solution.

10.5 Summary

As with any SAP project, if you spend time up front during project preparation, you are likely to alleviate many problems that may have been faced during implementation. Unless you have implemented an LMS before, whether Enterprise Learning or another LMS, you will encounter unique situations. The following is a list of things to keep in mind.

- ▶ Change Management is key to any LMS implementation. You are placing your learning in your employees' hands.
- ▶ Content integration is the trouble-spot for all LMS implementations, regardless of the LMS platform.
- ▶ If at all possible, begin your implementation with a pilot for content, so you have an opportunity to troubleshoot situations before they impact the entire employee base.
- ▶ Ensure that you have the right stakeholders in the room — not just your technical team and your HR team. You need all content owners and anyone involved in related Talent Management projects.

Now it's time to see everything we've covered so far at work in real-world situations. Chapter 11 provides two case studies to illustrate how it all can come together.

Case Studies provide insight into the paths other organizations have followed during their Enterprise Learning implementations. Although your exact requirements may not be mirrored in the following case studies, they may provide you with insight as you plan your implementation.

11 Case Studies

Every implementation of Enterprise Learning is different. As we discovered when we explored the Project Management aspect of Enterprise Learning, there are many different considerations that must be made when planning and implementing your project. Following are two case studies which highlight considerations that were made during two implementations. One case study follows an ALE implementation leveraging LSO200 in a regulated environment while the second covers a global implementation of the learning solution. As you read through the case studies, you will notice common threads even though the implementations are vastly different.

11.1 Case Study 1: Implementing a Standalone Learning Solution Using ALE

This case study walks through the execution of a standalone Learning Solution 2.0 implementation that uses Application Link Enabling (ALE) to pass HCM data from the core ERP solution. We will discuss some of the pros and cons and lessons learned using this solution.

11.1.1 Background

This case study focuses on a life sciences company (LSC) that required a Learning Management System (LMS) to manage its regulatory required training, as well as its employee development training. The organization had approximately 4,000 employees and planned to bring the solution live for their 1,000 home office employees initially. The organization had SAP 4.6C for both their financials and their HR master data. Because they had no formal learning organization, LSC requested an outside consulting firm to help them identify the LMS that would best meet their needs.

After looking at four other best-of-breed solutions as well as the SAP Learning Solution, they decided to implement Learning Solution release 1.0 as part of an integrated solution. But after this decision was made, SAP determined that they were not be able to back port the e-Signature functionality, which allows electronic confirmation of Course attendance to the 1.0 solution. Because e-Signature is an important requirement for training in life sciences organizations, the organization decided to implement Learning Solution 2.0 as a standalone solution on release 4.7 (a prerequisite for LSO200) and ALE HR Master Data from the 4.6C core solution to the standalone LSO200 implementation. As the organization began the implementation, LSO200 had not started ramp-up, so LSC decided to become a ramp-up customer.

11.1.2 Implementation Project Planning

Initially, LSC planned on starting its implementation in early January and going live in June. Because they now had to incorporate an ALE scenario into the implementation and because the ramp-up release date of LSO200 was not until early May, they pushed their project to an early August go-live date. The Learning Solution builds on the Training and Events Management solution so LSC decided to complete the bulk of their configuration prior to augmenting Training and Event Management with the Learning Solution 2.0 release by focusing on the TEM configuration.

Because the LSC was to be a ramp-up customer, they were required to have SAP consultants on-site to support their implementation. The implementation team consisted of the following members:

► An LSC Basis support person dedicated full time

► Two LSC ABAP support resources

► A full-time LSC functional support resource

► A team of two LSE part-time SMEs

► A full-time SAP functional HR consultant

► A part-time SAP Platinum HR consultant/project manager

► A part-time SAP Basis consultant

► A full-time change management consultant

- Two part-time education consultants
- A full-time validation consultant
- A part-time LSC Valuation resource

11.1.3 Blueprint

As LSC was one of the first organizations to implement the Learning Solution, no standard Blueprint format existed. The SAP consultants used existing Training and Event Management questions to create an outline for the Blueprint. Because they had access to internal SAP systems and because one of them had been involved in testing the LSO200 release, they were able to develop a complete questionnaire that captured all of the new functionality available with LSO200.

The Blueprint workshops took place over three weeks. Key team members of the HR group and the Quality group participated in the workshops. The SAP consultants were able to demonstrate possible solutions using an internal SAP demo system, because LSC had no "LSO" sandbox — only a "TEM" sandbox. Because the organization had not had a global training catalog in the past, a lot of time was spent determining how the catalog should be structured to best meet administrative and learner needs. Other areas that were given particular attention were reporting needs (particularly regulatory required reports), portal look and feel, and integration, both to the core SAP HR system and to the controlled documents management system, Documentum. Because there were few existing system-based processes to build on, LSC leveraged many of the best practices administrative solutions provided by the Learning Solution.

By the end of the Blueprint workshops, most of the end-user processes had been agreed on; a catalog structure had been identified; master data elements that would be leveraged had been identified; a process to access controlled documents directly from Documentum had been determined; reports had been outlined at a high level; and all other gaps had been identified with documented, high-level solutions. In addition, standard roles had been determined and authorizations had been documented at a high level. By the end of February, the project team was ready to begin implementing Training and Event Management.

11.1.4 Realization

As mentioned earlier, LSC planned to configure the Training and Event Management Solution first and then begin configuration for the LSO in early May, when the add-on solution was available. Phase 1 configuration was completed and unit tested easily by the end of April. The master data conversion plans, using the CATT tool, were also created during this time. In addition, the development team was able to start working on some of the gap solutions because the data structures used by TEM and LSO were very similar. An example of this was the completion of a custom infotype needed to store additional Course data for regulatory reporting. The only issue LSC ran into during Phase 1 configuration was the issue of replicating the Enterprise and Personnel structures. Because the Core HR system was on a 4.6C release and the LSO was on a 4.7 release, SAP would not officially approve a method to automatically move these structures from one system to the other. LSC decided to manually reconfigure their structures, rather than trying to transport them.

SAP delivered the ramp-up release of LSO200 on time and the LSC Basis team began installation. The initial installation and setup had been estimated to take a week, but LSC ran into installation problems. It turned out there was a support package issue related to the operating system, so the install took 12 days. This was the first major issue the implementation encountered.

Phase 2 configuration began in late-May. As LSC and their consultants had hoped, the LSO add-on had slipped seamlessly on top of the initial TEM configuration. All existing configuration was retested and worked as expected. The consultants carefully reviewed each step of the IMG to ensure that no steps were missed as they went back through the configuration, adding in the new functionality provided by the LSO.

At the same time that the configuration was going on, the team began to test the ALE solution. The plan from an ALE perspective was to pass only the master data required to support the LSO system from the core system. There was no plan to pass any data back to the core system, because the LSO system would become the system of record for all training records. The records identified as needing to be ALE'd from the core system were as follows:

- **Person Data**
  - Actions (Infotype 0000)
  - Organizational Assignment (Infotype 0001)
  - Personnel Data (Infotype 0002)

- ▸ Address (Infotype 0006)

- ▸ Communications (Infotype 0105, Subtypes 0001 and 0010)

▸ **Organizational Data**

- ▸ Organizational Units

- ▸ Jobs

- ▸ Positions

- ▸ Tasks

Most of the data previously listed is self-explanatory. LSC needed a record of the employee, including their name and organizational assignment, to ensure that training history was recorded correctly. The administrators used address information to send out orientation and training materials and, of Course, the communications data was needed for the employees to use the Portal and receive email confirmations. The organizational assignment information was used mostly from a reporting perspective. The only unusual item in the previous list is the "Task" object.

During Blueprint, LSC had decided that Qualifications would best help them meet their regulatory required training management needs. Qualifications provide simple reporting that allows a learner and an administrator to determine if someone is out of compliance. They also provide simple expiration functionality to track training certifications that need to be renewed on an annual basis. However, generally qualifications are maintained at the Job or Position level. Because the Job definition was based on compensation data at LSC, and maintaining detailed requirements profiles at the Position level was not a reasonable solution, LSC decided to use the Task object to maintain requirements profiles.

In SAP HR, tasks describe both jobs and positions, so creating a Task profile of qualifications provides one profile that can be linked to many jobs or many positions, as needed. Because LSC had never considered using the task object in this manner before, they were excited about the possibilities it offered in terms of an additional layer of reporting. They decided to maintain the task object in the core HR system. However, during ALE testing, it was determined that tasks could not be transported, most likely because they were once key Workflow objects.

> **Note**
>
> Workflow Tasks are now used to support Workflow. The HR Task has not been recommended by SAP since release 4.0.

In order to maintain tasks in the core HR system, LSC would have to manually create them twice — once in the core HR system and once in the LSO system. SAP was unable to provide them with any other solution.

The final major issue that LSC encountered during Realization had nothing to with the ALE solution; instead, it had to do with the e-Signature functionality. During implementation of the e-Signature solution, LSC discovered that e-Signature validated against the backend R/3 user ID rather than against the corporate LDAP. LSC escalated this issue to SAP as very few of their users knew their backend R/3 user password. Generally, it was a scrambled default password that was never used. LSC did not want to require that their entire employee user base log onto the backend system every 60 days to change their passwords in order to validate Course completion on the Portal. SAP was unable to provide a delivered solution and, instead, provided development support to create a custom solution that allowed the e-Signature functionality to validate against the corporate LDAP as opposed to the backend R/3 user.

The final phases of Realization included System Testing and User Acceptance Testing (UAT). There were over 125 integration tests written and close to as many UATs. Testing was fairly intensive because LSC had to ensure that the system was validated per FDA requirements.

11.1.5 Go-Live Preparation and Go-Live

The last two weeks of the implementation consisted of validating the data loads and loading them via CATT. LSC had explored a few different methods for loading the data and decided to use CATT. Neither the templates provided by SAP's Best Practices solution or by the data mapping program RHALTD00 contained all the LSO elements and because their master data load requirements were minimal, they decided to load training history data and catalog data using CATT. They loaded the qualifications catalog manually and used CATT to create qualifications profiles for all employees that showed only their current certifications.

Although go-live was scheduled for a Monday in early August, LSC turned the solution on the Friday prior to go-live. They were comfortable enough to take the weekend off and the official go-live the following week was fairly painless.

11.1.6 Team Education and Change Management

As part of LSC's agreement with SAP, they were provided customized training on the SAP Learning Solution. The SAP consulting team provided an initial, one-day overview of the entire suite of LSO functionality, using an SAP internal demo system, prior to the Blueprint. The consulting team also developed a custom, two-day workshop that was delivered in the early phases of Realization. This training session covered the solution based on the results of the customer's Blueprint workshop. It allowed the configuration team and the end users to understand the capabilities of the product and it also served to validate the requirements that were gathered during Blueprint. Toward the end of the Realization phase, a team of two education consultants began to create end-user training and documentation. These materials were delivered during end-user training workshops that took place during go-live preparation.

In addition to the team and end-user training that took place during the implementation, change management processes also occurred. Because the stakeholders (Quality and HR) were involved in the LMS purchasing decision making process, there was already administrative user buy-in. In addition, they were active participants in the Blueprint workshops and the training sessions (which also acted as proof-of-concept sessions). LSC did, however, need to involve the rest of their end-user population — their learner user base.

To do this, they performed periodic usability testing with a team of specifically selected end users that included IT personnel, HR personnel, and other local and remote users. This allowed LSC to understand from an educated user and a novice user perspective which elements of the solution were easily understandable and where changes, if at all possible, needed to be made. This feedback helped the development team focused on streamlining the BSP pages.

Additionally, toward the end of the testing phases, the communications team began marketing the solution to all LSC employees. The focus was to excite the users, so they would be eager to switch from paper-based controlled document training to application-based training. Early in the project, the team had branded the solution with an easily recognizable name and used that in all communications to employees. In addition to periodic announcements that included screenshots of the solution, they posted a link on the corporate intranet that showed a demo of the solution, incorporating examples of how to perform common activities on the Learning Portal. This link was later incorporated into the navigation panel of the Learning Portal, at the top, so learners could easily refer to it if they needed a refresher.

Finally, during the week of go-live, the implementation team and the stakeholder team members provided "drop-in" demos for anyone interested in viewing the solution. They had a barista who provided coffee and pastries to all employees during these demos. They also provided "roving" support the first two-weeks, to provide hands-on support to end users who might need it.

11.1.7 The Rest of the Story

Three years after going live with LSO200, LSC upgraded their core SAP system to ECC6.0. Less than one year after the upgrade, they migrated their LSO implementation from a standalone solution to an integrated solution. LSC IT had many discussions about the pros and cons of keeping the systems separate. Some of their concerns are listed below.

▶ **Security:** As a standalone solution, there were fewer security concerns from an administrative and end-user perspective. There was no need to restrict administrators out of the HR data because only infotypes they had view access to were migrated over. Because nothing was ever sent back to the core system, any data changes that were made to organizational objects were inconsequential because they were over-ridden on a nightly basis.

▶ **Validation:** Only the LMS was required to be validated by the FDA. Integrating the LSO with the rest of the systems might cause more oversight to be placed on the core system.

▶ **System Response:** Because the LSO backend was on its own server, it had no impact on the response of the core systems.

▶ **ALE issues:** Any changes made to the Enterprise and Personnel Structures, as well as to the Task catalog, had to be manually replicated in the LSO system. This led to additional testing requirements as well.

▶ **ALE issues:** The administrative team disliked having to wait 24 hours for employee updates.

After weighing these issues, as well as others, LSC decided to integrate the two systems. The entire process took almost eleven months. The project was not just an integration of two existing systems; instead, it was a reimplementation of the solution, including data migration from the LSO200 release to the LSO600 release, reconfiguration of the entire solution, and the addition of new functionality, such as request-based correspondence and new reports. Testing alone took close to four months of the implementation because of the system validation and data validation requirements in a regulated industry.

11.2 Case Study 2: Global Implementation

Implementing a Global Learning Management System is complex and requires a dedicated team. This case study walks through some of the challenges and shares some thoughts about implementing SAP Enterprise Learning globally across the organization citing specific examples from an Implementation.

11.2.1 Background

This case study focuses on a company that required a Learning Management System (LMS) to manage training across many offices around the globe. The organization had several different and competing legacy LMS systems, so they requested an outside consulting firm to help them identify the LMS that would best meet their needs. After looking at four other best-of-breed solutions as well as the SAP Learning Solution, they decided to implement Learning Solution company-wide, using a Global Implementation strategy.

11.2.2 Global Implementation Readiness

As with any other implementation, the first question that should be raised in a global learning implementation project is the readiness of the organization for such a change. Often, the success of the implementation depends on the readiness of the organization.

A Learning Management System implementation is unique because it involves many aspects within an organization. So, analysis of the current state for readiness becomes very important before the implementation. This section explains some of the readiness items that need to be checked off before an implementation.

11.2.3 Learning Systems

The first step is to identify the various Learning Systems that exist in the current organization. Information on the current state of Learning Systems will provide clarity on how best to plan the future state. In the case of this implementation of SAP Enterprise Learning, there were at least three different Learning Management Systems with multiple individual instances deployed in multiple locations across the globe. Some of these learning systems were not built to standards. We analyzed the type of content supported all three learning systems.

> **Note**
>
> Information about the Learning System should include: type of content supported, number of users supported, size of the system, reports provided, etc. This information was helpful in data gathering and planning a phased approach in rolling out the Global Learning System.

Business Processes and Requirements

If different departments of the organization use different Learning Management Systems or even different instances of the same LMS, chances are that these departments follow different business processes for learning. This is critical information when designing a global system, because this will impact the way the new system is configured. In the case of this implementation, some business processes were specific to a location. During design, the team had to identify the best practices, implement the processes globally, and eliminate the processes that were too location-specific to implement across the organization. At the same time, the team had to maintain end-user buy-in. To accomplish this, they continued to educate the stakeholder team members and explain the business drivers behind the implementation.

Apart from eliminating localized processes, there is also a need to harmonize learning requirements from various stakeholder groups in the organization and evaluate these against the LMS functionality during the decision making processes. This harmonization process should focus on developing centralized governance for the organization. It should not only act as a guide for the LMS selection process but again, educate the stakeholder groups about the implementation's objectives, from a global perspective. This process is discussed in more detail in the requirements gathering section.

Interfaces and Dependencies

Apart from identifying business processes, the readiness exercise also includes the identification of dependencies and interfaces for the current learning systems. Learning systems are typically integrated with HR-related systems. It is important to ensure that these interfaces are identified and maintained in the future-state if necessary, or addressed in the new solution and eliminated, if possible. In our project, we compiled a list of the current interfaces and during the requirements and design phases, we performed analysis to determine if there was a need for each interface or it could be met by a different solution. In some cases, there was no need to maintain the interface, or the data stream was replaced by reports.

Technology

Technology is a key aspect in any Learning Implementation. The current state of technology will give a good understanding of where the organization is in terms of its readiness. This includes server infrastructure as well as standard IT desktop configuration policy.

The location of offices and potential users will also need to be analyzed because bandwidth constraints need to be taken into account for content. Gathering this information is critical for the sizing of the system as well.

11.2.4 Planning the Future State

Planning for the future state provides a road map for the implementation. If the future state is well laid out, the design of the system becomes simpler because the goal is clear. Here are some of the areas that need to be looked into when planning for the future state.

Learning Methodology

Learning Methodology depends not only on the type of content but also on the audience. There is also a need to develop an instructional design strategy for the future state. Setting a realistic and tangible goal often helps. In this implementation, the organization decided that they would like to deliver 80% of their content in the form of Web-based Courses in the future as opposed to the current 40%. The goal was arrived at based on the feedback they had received from the end users through various surveys. This goal was tangible and had a timeline of two years from the time the new Learning Management System (SAP Enterprise Learning) was launched. This decision largely influenced the design of the SAP Enterprise Learning implementation for this client.

Learning Standards Adoption

Learning Standards are critical in any implementation involving e-learning content. Adopting standards for the content ensures reusability, predictability, and interoperability. There are currently two Learning Content Standards — AICC and SCORM. There are multiple versions within these standards such as levels within AICC and 1.1, 1.2, and 2004 versions in SCORM. The current widely adopted standard is SCORM 1.2; however, the next version, SCORM 2004, is catching up quickly and the standards world is moving rapidly toward SCORM 2004, SAP Enterprise Learning supports all levels in AICC and also supports 1.2 and 2004 versions of SCORM. The decision point for this organization was to arrive at the standards the content should adhere to in the future state. Our implementation team recommended

SCORM 1.2 for this organization. Some of the key decision points that our implementation team had in recommending this standard are listed below.

▶ Ease of converting the existing content to the recommended standard. In this case, we utilized a tool to convert the existing content to SCORM 1.2.

▶ Complexity of the content. Most of the content available will not utilize the functionality available in SCORM 2004.

Infrastructure Support

Infrastructure support needs to be factored in for the future state. The organization's IT team needs to be consulted for planning this. There are two aspects that need to be defined here: Desktop Configuration and System Landscape.

Desktop Configuration

Desktop Configuration of the end users is critical for the user experience. Apart from the requirements of the Learning Management System, the Course content requirements will drive the end-user configuration. The primary components that need to be taken into account are:

▶ Browser Support

▶ Flash for animations

▶ Multimedia support (Audio and Video)

It is always good to build a diagnostics page within the content or in the LMS. This diagnostics page can run a simple JavaScript-based validation that tests an end user's configuration and displays results. This has been an effective tool in many implementations. The support team often requests the users run this diagnostics page so they can offer solutions. In a global implementation, IT policies generally vary across multiple locations, so a solution of this type becomes very important.

System Landscape

Typically, an implementation will involve multiple environments. In our implementation for SAP Learning Enterprise, the following environments were in place:

▶ Development Environment — Used primarily for development and Unit Testing

▶ Quality Environment — Used primarily for Quality Assurance Testing

▶ UAT Environment — Used during the User Acceptance Testing phase by the client

▶ Production Environment — Live Environment

▶ Disaster Recovery Environment

Each environment had its own instance of Content Player and CMS server for hosting the content. Apart from these environments, because of the locations of the end-users, the organization considered using Content Caching servers. A Content Caching server installed at the end-use location (for instance, an offshore location) may greatly improve the user experience in that location. Content Caching allows feature rich-content to be played without any disruption in locations where the internet connection may not be optimal. However, Content Caching requires an investment from IT. In this implementation, due to the costs associated with Content Caching, the solution arrived at was to use the Offline Player. Because the Offline Player runs content from the local machine, low bandwidth is no longer an issue. The content is downloaded once and played from the local repository. All of the previously mentioned points should be considered when deciding on the future state, because some of these decisions affect content design.

Governance Team

In a Learning Implementation, the ongoing governance team that supports the Learning Management System's activities is critical to the success of the whole project. Ongoing support not only includes technical resources, but also resources related to Learning and Performance. The broad functions of the ongoing team are:

▶ Defining a learning road map for the organization

▶ Providing third-party vendor Management

▶ Conducting organizational development programs

▶ Providing training investment analysis

Additional drivers often come into play as well. In this case, the organization had a vision to have all levels of evaluation (Kirkpatrick's model) implemented. This vision helped in structuring the post implementation support model. Apart from the global committee to oversee the ongoing activities, the team composition included Regional Performance Consultants (one per region). The role of these performance consultants was to design and execute the organizational assessments and program evaluations within the region and provide recommendations to the global committee.

11.2.5 Requirements Gathering

The Requirements Gathering phase is the most important for any implementation. The guidelines for requirements gathering for global implementation are similar to that of any learning implementation. This section highlights some of the key guidelines and processes to consider during a global implementation.

It is important that all process requirements are analyzed to ensure that the requirements have a global fit. During our implementation, the most important guideline the implementation team agreed upon was to keep the processes global. Variations were allowed only when there was a regulatory requirement enforced by the local government. This principle was always kept in mind and it helped to keep the design simple and to keep local variations to less than 10% of the global requirements.

In a global operation environment, the level of access that employees have to a system is always a priority, particularly as you consider the need to keep data private in certain countries. Obviously, the design of roles requires attention in this situation. A business benefit of implementing SAP Enterprise Learning is the robust security functionality to support these requirements. Most other LMS' provide the ability to customize roles and provide security functions. But when the requirements get complex, as in a global implementation, SAP Enterprise Learning has an edge in terms of customizing. In our global implementation, we were able to customize the roles to a large extent and in some cases, even restrict access down to the transaction level. A limitation of this customization, of course, is the maintenance of these roles during the post-implementation phase.

Documenting the requirements plays a vital role if the plan is to use third-party vendors for content services. The most crucial areas to understand from this perspective is the web-based learning content. Large organizations often have a number of vendors who provide content and this organization was no exception. When such an organization decides to implement an LMS, it is important to make the vendors aware of the changes and how the new system will affect their services.

In the case of this implementation, a number of vendors provided content for various departments. The content requirements were different for each vendor as they were tailored to the existing LMS'. When the organization decided to implement SAP Enterprise Learning across the company, the need to harmonize vendor requirements became critical. Some of the activities our implementation team did were:

- ▶ Consolidate a list of third-party vendors who would continue to provide content in the future. One best practice is to limit the number of third-party vendors who provide content. A good method to follow to determine the "best-of-breed" vendors is to evaluate the vendor-provided content by playing the content in SAP Enterprise Learning to identify content readiness.

- Document the system behavior for standards-compliant content. In our case, we had decided to adopt SCORM 1.2 as the standard for all Web-based learning courses.

- Document the characteristics of the Content Player in terms of size of the window, properties of the window, etc.

- Gather sample content from each vendor and provide a test system to test the content behavior. Report issues, so the vendor can fix the content.

These activities during the initial stages of the implementation eliminated many risks that we would have run into at the later stages of the implementation. For example, one of the content vendors did not have SCORM 1.2 compliant content. The vendor converted the existing Courses using a tool. When the sample content was run, there were some custom data elements that were not built to the standards specification. The SAP Authoring tool provides a local player to test the content before publishing the Course on the server. This player has an option to enable logs that will identify errors that occur during the transactions for recording the data. With the help of these logs, these errors were identified and eliminated. Because these errors were identified at an earlier stage, the third-party vendor had enough time to fix the content.

These activities also set expectations for the client in terms of the behavior of the system and the data that can be stored. When the sample Courses were tested, the logs also provided information about the type of transactional data (in terms of content tracking) that can be provided by the vendor Courses.

These activities also set expectations in terms of the behaviors of the system and the data that is stored. This helped the team determine the vendors they would continue to work with post-implementation. When the sample courses were tested, the logs provided information about the type of transactional data (in terms of content tracking) that is provided by the vendor courses. This type of information is useful when determining which vendor to use in the future for a particular type of course. For instance, one vendor may provide more tracking information than another vendor, which may be important for a compliance-related course.

These activities will extend beyond the requirements gathering phase; however, it is important to start these activities in this phase due to the nature of the errors encountered and the time needed to address content issues. Typically, all content errors should be identified and fixed before the end of the development phase.

Reports

Without reports, the success of any implementation cannot be measured. If implemented correctly, reports provide qualitative as well as quantitative data regarding the usage and effectiveness of the Learning Initiatives. SAP Enterprise Learning provides a number of reports pre-packaged that offer a variety of meaningful information. During the requirements gathering phase of our project, the team listed the reports by process. From the process flow, the areas where reports were needed were identified. This can be achieved by looking at the data flow in the process. If a dataflow needs to be tracked, it could potentially lead to a report.

In our project we identified the reporting needs and listed all reports required by the client. We broadly categorized these reports into:

- Standard SAP Report
- Custom SAP Report
- Non-SAP Report

There were some reports that were close to standard reports with some minor variations. In such cases, unless there was a business reason that mandated the change, the decision was to provide the standard reports. For reports that needed to be custom built, the team analyzed the nature of the reports to decide if SAP was the right tool to build the report in. In some cases, such as results of the Level 3 and Level 4 evaluation, the team decided that it was better to use a third-party tool to provide the data. In this case, the decision was made keeping in mind the amount of customization it would take to get the same report out of SAP. A good rule of thumb is to keep custom reports to a minimum because maintenance becomes an issue later with upgrades. Such decisions helped us reduce the time frame of the implementation.

11.2.6 Design

After the requirements are documented and signed off, the design phase begins. The design of a global system should be robust. The design dictates the behavior of the system. A well-designed system undergoes minimal change during the post implementation phase. The design should take into consideration the potential changes that could occur and be flexible enough to accommodate changes without a major redesign. This section discusses the main areas that are specific to a global SAP Enterprise Learning Implementation.

Global vs. Local

As expected in any global implementation, the design of the system should be flexible enough to accommodate any local requirements that may arise during the local design sessions. In our project, we had our global and local requirements documented before the design stage. However, some local requirements did get added at a later stage. This could not be avoided due to various reasons. However, our design was solid, since it could accommodate changes without a major redesign of the system. For instance, one of the global requirements was to let the student add external Course completion results. When we were designing the solution for Europe, France had a government-enforced requirement that required us to make a change to the form where the student entered the external Course completion data. We had utilized a custom-built framework that allows employees to enter data and subsequently had a workflow for approval that was optional. The requirement for France required a change to the approving authority as well. Rather than redesign the form, we extended the functionality of the form to provide a different flow in case the submitting employee was from France. The solid design of our framework enabled us to make this change with relatively little effort.

11.2.7 Catalog Design

The Learning Catalog gives life to any LMS. The success of any implementation depends largely on the design of the catalog because this is the first thing a Learner looks at and the tool an administrator leverages every day. The catalog design affects the way the end-users use the system. One method we adopted to understand how the learners were using their current system and their likes and dislikes was to conduct formal surveys. The feedback we received from these surveys was very useful as we determined how to best structure the catalog. Because SAP Enterprise Learning provides a wide variety of options when it comes to catalog design, there is no one right way to create the catalog. Its structure depends on the needs of the organization.

The SAP Enterprise Learning Catalog is hierarchical in nature. The user has to navigate from the top-level node down to the course level details. It becomes important to ensure the classification of the courses is usable in order to achieve the correct hierarchy. Here are some of the options that we considered during our implementation:

- Functional classification
- Location/Region-based classification

- Language-based classification
- Competency-based classification
- Audience Type–based classification

Each option has its own advantages and limitations. For instance, the Competency-based classification was straightforward when classifying the Courses but became increasingly complex as the number of competencies a Course imparts increased to more than two. The implementation team had multiple discussions and went through multiple catalog iterations before deciding on the final catalog design: a functional classification at the top level with occasional location-based classification (usually the last level of node) in case of any location-specific Courses. As mentioned previously, there is no one correct classification that works for all organizations. Here are some points to be kept in mind when designing the catalog for SAP Enterprise Learning:

- Guiding Principle: It is good to have a guiding principle for the design of the catalog. This will enable the team to remain on focus. In our case, this was derived from our survey results.

- End-User Involvement: Involve end users when designing the catalog. The end users are the ultimate users of the system. Their feedback must be incorporated.

- Phased Rollout: If possible, have a phased rollout of the Courses. In our case, our client went live with about 20% of their entire catalog and added Courses in a phased manner. This approach helped us design the best possible catalog because minor tweaks were possible even after the project went live.

- Navigation Depth: Because the catalog is hierarchical in nature, the end user has to navigate the nodes. This could potentially lead to a usability issue. In our project, we decided to restrict the level of the nodes to three. Any Course should be reached within three levels starting from the top node.

- Relevance of classification: This depends on the organization and the end users. The classification naming must be user friendly. In our case, we used terms in the nodes that were widely used in the client organization. This increased the familiarity factor for the end users.

- Ease of Search: The majority of the users will choose to search for the Course rather than go through the hierarchy. Appropriate keywords will have to be used in the Course title and description to enable search.

11.2.8   Realization

Realization is the phase where the design begins to take a tangible form. The requirements transform into reality and it is the most rewarding phase. In this section, we will highlight some of the activities that helped us in our project.

Data Automation

SAP Enterprise Learning has many data elements and fields stored in a variety of infotypes. These form the backbone of the solution. Based on the requirements and the design, the implementation team determines the infotypes that will be utilized.

In our implementation, there were many legacy courses (more than 50,000) stored in different systems. Even though the use of conversion programs would make the upload process easier, it was difficult to create the data files in a form that conversion programs could read. The team realized that the best way to execute this activity was by automating the whole process. We designed an Excel spreadsheet that the client used to collect data for the courses. We also designed a simple Access database that would take the spreadsheet as the input and create multiple files (one for each infotype). The access database also ensured a basic level of error checking, such as missing required data for an infotype, data violation in terms of number of characters used for an element, etc. This automation served multiple purposes:

▶ The client used a user friendly spreadsheet to input data.

▶ The implementation team created infotype format files in less than one hour (for any number of courses).

▶ The infotype format files were error free due to the error checks that were built in.

It took approximately three weeks to build this database and create the scripts to perform the error checking, but this reduced the conversion effort by about 90%.

Learning Content Automation

As mentioned, the team decided to use SCORM 1.2 compliant content only with the SAP Enterprise Learning implementation. However, the client had legacy content in multiple formats. Some of the content was available in the SCORM 1.2 format but much of it was in other formats (Word, PDF, etc.). SAP Enterprise Learning provides the capability to import these types of files directly. However, for consistency of look and for content tracking and analytics purposes, the team decided to convert these files to SCORM 1.2 format prior to publishing. Rather than convert the client files to .html format and then to SCORM 1.2 format, which would have required enormous effort, we built a tool that will take any file and create a shell SCORM 1.2 course by building a manifest file and the necessary JavaScript files. The node in the manifest file pointed to the client file. So, when the end-user launched the course, it launched the contents files and maintained the SCORM 1.2 tracking. This automation also saved the team a lot of time and work effort.

Translation

Translation is a challenge in any global implementation due to the number of languages that need to be supported for the end users. In our project, we rolled out initially in English and added languages in phases. This reduced the complexity of translation. SAP offers language packs, but as with any implementation, all custom elements need to be translated. Here are some common areas that need to be translated in the system:

▶ Custom infotypes and tables

▶ Custom forms and screen elements

▶ Custom report elements

▶ Notifications

▶ Course Group titles

We created a list of items that need to be translated for the implementation. For the infotypes and tables, the development team wrote a program to extract the data elements in an Excel spreadsheet so they could be sent for translation. A similar program was written to upload these translations. We had two approaches for the translation:

▶ Machine-based translation using translation software

▶ Professional translation using a translation vendor

Our guideline was to use the translation software when the need was to translate just one or two standalone words (such as data elements) and to use the professional translation for items that contained phrases or sentences (such as Notifications). The guideline was based on two factors:

▶ Cost for translating using a vendor is expensive

▶ Machine translation is not accurate for phrases or sentences

We encountered a couple of challenges during the translation phase. Even though the translation was performed by an expert team, there were times when having an internal team member who could read the language in question was important. This was especially important when loading the translations. For example, the standard notifications have system variables with *If...Else* loops. A team member who can read the language and understand the business requirements can ensure that the final notifications are formatted correctly for each scenario. If no such team member is available, ensure you send the text to be translated along with the variables for translation. This will reduce the chance of error.

Other than cost, there are other reasons it is a good practice to include language experts and end-users from the client team during translation. Involving the client language experts before the final translations are complete reduces rework. These users are familiar with terms used within the organization that may translate differently internally, that an outsider would not be aware of. They are also able to catch variations in translations for the same language from different countries (e.g., Canada and France). These team members can work together to find a translation that fits both countries' business needs. It is also a good practice to run a pilot and confirm the approach and the translations from the vendor with a subset of the project translation requirements, before allowing the vendor to translate all of your requirements. This serves as a validation of the vendor's techniques.

11.2.9   End-User Education

A global learning implementation implies change for the organization. Any change should be rolled out with appropriate support and *end-user education*. This section explains some of the experiences that we faced in creating and rolling out our end-user education.

Creating End-User Education

End-user education is often given lower priority during the implementation, even though it is key to the success of an implementation. End-user education reduces resistance to change among users. In a large-scale implementation, it is best to have a separate team that is responsible for creating end-user education materials. There are two types of end-user education Courses that need to be created:

▶ Process-related end-user materials

▶ System-related end-user materials

Process-related materials are system independent and can be created once the design is complete. The system-related materials have a dependency on the system, so these materials cannot be created until the entire system has been created and signed off. This poses an issue because it may delay the creation and rollout of the end-user education program. Here are some steps that our team took to avoid such potential roadblocks.

▶ Engaging the end-user education team from the beginning of the project was one of the keys to the success of the project. This ensured that the end-user education team was aware of the design and helped them in preparing for the content. The end-user education lead worked closely with the core implementation team to determine the scope of work.

▶ Treat end-user education content creation as a mini-project. Create a template for the content that can be reused for consistency and ease creation of content. A good rule is to create the template so that it is easy to swap out images for system-related materials. Even after the User Acceptance phase, there may some changes that will be made to the system. If the content template can handle such changes, it makes life easier for the end-user education team.

Rolling Out End-User Education

The roll-out strategy for the end-user education is equally important when it comes to the success of the project. End-user education content does not always mean Courses. We created support documents in multiple for the user, such as job aids. These were made available from a central location the user has access to. The end-user education team also conducted several sessions for the end users to help them understand the new system. The sessions were conducted about two weeks prior to go-live.

11.2.10 Rules of Thumb

Global learning implementation is similar to any other learning implementation; however, certain aspects of the implementation need more attention. In summary, here are some of the main points:

▶ Organizational readiness

▶ Global requirements for the new system where possible

▶ Consolidation of content and a clear future content strategy and content

▶ Third-party vendor management consolidation

▶ End-user education

▶ Governance team for ongoing improvement and support

11.3 Summary

Case studies provide guidance as to how other organizations have implemented Enterprise Learning in the past. Each of these case studies illustrates an implementation that followed ASAP or a similar project implementation methodology and highlighted the importance of project preparation, SME involvement, and change management throughout the project. These key takeaways, as well as other lessons learned described in these implementation studies should help you begin your Enterprise Learning implementation with an understanding of the variances that can occur in these projects.

Evolution is necessary for any product. A good product evolves as the market needs change. Understanding and adapting to the market needs is the key to the success of any product. The implementation team must be aware of the functionality provided in the different versions in order to have a successful implementation.

12 Functionality Comparison by Version

Functionality in SAP Enterprise Learning has increased and improved significantly since the first release, and the underlying technical architecture has evolved as well. SAP Enterprise Learning has many components such as the Portal and Authoring Environment, which have also improved functionality with every version.

In this chapter, we will provide a detailed overview of the supported technical components and the features available by version. This is important information to keep in mind when making your purchase and implementation decisions.

12.1 System Architecture Compatibility

Table 12.1 is a system compatibility chart for various versions of SAP Learning Solution. Within the table, you will see reference to the keyword ALE, which as a reminder stands for Application Link Enabling. ALE is a middleware tool that enables integration of business processes between SAP systems and between SAP systems and non-SAP systems.

> **Tip: Key Things to Check in System Architecture Compatibility**
>
> If you want to run the SAP Learning Solution 600 or SAP Enterprise Learning, you need ECC 6.0 to keep implementation simple and costs low. You may be running Backend HR 4.6c or Backend HR 4.7. If that is the case, please look at the versions supported and take appropriate decisions. Versions that require connection via ALE are practical solutions; however, you need to consider implementation and migration costs before making a decision.

Product Version of SAP Learning Solution	1.00	2.00	3.00	6.00	6.02	6.04
SAP Backend and NetWeaver						
Backend HR 4.6c	Y	ALE	ALE	ALE	ALE	ALE
Backend HR 4.7 (Extension 1.10)		Add On	ALE	ALE	ALE	ALE
Backend HR 4.7 (Extension 2.00)		Add On	ALE	ALE	ALE	ALE
ECC 5.0			Y	ALE	ALE	ALE
ECC 6.0				Y	Y	Y
SAP NetWeaver 04			Y			
SAP NetWeaver 04s				Y	Y	Y
Enterprise Portal 5.0	Y	Y				
Enterprise Portal 6.0		Y	Y	Y		
Enterprise Portal 7.0			Y	Y	Y	Y
Web Browser Support						
Internet Explorer 5.X	Y	Y				
Internet Explorer 6.0		Y	Y	Y	Y	Y
Internet Explorer 7.0					Y	Y
Firefox				Y	Y	Y
WebAs and J2EE						
WebAs 6.20	Y	Y				
WebAs 6.40			Y			
WebAs 7.00				Y	Y	Y
J2EE 6.20	Y	Y				
J2EE 6.30		Y	Y			
J2EE 6.40			Y			
J2EE 7.00				Y	Y	Y
BW and Security						
SAP BW Content for Learning Solution		Y	Y	Y	Y	Y

Table 12.1 System Architecture Compatibility

Product Version of SAP Learning Solution	1.00	2.00	3.00	6.00	6.02	6.04
TREX 6.0		Y				
TREX 6.1			Y			
TREX 7.0				Y	Y	Y
HTTPS support				Y	Y	Y

Table 12.1 System Architecture Compatibility (Cont.)

Note

In Table 12.1, and in all tables in this chapter, Y indicates that the product version is compatible. A blank indicates that the combination is not applicable.

12.1.1 Portal Functionality Comparison

Portal Functionality is critical for learners and administrators. Table 12.2 compares the functionality in the various versions.

There are two key things to check in your portal functionality comparison.

1. If you have a large number of training administrators in one location or a distributed set of training administrators working from multiple locations, the Training Administrator Portal is a key feature that will help. Using the Training Administrator Portal will significantly simplify training administration. This feature was released in SAP Enterprise Learning 6.04 or enhancement pack 4.

2. If you have a large number of instructors in your organization and if they are spending a lot of time on administrative activities, the Instructor Portal will be a critical tool for you. This was released as part of SAP Enterprise Learning 6.02 or enhancement pack 2.

Product Version of SAP Learning Solution	1.00	2.00	3.00	6.00	6.02	6.04
Learning Portal						
Participant Self-Booking for instructor-led Courses	Y	Y	Y	Y	Y	Y
Participant Self-Booking for Web-based Courses	Y	Y	Y	Y	Y	Y
Process to notify learners about newer versions of content					Y	Y	Y
Process to update to the newer version					Y	Y	Y

Table 12.2 Portal Functionality

Product Version of SAP Learning Solution	1.00	2.00	3.00	6.00	6.02	6.04
Filter catalog by authorization profiles	Y	Y	Y	Y	Y	Y
Apply user preference to the order of search results		Y	Y	Y	Y	Y
Asynchronous collaboration		Y	Y	Y	Y	Y
Synchronous collaboration		Y	Y	Y	Y	Y
Third-party integration via Web services		Y	Y	Y	Y	Y
Third-party integration via Web services based on XI			Y	Y	Y	Y
Ability to move between different language views	Y	Y	Y	Y	Y	Y
Qualification Profile activated by the learner	Y	Y	Y	Y	Y	Y
Course Appraisal by the learner		Y	Y	Y	Y	Y
Learner Preferred Learning Strategy	Y	Y	Y	Y	Y	Y
Offline learning and synchronization of learning progress		Y	Y	Y	Y	Y
Access Virtual Learning Room Courses					Y	Y
Training Administrator Portal						Y
▶ Schedule Courses and manage participation						Y
▶ Monitor resources and capacities						
▶ Manage correspondences						
▶ Follow-up Courses						
▶ Manage mandatory Courses						
Instructor Portal						
View Course catalog					Y	Y
View Courses assigned to the instructor					Y	Y
View details of Courses assigned to the instructor					Y	Y
Manage Course participation					Y	Y
Perform Course follow-up					Y	Y
Access virtual learning rooms					Y	Y
Manage virtual learning rooms					Y	Y
Run Instructor Portal with SAP NetWeaver Business Client					Y	Y

Table 12.2 Portal Functionality (Cont.)

12.1.2 Training Management Functionality Comparison

Now let's look at Table 12.3, which lists the Training Management Functionality availability by version.

Tip: Training Management Functionality to Check For

You may be in the process of turning most of your classroom training into Web-based Courses or Virtual Learning Room Courses. If that is the case, watch for the versions that support the Virtual Learning Room delivery method. The cost reduction achieved by conducting a few of your Courses in Virtual Learning Rooms may be more than the cost of upgrade or cost of license.

If you have a lot of content that is compliant with SCORM 1.2, SCORM 2004 or AICC standards, pay attention to the particular versions that support AICC, SCORM 1.2, or SCORM 2004 content. The cost of upgrading to these versions may reduce your content conversion costs.

Product Version of SAP Learning Solution	1.00	2.00	3.00	6.00	6.02	6.04
Training Management						
Update learner profile based on Course completion	Y	Y	Y	Y	Y	Y
Impart qualifications	Y	Y	Y	Y	Y	Y
Input individual development needs	Y	Y	Y	Y	Y	Y
Post Course catalog and schedule on Web	Y	Y	Y	Y	Y	Y
Create and maintain individual Course syllabi	Y	Y	Y	Y	Y	Y
Automatically identify learning Courses and proposed schedule based on development plan		Y	Y	Y	Y	Y
Generate and publish Course enrollment wait list and cancellation	Y	Y	Y	Y	Y	Y
Automatic correspondence when business processes are carried out	Y	Y	Y	Y	Y	Y
Automatic correspondence based on Adobe Forms, Short Message Service, Worklist-based					Y	Y
Notify training coordinator of Courses that do not have minimum number of attendees enrolled	Y	Y	Y	Y	Y	Y
Assign instructors and resources, if necessary	Y	Y	Y	Y	Y	Y

Table 12.3 Training Management Functionality Availability by Version

Product Version of SAP Learning Solution	1.00	2.00	3.00	6.00	6.02	6.04
Assigning tutors to Course Types of any delivery method						Y
Collect and store evaluation information by Course	Y	Y	Y	Y	Y	Y
Ability to return to beginning of module if learner does not meet "Pass rate"	Y	Y	Y	Y	Y	Y
Ability to create a Curriculum of specific Courses	Y	Y	Y	Y	Y	Y
Create Course Programs					Y	Y
Integration with PD Qualifications catalogue	Y	Y	Y	Y	Y	Y
Ability to push Course out to Organizational Units		Y	Y	Y	Y	Y
Ability to push Course out to Jobs	Y	Y	Y	Y	Y	Y
Ability to push Course out to Positions	Y	Y	Y	Y	Y	Y
Ability to push Course out to Persons	Y	Y	Y	Y	Y	Y
Creation of Course appraisals		Y	Y	Y	Y	Y
Ability to push Courses out based on development plan		Y	Y	Y	Y	Y
Ability to push Courses out based on company-specific rules		Y	Y	Y	Y	Y
Delivery method for taking a WBT in a classroom				Y	Y	Y
Create Course Types with delivery method as Virtual Learning Rooms					Y	Y
Set access time restrictions to Virtual Learning Rooms					Y	Y
Offline Course distribution						Y
Support for Concurrent Employment and Global Employment						Y
Rapid Content Publishing from Portal						Y

Table 12.3 Training Management Functionality Availability by Version (Cont.)

12.1.3 Authoring Functionality Comparison

Table 12.4 lists the features available in the Authoring Environment and the Content Management System by version.

Product Version of SAP Learning Solution	1.00	2.00	3.00	6.00	6.02	6.04
Authoring Environment	Y	Y	Y	Y	Y	Y
Build pre- and post-assessments	Y	Y	Y	Y	Y	Y
Test out of an entire Course or specific modules	Y	Y	Y	Y	Y	Y
Use of third-party Course Development Tools	Y	Y	Y	Y	Y	Y
Import third-party Course content	Y	Y	Y	Y	Y	Y
Repository Explorer	Y	Y	Y	Y	Y	Y
Template Manager	Y	Y	Y	Y	Y	Y
Learning Objectives Manager	Y	Y	Y	Y	Y	Y
Randomization of questions		Y	Y	Y	Y	Y
Dynamic question selection		Y	Y	Y	Y	Y
Rich text editing and use of HTML tags for test					Y	Y
Optional Learning Objectives in a test		Y	Y	Y	Y	Y
Wizards to configure Wizard and import content			Y	Y	Y	Y
Learning strategy preview			Y	Y	Y	Y
Meta-data maintenance and search				Y	Y	Y
Process for managing outdated content				Y	Y	Y
Batch import				Y	Y	Y
Import as new version of existing content				Y	Y	Y
Option for learners to accept new content				Y	Y	Y

Table 12.4 Comparison of Authoring Features

12.1.4 Content Management System Functionality Comparison

All versions of SAP Learning Solution and SAP Enterprise Learning support a Content Management System. If you are using or planning of using Web-based Courses, content management functionality is critical (see Table 12.5).

Product Version of SAP Learning Solution	1.00	2.00	3.00	6.00	6.02	6.04
Store Courses in a central information repository	Y	Y	Y	Y	Y	Y
Changes to online Courseware updated in the Authoring Environment automatically	Y	Y	Y	Y	Y	Y

Table 12.5 Content Management System Functionality Comparison

12.2 Workflow, Courseware, and Reporting Functionality Comparison

Table 12.6 lists the workflow, Courseware, and reporting functionality.

Product Version of SAP Learning Solution	1.00	2.00	3.00	6.00	6.02	6.04
Workflow						
Approval and rejection of classroom Course booking		Y	Y	Y	Y	Y
Approval and rejection of classroom Course cancellation		Y	Y	Y	Y	Y
Approval and rejection of Web-based Course booking		Y	Y	Y	Y	Y
Approval and rejection of Web-based Course cancellation		Y	Y	Y	Y	Y
Courseware						
Integration link to static content		Y	Y	Y	Y	Y
Launch content hosted in another LMS		Y	Y	Y	Y	Y
Launch and track content hosted in another LMS			Y	Y	Y	Y
Reporting						
Ability to report on participation and time spent in Course	Y	Y	Y	Y	Y	Y
Ability to report on training costs by employee	Y	Y	Y	Y	Y	Y
Ability to report on training charged to projects	Y	Y	Y	Y	Y	Y
Ability to track learner progress for all online Courses	Y	Y	Y	Y	Y	Y
Track pre- and post-assessments results	Y	Y	Y	Y	Y	Y
Ability to report on SCORM 2004 and AICC Courses					Y	Y
Integration with Business Warehouse 3.2		Y	Y	Y	Y	Y
Reporting for managers		Y	Y	Y	Y	Y

Table 12.6 Workflow, Courseware, and Reporting Functionality

12.2.1 Support for External Learners

External learners, as we learned earlier, are people who are not employees of the company but are critical to the success of the company.

In many industries and companies, it is essential to train people who are not employees of the organization. For example, a car manufacturer may want to train its dealers or a computer chip manufacturer may want to train its channel partners on how to sell its products. There are several options within the SAP Learning Solution for training those outside of your organization, as shown in Table 12.7.

Product Version of SAP Learning Solution	1.00	2.00	3.00	6.00	6.02	6.04
Integration to Sales and Distribution module for billing		Y	Y	Y	Y	Y
Charge training fee to credit cards		Y	Y	Y	Y	Y
Access to Learning Portal for external learners		Y	Y	Y	Y	Y

Table 12.7 External Learner Support Offerings

12.3 Standards and Compliance

If you have a lot of e-learning Course content that is compliant with SCORM 1.2, SCORM 2004, or AICC standards, pay attention to the particular versions that support AICC, SCORM 1.2, or SCORM 2004 content. The cost of upgrading to these versions may reduce your content conversion costs.

Table 12.8 lists the standards compliance by version.

Product Version of SAP Learning Solution	1.00	2.00	3.00	6.00	6.02	6.04
Courseware						
AICC 4.0					Y	Y
SCORM 1.1	Y	Y	Y	Y	Y	Y
SCORM 1.2	Y	Y	Y	Y	Y	Y
SCORM 2004					Y	Y
LMS-RTE2	Y	Y	Y	Y	Y	Y
FDA (CFR Part 11)		Y	Y	Y	Y	Y

Table 12.8 Standards and Compliance

12.4 Virtual Learning Room

This section details the versions that support the integrated Virtual Learning Room powered by Adobe Connect.

The Virtual Learning Rooms powered by Adobe Connect are available as part of SAP Enterprise Learning for SAP Learning Solution 600 customers who own deployed enhancement pack 2. Customers who won SAP Learning Solution 600 have to buy a separate license to use this feature. It is not available as part of the standard maintenance (Table 12.9).

Virtual Learning Rooms Can Reduce Training Costs Significantly

If you are planning to save training delivery costs by moving some of your classroom Courses to a Virtual Classroom, or if you are considering expanding your training programs to other countries or regions using Virtual Learning Rooms, you need SAP Enterprise Learning 6.04.

Product Version of SAP Learning Solution	1.00	2.00	3.00	6.00	6.02	6.04
Virtual Learning Room						
Built-in Virtual Learning Rooms powered by Adobe Connect					Y	Y
Course Types with delivery method "Virtual Learning Rooms"					Y	Y
Set access time restrictions to enter virtual learning rooms					Y	Y
Access virtual learning rooms from the Instructor Portal					Y	Y
Manage virtual learning rooms					Y	Y
Participate in Courses conducted in Virtual Learning Rooms					Y	Y

Table 12.9 Virtual Learning Room

12.5 Integration

SAP Enterprise Learning and SAP Learning Solution are integrated with external content providers and hosted assessment providers.

It is important to pay attention to integration support for various reasons. First, you need to consider whether you have advanced assessments creation and delivery needs in your company or not. If you do, you may already be using Questionmark Perception in your company to deliver assessments. If this is the case, make sure you the version, or upgrade to the version, that supports the integration with Questionmark Perception.

Second, if you are already using content from SkillSoft or plan to buy e-learning Courses from SkillSoft, make sure that you select or upgrade to the version that supports SkillSoft integration.

Finally, if you own SAP ERP HCM Employee Performance Management software and want to empower your appraisers to assign mandatory Courses directly to employees, pay attention to enhancement pack 4 or SAP Enterprise Learning 6.04. See Table 12.10 for an over of integration with external products by version.

Product Version of SAP Learning Solution	1.00	2.00	3.00	6.00	6.02	6.04
Integration with SAP Performance Management						Y
Questionmark Perception Integration			Y	Y	Y	Y
Integration with hosted SkillSoft content				Y	Y	Y

Table 12.10   Integration with Other Systems

12.6   Learning Services for Managers

Empowering your managers to drive training adoption is critical to the success of your training program, because your managers play a key role in the adoption of training by your employees. SAP Enterprise Learning 6.04 has significant features that empower managers to drive training adoption. Pay attention to the features and deploy this version if training adoption is a key issue for you (see Table 12.11).

Product Version of SAP Learning Solution	1.00	2.00	3.00	6.00	6.02	6.04
View training history of learners				Y	Y	Y
Assign mandatory Courses to learners						Y
Book learners in a Course						Y
Assign mandatory Courses to Jobs, Positions, and Org units						Y

Table 12.11   Learning Services for Managers

12.7 Summary

Choosing the correct version is critical for any implementation. Knowledge of the functionality provided in the versions of the system is also key to the decision making process. In this chapter, we discussed the functionality available in the different versions of SAP Learning Solution and SAP Enterprise Learning. These are very important to understand and consider when planning your training implementations or upgrades, so you can get the best possible return on your investment.

12.8 Conclusion

This chapter also concludes the book. We hope that this book gave you a good overview of SAP Learning Solution and SAP Enterprise Learning and prepared you for your Learning Management System decisions and implementations.

As you can see from the case studies, a successful implementation depends not just on the Learning Management System technology but also on the preparation, planning, and maturity of the organization. It is always good to start small, have a clear goal, keep processes simple, and create solutions before scaling the solution for the entire organization.

It is also important to employ or hire the services of experienced SAP Enterprise Learning implementation consultants either from SAP or from one of the several partners who implement SAP Enterprise Learning.

The Authors

Sharon Wolf Newton is principal and CEO of hyperCision Inc. She has over 12 years experience in the management and implementation of SAP HCM solutions, particularly SAP Enterprise Learning and the SAP Learning Solution. She has worked with over seventy customers, including twenty-five Fortune 500 and Global 500 organizations, both from an implementation and a support standpoint, and has supported more than 20 clients in their SAP Enterprise Learning implementations. Ms. Newton was a Platinum Consultant at SAP America for 10 years.

Prashanth Padmanabhan is the topic lead and Product Manager for SAP Enterprise Learning. He is responsible for the product strategy and roadmap of SAP Enterprise Learning, and has over 15 years of experience in the training industry in the areas of content development, learning management system design, and implementation and management of on-demand learning platforms.

Shankar Bharathan is the product manager for SAP Enterprise Learning. He has over 8 years of experience in the HCM domain. Before joining SAP, Shankar worked for Ramco Systems Ltd., an India-based ERP vendor.

 **Christian Hochwarth** has been the development project manager for SAP Enterprise Learning since 2004. He is responsible for the overall design, development and delivery of SAP Enterprise Learning, and is also the leader of the global SAP Enterprise Learning development team. Christian holds an US patent for the design of SAP Learning Solution.

 **Manoj Parthasarathy** is a Senior Manager responsible for Learning and Performance Implementations at Convergys Corporation. Manoj has over 10 years of experience in the Learning Industry specializing in the areas of Learning Management Systems implementation and content design and development. He has successfully implemented a wide variety of Learning Management Systems including SAP enterprise Learning for various customers.

Index

A

Activity Allocation, 158
ABAP Resource, 292
ABAP support resources, 304
Action Infotype, 75
Actions (Infotype 0000), 306
Active List Viewer (ALV), 175
Activity Allocation, 158
ADDIE model, 222
Address (Infotype 0006), 307
Administrator Portal, 209, 223
Adobe Connect, 68, 287, 336
Adobe Connect database, 210
Adobe Connect Professional, 28, 206
Adobe Connect servers, 216
Advanced Distributed Learning (ADL), 237
AICC, 227, 229, 313, 331, 335
AICC-based solution, 290
AICC-compliant format, 237
ALE (Application Link Enabling), 303, 327
A learning management system, 25
ALE HR Master Data, 304
ALE issues, 310
ALE testing, 307
Application Link Enabling, 327
Approval Workflow, 148
Articulate, 300
Asset Safety and Compliance, 32
Attendee Types, 143
Attract And Acquire, 31
Authoring Environment, 58, 66, 111, 300, 332
Authoring Environment (AE), 219
Authoring Environment (LSOAE), 59
Aviation Industry CBT Committee (AICC), 105

B

Backend HR 4.6c, 327
Backend HR 4.7, 327

BAdI, 149
  Change Output Control Options, 150
  Determine Sender, 150
  Specify Access to Communication Data, 149
  Specify Correspondence Control Options, 149
Basis Resource, 293
BI Resource, 292
blended learning, 163
Blueprint, 291, 294, 307
blueprinting, 291
Blueprint workshop, 309
Blueprint workshops, 305
Booking, 143
Book List, 80
Book Marking, 111
Browser Support, 314
BSP, 106
BSP Resource, 292
Budget Management, 157
Business Add-In, 107
Business Intelligence, 29, 179
Business Package, 63
Business Server Pages (BSP), 106, 273
business stakeholders, 288
Business/Systems Analyst, 292
BWI Reports, 182

C

Cancellation Reasons, 271
Cancel participation, 46
Capacity Monitor, 192
Catalog Design, 319
Catalog settings, 103
CATs, 306, 308
Central Repository, 233
Certifications, 96
Change Management, 299, 302, 308
Change Management Lead, 291
Classroom Training, 127

Collaboration, 156
Collaboration Features
    Application Sharing, 210
    Chat, 210
    Polls, 210
    Questions and Answers, 211
    Video or Image of Speakers, 211
Collaboration Functions, 269
Collaboration Rooms, 131, 160
Communications Infotype, 76, 108
Communications (Infotype 0105, Subtypes 0001 and 0010), 307
Compensation Management, 157
Concurrent users, 69
Conducting the Course, 114
Configuring Structural Authorizations, 278
Confirm participation, 46
Content administrators, 58
Content Architect, 221
content author, 56
Content/Instructional Design Resource, 292
Content Management, 298
Content Management System (CMS), 57, 66, 68, 223, 332
Content packages, 57
Content Player, 59, 64, 69, 106, 111, 228, 232, 247, 277
Content versioning, 233
Copy-Writer, 221
Correspondence, 148
Correspondence BAdIs, 271
Correspondence Work List, 193
Cost Accounting, 29, 73
Course author, 51
Course Catalog, 46, 98, 101
    Course Groups, 122
    Courses, 125
    Course Types, 125
    Delivery Method, 126
Course Completion Specification Infotype, 131
Course Details, 52
Course Follow-Up, 52, 114
Course Offering phase, 131
Course Preparation, 113
Course Program, 170, 172
Courses schedules, 59

Course Type, 90, 161
Course Type Attributes, 129
Course Type Content Infotype, 131
Course Types, 59
    Course Program, 128
    Curriculum Type, 128
Course Work List, 191
Create Course Schedule, 195
Curriculum, 172
Curriculum Types, 161, 172

D

Data Automation, 321
DataSources, 182
Day-to-Day Activities, 142
Delivery method, 102
Deployment Option, 69
Depreciation Meters, 85
Depth, 280
Design, 318
Desktop Configuration, 314
Development Plan Groups, 90
Development Plans, 90, 196
Documentum, 305
Dynamic Course Menu, 132
Dynamic Menu Enhancements, 267
Dynamic Participation Menu, 132
Dynamic Planning Menu, 126
Dynamic Reporting Menu, 268

E

Educate and Develop, 30
Education Consultant, 292
e-learning, 105, 126
e-Learning content, 105
e-learning course content, 335
Electronic signature, 46
End-To-End Business Process, 32
End-User Education, 323
Enhancement Pack 2 [2007], 33, 329
Enhancement Pack 4 [2008], 33, 223, 225, 329, 337

Enhancement Package Strategy, 32
Enterprise Extension EA-HR, 135
Enterprise Learning, 59
Enterprise Learning Request-Based
Correspondence, 149
Enterprise Portal, 68
Enterprise Structure, 76
E-Recruiting, 59
e-Signature functionality, 308
Evaluation Path, 280
Exchange Infrastructure (XI), 237, 255
Expert Mode Detailed Maintenance, 78
Extended Search, 102
External Course Catalog Connection Infotype
(IT5042.), 138
External Delivery Methods, 220
External Learners, 335
External Persons (object type H.), 276

F

Facilities management, 51
Federation for Learning-Education-Training-
Systems-Interoperability (LETSI), 237
Fee Handling, 270
Flash for animations, 314
Functional Requirements Matrix (FRM), 296
Function Module, 280

G

GET_LEARNER, 108
Global Implementation, 310
Global vs. Local, 319
Go-Live, 301, 308
Governance Team, 315

H

HR InfoSet Query, 183
HTTP, 60
HTTP AICC Communication Protocol (HACP),
255

Human Capital Management (HCM), 26

I

Independent Authoring, 225
Individual Development Plans, 90, 197
Infocubes, 182
InfoSets, 184
Infotype, 74
Infrastructure Support, 314
Institute of Electrical and Electronic Engineers
(IEEE), 238
Instructional Designer, 221, 224
Instructional Element, 226
Instructional Management Systems Project
(IMS), 238
Instructor, 63
Instructor Portal, 45, 51, 59, 112, 207, 329
Integrated Authoring, 225, 227
Interfaces and Dependencies, 312
Item Groups, 230, 232
iView, 61

J

J2EE, 106
JavaScript, 111

K

Keyword Search, 102
Kirkpatrick's Four Levels of Evaluation, 153
Kirkpatrick's model, 315
Kirkpatrick Level Three Evaluation, 188
Knowledge Categories, 227
knowledge tags, 232
Knowledge Types, 229

L

Learner enrollments, 59
Learner Portal, 59, 61, 64, 255

Learning Content Automation, 321
Learning Management System (LMS), 219, 303
Learning Methodology, 313
Learning Net, 226, 229, 232, 240
Learning Nets (Content), 254
Learning Objectives, 232, 254, 277
Learning Objects, 226, 232, 254
Learning Paths, 129
Learning Portal, 45, 89, 95, 102, 106, 206, 273, 290
Learning Portal, 111
Learning Portal View, 273
Learning Solution 2.0, 304
Learning Solution Content Player, 222
Learning Solution Course Catalog, 260
Learning Standards, 313
Learning Strategies, 227
LMS, 25
Local Repository, 232
LSO, 306
LSO200, 306, 310
LSOAE, 66
LSOCP, 64
LSOFE, 61, 106
LSO Functional Consultant, 292
LSO_LEARNER, 108
LSO_PRICES, 270

M

Macro-strategy, 228
Maintenance Flag, 280
Manage Mandatory Assignments, 116
Manage Participation, 114
Manager Self-Service (MSS), 93, 95
Manager Self-Service Portal, 55, 115
Manage Virtual Learning Room, 113
Mandatory courses, 46, 97
manifest file, 240
Master Data, 138
Materials Management (MM), 29, 51, 74, 157
Media Development Specialist, 221
Messages and Notes, 89, 99, 106
Micro-strategy, 228
Multimedia support, 314

Multiple Sequencing with API Content Example (MSCE), 118
My Favorites, 103
My Learning Account, 102
My Training Activities, 100, 104

N

NetWeaver Portal, 287
Notifications, 46

O

Object ID, 280
Object Type, 280
Offline Content Player, 45, 47
Offline learning, 105
Offline Player, 59, 66, 118
Offline Player (LSOOP), 65
OM, 74
Online Content Player, 45
Online Publishing Tool, 234
Online test, 46, 111, 220
OOQA, 83
Organizational Assignment Infotype, 75
Organizational Assignment (Infotype 0001), 306
Organizational Data, 307
    Jobs, 307
    Organizational Units, 307
    Positions, 307
    Tasks, 307
Organizational Management (OM), 28 59, 73, 287
Organizational object
    cost center, 78
    jobs, 78
    organizational unit, 78
    positions, 78
Organizational object
    units, 78
Organizational Structure, 76, 77
Organizational Unit, 79, 157
Organization and Staffing Interface, 78

P

PA, 74
Participation, 52
Pay For Performance, 30
Payroll, 29, 59
PD, 74
Performance Management (PM), 90, 200
Period, 280
PERNR, 276
Person, 108
Personal Data Infotype, 76
Personal development, 59
Personalizing Work Lists, 193
Personnel Administration, 28, 59, 73, 287
Personnel Data (Infotype 0002), 306
Personnel Development, 28, 73, 83, 287
Personnel Planning, 83
Planning, 131
Plan Version, 280
Portal Functionality, 329
Portal Resource, 292
Pre-book, 46
Preferred Learning Strategy, 103
Prerequisite, 102
Pretest, 232
Proficiency Scale, 84
Profile, 280
Profile match-up, 46
Project Manager - Business, 291
Project Manager - Technical, 291
project sponsor, 288
Project Timeline, 293
Proof of Concept, 301
Publish Course Content, 58

Q

Qualification gaps, 96
Qualification profile, 95
Qualifications, 46, 83, 95, 254, 307
Qualifications Catalog, 83, 86
Qualifications Groups, 83
Questionmark Perception, 257
Questionmark Perception, 337
Questionmark₍ Perception₍ Assessments, 261

R

Rapid Content Publishing (RCP), 232
Rapid Content Publishing (RCP), 234
Rapid Content Publishing Tool, 219
Rapid Prototyping, 222
Rapid Publishing, 225
Realization, 298, 321
Realization phase, 309
Regulatory Required training, 303
Relationships, 227
Reporting, 268
Reports, 318
    Custom, 318
    Non-SAP, 318
    Standard, 318
Repository Explorer, 45, 232, 236
Repository Explorer, 233
Request-Based Correspondence (RBC), 271
Requirements Gathering, 315
Requirements Profile, 87
Resource Management, 270
RFC, 60
roll-out strategy, 324

S

Sales and Distribution, 29, 73
SAP 4.6C, 303
SAP Accelerated Methodology (ASAP), 287
SAP Ad Hoc Query, 183
SAP Appointment Calendar, 74
SAP Authoring tool, 317
SAP Business Suite, 31
SAP Customer Relationship Management (CRM), 31
SAP Enterprise Learning 6.02, 329
SAP Enterprise Learning 6.04, 336, 329, 337
SAP Enterprise Portal, 63
SAP ERP (Enterprise Resource Planning), 31
SAP ERP Financials, 79
SAP ERP HCM, 71
SAP Exchange Infrastructure (SAP XI), 256
SAP_HR_LSO_INSTRUCTOR, 63
SAP Knowledge Warehouse, 74
SAP Learning Solution, 28

SAP Learning Solution 600, 327, 336
SAP NetWeaver, 68
SAP NetWeaver Enterprise Portal, 160
SAP Product Lifecycle Management (PLM), 31
SAP Sales and Distribution, 158
SAPScript-based notifications, 149
SAP Supplier Relationship Management (SRM), 31
SAP Supply Chain Management (SCM), 31
SAP Training and Event Management, 119
SCORM, 227, 229, 313
SCORM 1.1, 238
SCORM 1.2, 111, 238, 331, 335
SCORM 2004, 111, 219, 237, 227, 238, 313, 314, 331, 335
SCORM/AICC-compliant content, 223
SCORM API, 111
SCORM compliance, 300
SCORM compliant, 298
SCORM-compliant content, 237
SCORM Course Delivery, 237
SCORM Data Elements, 239
SCORM Navigation Strategies, 118
SCORM Tests, 242
Search Options, 103
Section, 230
Security, 310
Security Resource, 292
Sequence Number, 280
Settings, 103
Sharable Content Object Reference Model (SCORM), 108
Sharable Content Object (SCO), 108
Shareable Content Object Reference Model (SCORM), 105
Shareable Content Object. (SCO), 226
SkillSoft, 257, 337
Status Vector, 280
Stopmark customizations, 193
Structural Authorizations, 267, 278
Subject area, 102
Subject Matter Expert (SME), 51, 221, 224, 292
Succession Planning, 31
Sun Java Plug-In 1.4.2, 111
synchronous events, 205

System Landscape, 314
System Response, 310

T

Talent Management, 44, 198, 287
Target group, 102
Task object, 307
Team Education, 308
TEM, 306
Test Editor, 229
Tests, 230, 254
Time Management, 28, 59, 73, 156
Top 10 Courses, 107
Training Activities, 99
Training Administrator, 52, 209
Training Administrator Portal, 45, 189, 287, 329
Training Administrators, 233
Training and Event Management (HR-TEM), 27, 34, 304, 305, 306
Training history, 46, 59
Training Home, 98
Training Management, 119, 267, 287
Translation, 322
TREX, 68
TREX 6.0, 329
TREX 6.1, 329
TREX 7.0, 329
TREX configuration, 236

U

Usability Analyst, 292
User Acceptance Testing (UAT), 301, 308
User Groups, 186
User ID, 276

V

Validation, 310
Validity Periods, 85

Version Control Options Infotype (IT5049), 146
Versioning, 145
Virtual Classrooms, 138
Virtual Learning Room, 28, 52, 60, 68, 113, 156, 196, 203, 330, 331, 336
Visual Designer, 221

W

WBT, 332
Web Application Server, 106
Web AS, 61
Web-based courses, 57
Web-based courses, 331

Web-Based Learning, 105
Web-Based Training, 129, 220
WebDAV, 68
WebDynpro Resource, 292
Wizards, 225, 240
Work Centers, 190
Workflow, 287, 291
Workflow objects, 307
Workflow Resource, 293

X

XI Resource, 292
XI services, 138

Completely updated and revised edition of complete guide to SAP ERP HCM

Explains how to meet your business needs using HCM

Covers all core areas from recruiting personnel to transferring HR data to accounting

Up to date for ERP 6.0

Sven Ringling, Jörg Edinger, Janet McClurg

Mastering HR Management with SAP ERP HCM

This new updated and enhanced edition of the definitive guide to SAP ERP HCM, is written to teach HR managers, functional users, project managers, and others working with HCM about how to use and customize it throughout the entire HR process. From recruiting personnel to transferring HR data to accounting are all covered based on the current release SAP ERP 6.0. This is the one resource the HR team needs to get the most out of their HCM implementation.

664 pp., 2. edition 2009, 69,95 Euro / US$ 69.95
ISBN 978-1-59229-278-3

>> www.sap-press.de/2065

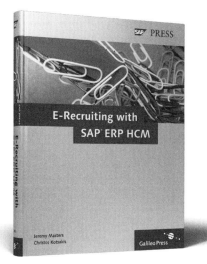

Provides a complete guide to the functionality of E-Recruiting

Teaches how to configure and use E-Recruiting with other HCM components

Uses a real-world workflow approach

Jeremy Masters, Christos Kotsakis

E-Recruiting with SAP ERP HCM

This book provides a practical guide to configuring and using SAP E-Recruitment effectively in the real-world. It is written to teach SAP ERP HCM users and the implementation team what the E-Recruiting tool is so that they can use it effectively in their recruitment process and integrate it easily with other HCM components. Beginning with an overview, the book progresses through the configuration process from a real workflow perspective. And all of the processes are covered in the order in which they are used in a real recruiting project. The book also details how to integrate E-Recruiting with other SAP components, and, as applicable, examples of companies using E-Recruiting successfully will be integrated throughout.

approx. 320 pp., 69,90 Euro / US$ 69.95, ISBN 978-1-59229-243-1, Dec 2009

>> www.sap-press.de/1957

Provides a complete guide to Organizational Management (OM) with SAP ERP HCM

Teaches all functions of OM from a global perspective

Includes practical integration and customizing tips and techniques

Sylvia Chaudoir

Mastering SAP ERP HCM Organizational Management

This book teaches the HCM team how to maximize the organizational management (OM) component of SAP ERP HCM. It takes readers beyond the basics, by delving into all aspects of the component as well as the little-known concepts. It teaches all of the key OM functions, their purpose, and how to use and customize them. Numerous examples from customers are used to provide context for decisions and to explain the benefits of the choices that can be made. And in-depth explanations and practical examples are used to help readers leverage the many available organizational objects to get the most out of their SAP HR implementation.

348 pp., 2008, 69,95 Euro / US$ 69.95
ISBN 978-1-59229-208-0

>> www.sap-press.de/1796